C000090788

1 MONTH OF
FREE
READING

at
www.ForgottenBooks.com

By purchasing this book you are eligible for one month membership to ForgottenBooks.com, giving you unlimited access to our entire collection of over 1,000,000 titles via our web site and mobile apps.

To claim your free month visit:
www.forgottenbooks.com/free977655

* Offer is valid for 45 days from date of purchase. Terms and conditions apply.

ISBN 978-0-260-86096-5
PIBN 10977655

This book is a reproduction of an important historical work. Forgotten Books uses state-of-the-art technology to digitally reconstruct the work, preserving the original format whilst repairing imperfections present in the aged copy. In rare cases, an imperfection in the original, such as a blemish or missing page, may be replicated in our edition. We do, however, repair the vast majority of imperfections successfully; any imperfections that remain are intentionally left to preserve the state of such historical works.

Forgotten Books is a registered trademark of FB &c Ltd.
Copyright © 2018 FB &c Ltd.
FB &c Ltd, Dalton House, 60 Windsor Avenue, London, SW19 2RR.
Company number 08720141. Registered in England and Wales.

For support please visit www.forgottenbooks.com

Illinois Institute of Technology

E 31

Information Center

1997

Illinois Register

Rules of Governmental Agencies

Volume 21, Issue 52—December 26, 1997

Pages 16,941 - 17,218

published by

George H. Ryan

Secretary of State

PROPOSED RULES

ADOPTED RULES

i

ii

Editor's Note: The Cumulative Index and Sections Affected Index will be printed on a quarterly basis. The printing schedule for the quarterly and annual indexes are as follows:

April	18, 1997 - Issue 16:	Through	March	31, 1997
July	18, 1997 - Issue 29:	Through	June	30, 1997
October	17, 1997 - Issue 42:	Through	September	30, 1997
January	16, 1998 - Issue 3:	Through	December	31, 1997 (Annual)

BOARD OF SAVINGS INSTITUTIONS

NOTICE OF PROPOSED AMENDMENT

1) <u>Heading of the Part</u>: Board of Savings Institutions

2) <u>Code Citation</u>: 38 Ill. Adm. Code 500

3) <u>Section Number</u>:   <u>Proposed Action</u>:
   500.200   Amendment
   500.230   Amendment

4) <u>Statutory Authority</u>: Implementing and authorized by Section 7-20 through 7-27 of the Illinois Savings and Loan Act of 1985 [205 ILCS 105/7-20 through 7-27] and Section 9018 of the Savings Bank Act [205 ILCS 205/9016].

5) <u>A complete description of the subjects and issues involved</u>: On October 23, 1997, the Board of Savings Institutions approved reducing its annual schedule of regular meetings from four meetings to two meetings. This rulemaking amends Section 500.200 to implement that change. (In addition to its regular meetings, the Board may call special meetings when necessary pursuant to Section 500.210 of the rules.) The proposed rulemaking also amends Section 500.230 to correct a misspelling.

6) <u>Will these proposed amendments replace emergency amendments currently in effect</u>? No

7) <u>Does this rulemaking contain an automatic repeal date</u>? No

8) <u>Do these proposed amendments contain incorporations by reference</u>? No

9) <u>Are there any other proposed amendments pending in this Part</u>? No

10) <u>Statement of Statewide Policy Objectives</u>: This rule will not affect local government.

11) <u>Time, place and manner in which interested persons may comment on this proposed rulemaking</u>: Interested parties should submit written comments or views concerning the proposed rulemaking to the attention of:

    John Arthur, Legislative Liaison
    Office of Banks and Real Estate
    500 East Monroe, Suite 900
    Springfield, IL 62701
    Telephone: (217) 782-3000
    Fax: (217) 524-5941

    The Agency will consider all written comments it receives in writing within 45 days after the date of publication of the *Illinois Register*.

12) <u>Initial Regulatory Flexibility Analysis</u>:

BOARD OF SAVINGS INSTITUTIONS

NOTICE OF PROPOSED AMENDMENT

A) <u>Types of small businesses affected</u>: None

B) <u>Reporting, bookkeeping or other procedures required for compliance</u>: None

C) <u>Types of professional skills necessary for compliance</u>: None

13) <u>Regulatory Agenda on which this rulemaking was summarized</u>: This rulemaking was not included on either of the 2 most recent agendas because: The Board did not consider and approve the proposed change in its meeting schedule until its October 23, 1997 meeting, which was after the most recent Regulatory Agenda filing period.

<u>The full text of the Proposed Amendments begins on the next page:</u>

BOARD OF SAVINGS INSTITUTIONS

NOTICE OF PROPOSED AMENDMENT

TITLE 38: FINANCIAL INSTITUTIONS
CHAPTER IV: BOARD OF SAVINGS INSTITUTIONS

PART 500
BOARD OF SAVINGS INSTITUTIONS

SUBPART A: GENERAL PROVISIONS

Section
500.100   Applicability

SUBPART B: MEETINGS

SUBPART C: OFFICERS AND COMMITTEES

SUBPART D: HEARINGS BEFORE THE BOARD OF SAVINGS INSTITUTIONS

BOARD OF SAVINGS INSTITUTIONS

NOTICE OF PROPOSED AMENDMENT

AUTHORITY: Implementing and authorized by Sections 7-20 through 7-27 of the Illinois Savings and Loan Act of 1985 [205 ILCS 105/7-20 through 7-27] and Section 9018 of the Savings Bank Act [205 ILCS 205/9018].

SOURCE: Filed August 15, 1973; codified at 8 Ill. Reg. 17916, September 14, 1984; old Part repealed, new Part adopted at 15 Ill. Reg. 17376, effective November 14, 1991; recodified from Chapter IV, Savings and Loan Board, to Chapter II, Office of Banks and Real Estate, pursuant to PA 89-508, at 20 Ill. Reg. 14947; amended at 22 Ill. Reg. _____, effective

SUBPART B: MEETINGS

Section 500.200   Regular Meetings

The Board of Savings Institutions shall hold two regular meetings each year on the first Wednesday of every March, June, September and December. One meeting shall be in the first calendar quarter of the year and the second meeting shall be in the fourth calendar quarter of the year. The Board shall designate the time and place for holding regular meetings.

(Source: Amended at 22 Ill. Reg. _____, effective _____)

Section 500.230   Quorum Quorum

A majority of the members of the Board of Savings Institutions shall constitute a quorum provided, that if less than a majority of such number of members are present at said meeting, a majority of the members may adjourn the meeting. The Board or any committee of the Board may participate in and act at any meeting of such Board or committee, through the use of telephone or other communications equipment by means of which all persons participating in the

OF SAVINGS INSTITUTIONS

OF PROPOSED AMENDMENT

Participation in such meeting shall constitute
on at the meeting of the person or persons so

22 Ill. Reg. _____, effective

DEPARTMENT OF INSURANCE

NOTICE OF PROPOSED RULES

1) Heading of the Part: Investment Fee Disclosure Requirements For Pension
    Funds

2) Code Citation: 50 Ill. Adm. Code 4430

3) Section Numbers: Proposed Action:
    4430.10   New Section
    4430.20   New Section
    4430.30   New Section
    4430.40   New Section

4) Statutory Authority: Implementing Section 1-113.5(b)(3), (d) and (e) and
    also 1-113.6, and authorized by Section 113.11 of the Illinois Pension
    Code [40 ILCS 5/1-113.5(b)(3), (d) and (e), 1-113.6 and 1-113.11, as added
    by P.A. 90-507, effective August 22, 1997].

5) A Complete Description of the Subjects and Issues Involved: Beginning
    January 1, 1998, police and firefighter pension funds established under
    either Article 3 or 4 of the Pension Code may now draw pension funds out
    for investment purposes. Pursuant to the requirements of this Part,
    pension funds must obtain a fee disclosure statement from any investment
    advisor, registered broker-dealer, bank, insurer or any other person used
    for investment-related services. This rule sets forth what elements must
    be contained in a disclosure statement and further identifies what
    recordkeeping requirements pension funds must meet to be in compliance
    with this Part.

6) Will this proposed rule replace an emergency rule currently in effect?
    Yes

7) Does this rule contain an automatic repeal date? No

8) Does this proposed rule contain incorporations by reference? No

9) Are there any other proposed amendments pending on this Part? No

10) Statement of Statewide Policy Objectives: This new Part will not require
    a local government to establish, expand or modify its activities in such a
    way as to necessitate additional expenditures from local revenues.

11) Time, Place, and Manner in which interested persons may comment on this
    proposed rulemaking: Persons who wish to comment on this proposed
    rulemaking may submit written comments no later than 45 days after the
    publication of this Notice to:

        Eve Blackwell   Denise Hamilton
        Staff Attorney   Rules Unit Supervisor
        Department of Insurance Department of Insurance

DEPARTMENT OF INSURANCE

NOTICE OF PROPOSED RULES

320 West Washington   (or)   320 West Washington
Springfield, IL 62767   Springfield, IL 62767
(217) 524-1634   (217) 785-8560

12) Initial Regulatory Flexibility Analysis:

   A) Types of small businesses, small municipalities and not for profit
      corporations affected: This rule will not affect small
      municipalities, as that term is defined in Section 1-80 of the
      Illinois Administrative Procedure Act [5 ILCS 100/1-80].

   B) Reporting, bookkeeping or other procedures required for compliance:
      Please see Section 4430.30 of this Part.

   C) Types of professional skills necessary for compliance: Clerical and
      organizational skills will be necessary to comply with this Part.

13) Regulatory Agenda on which this rulemaking was summarized: This
    rulemaking was not included on either of the two most recent agendas
    because: The Department did not anticipate the passage of HB 23.

The full text of the Rule is identical to the Emergency Rule being published in
this issue of the Illinois Register on page _____:

DEPARTMENT OF NATURAL RESOURCES

NOTICE OF PROPOSED AMENDMENT(S)

1) Heading of the Part: Commercial Fishing and Musseling in Certain Waters
   of the State

2) Code Citation: 17 Ill. Adm. Code 830

3) Section Numbers: Proposed Action:
   830.20   Amendments
   830.30   Amendments
   830.40   Amendments
   830.60   Amendments
   830.70   Amendments
   830.90   Amendments

4) Statutory Authority: Implementing and authorized by Sections 1-60, 1-65,
   1-120, 10-120, 15-35, 15-40, 20-35, and 25-5 of the Fish and Aquatic Life
   Code [515 ILCS 5/1-60, 1-65, 1-120, 10-120, 15-35, 15-40, 20-35, and
   25-5].

5) A Complete Description of the Subjects and Issues Involved: Amendments to
   this Part include eliminating harvest of washboard mussels on the
   Mississippi River to provide needed protection and correspond with
   proposed closures in Missouri and Iowa, changing the opening date for
   mussel season on the Mississippi River and Ohio River to April 2, adding
   language requiring at least a 4" bar mesh in trammel nets on the Ohio
   River, making the use of hand forks illegal, exempting the Ohio River from
   the 15" catfish limit, raising the limit on threeridge mussels to 3" and
   requiring monthly harvest reporting for commercial fishermen on the Ohio
   River.

6) Will this rulemaking replace any emergency rulemaking currently in
   effect? No

7) Does this rulemaking contain an automatic repeal date? No

8) Does this rulemaking contain incorporations by reference? No

9) Are there any other proposed rulemakings pending on this Part? No

10) Statement of Statewide Policy Objectives: This rulemaking does not
    affect units of local government.

11) Time, Place and Manner in which interested persons may comment on this
    proposed rulemaking: Comments on the proposed rule may be submitted in
    writing for a period of 45 days following publication of this notice to:

    Jack Price
    Department of Natural Resources
    524 S. Second Street

97

ENT OF NATURAL RESOURCES

OF PROPOSED AMENDMENT(S)

A-1787

sis:

    1 mun'c'alities and not for rofit
                                    d
                                    s
                                    y

                        None

    A summarized: This rule was not
ent agendas because: The Department
on this Part.

gins on the next page:

DEPARTMENT OF NATURAL RESOURCES

NOTICE OF PROPOSED AMENDMENT(S)

TITLE 17: CONSERVATION
CHAPTER I: DEPARTMENT OF NATURAL RESOURCES
SUBCHAPTER b: FISH AND WILDLIFE

PART 830
COMMERCIAL FISHING AND MUSSELING IN CERTAIN WATERS OF THE STATE

Section
830.5   Definitions
830.10   Waters Open to Commercial Harvest of Fish
830.20   Waters Open to Commercial Harvest of Mussels and Seasons
830.30   Special Regulations
830.40   Devices
830.50   Permission
830.60   Species
830.70   Size Limit
830.80   Commercial Fishing and Musseling in Additional Waters
830.90   Revocation and Suspension of Commercial Fishing and Musseling
          Privileges, Hearings and Appeals and Reporting Requirements

AUTHORITY: Implementing and authorized by Sections 1-60, 1-65, 1-120, 10-120,
15-35, 15-40, 20-35 and 25-5 of the Fish and Aquatic Life Code [515 ILCS
5/1-60, 1-65, 1-120, 10-120, 15-35, 15-40, 20-35, and 25-5].

SOURCE: Adopted at 5 Ill. Reg. 6809, effective June 16, 1981; codified at 5
Ill. Reg. 10648; emergency amendment at 6 Ill. Reg. 6468, effective May 18,
1982, for a maximum of 150 days; amended at 6 Ill. Reg. 10680, effective August
20, 1982; amended at 7 Ill. Reg. 2707, effective March 2, 1983; amended at 10
Ill. Reg. 6926, effective April 15, 1986; amended at 11 Ill. Reg. 9513,
effective May 5, 1987; amended at 12 Ill. Reg. 11714, effective June 30, 1988;
amended at 15 Ill. Reg. 8544, effective May 24, 1991; amended at 16 Ill. Reg.
5257, effective March 20, 1992; amended at 17 Ill. Reg. 3177, effective March
2, 1993; emergency amendment at 18 Ill. Reg. 4671, effective March 14, 1994,
for a maximum of 150 days; amended at 18 Ill. Reg. 9985, effective June 21,
1994; amended at 19 Ill. Reg. 5250, effective March 27, 1995; recodified by
changing the agency name from Department of Conservation to Department of
Natural Resources at 20 Ill. Reg. 9389; amended at 21 Ill. Reg. 4700, effective
April 1, 1997; amended at 22 Ill. Reg. _____, effective
_____.

Section 830.20 Waters Open to Commercial Harvest of Mussels and Seasons

    a) Mississippi River and backwaters, April 1 15 to August 31 inclusive,
        except for the following areas:
        1) All of the area directly above Lock and Dam 12 (RM 556.7) from
            the center of the navigation channel east to the Illinois
            shoreline and northward to a line extending from RM 558.4 to the
            Blanding's Landing boat ramp, including but not limited to all of

DEPARTMENT OF NATURAL RESOURCES

NOTICE OF PROPOSED AMENDMENT(S)

the area contained within the designated U.S. Military Reservation area.
2) All of the waters contained within Sylvan Slough from the Interstate 74 highway bridge (RM 485.8) west to the lower tip of Arsenal Island (RM 482.6).
3) All of the area north of and perpendicular to the center line of the navigation channel to the Illinois shoreline lying between RM 433.0 (New Boston Boat Launching Ramp) to RM 433.8 (lower tip of the first upstream island along the Illinois shoreline).
4) Pontoosuc Bay contained within and described as that area from the center of the main navigation channel and perpendicular to the Illinois shoreline located between RM 388.0 (Pontoosuc light and daymark) and RM 390.2 (Dallas City boat access area).
5) All of the area southward of the center of the navigation channel and perpendicular to the Illinois shoreline on a line from the Des Moines River daymark (Iowa side) and the Des Moines River lighted buoy (Illinois side), both of which are at RM 361.7, to Lock and Dam 19 (RM 364.5) including any slough channels of the Mud Island area along the Illinois side.
6) All of the area east of the center of navigation channel and perpendicular to the Illinois shoreline between RM 314.0 (Whitney light and daymark) and RM 316.0 (Hadley Island Goale light and daymark).
7) All of the area east of the center of navigation channel and perpendicular to the Illinois shoreline between River Mile 238.4 (Hasting's Landing light and daymark) and River Mile 246.8 (Turner Landing light and daymark).
8) Mark Twain U.S. Fish and Wildlife Service National Wildlife Refuge Waters.
b) Ohio River and backwaters, April 1 15 to September 30 inclusive.

(Source: Amended at 22 Ill. Reg. _____, effective
_____)

Section 830.30 Special Regulations

a) Commercial fishing and musseling will not be permitted in any streams, ditches, or tributaries connected to the backwaters of the aforementioned waters.
b) Any person harvesting mussels for commercial use may possess during the open season only those mussels identified in Section 830.60 of legal size. Mussels smaller than the legal size and all mussels not identified in Section 830.60 must be immediately returned to the mussel bed or location from which they were taken.
c) It shall be illegal to possess mussel shell more than 15 days after the close of the season without a mussel dealer license.
d) Paddlefish may not be commercially harvested except in the Ohio River, the Illinois River below Route 89, and in the Mississippi River below

DEPARTMENT OF NATURAL RESOURCES

NOTICE OF PROPOSED AMENDMENT(S)

Lock and Dam 19.
e) Commercial fishing devices must be checked and emptied of catch at the following time intervals:
1) Hoop nets and basket traps must be attended at least once every 48 hours during open water conditions. During ice cover conditions, hoop nets and basket traps must be attended at least once every 20 days.
2) Trammel and gill nets must be attended at least every 24 hours during open water conditions. During ice cover conditions, trammel and gill nets must be attended at least every 96 hours.
3) Trotlines and other hook and line devices must be checked at least every 24 hours.
4) Seines and trammel or gill nets fished by driving or drifting methods must be constantly attended.
5) Commercial gear containing dead or moribund fish as a result of failure to check gear and empty catch shall be considered an illegal device.
f) Washboard mussels may not be taken on the Mississippi River.

(Source: Amended at 22 Ill. Reg. _____, effective
_____)

Section 830.40 Devices

a) Commercial fishing devices used in the aforementioned waters shall conform to all regulations as outlined in Article 15 of Chapter 515 56 of the Illinois Compiled Revised Statutes. Hoop nets, basket traps, trot lines and dip nets may be used in all of the aforementioned waters.
b) It shall be unlawful:
1) To use trammel nets and gill nets except in the Illinois River up to Route 89 Highway bridge, the Ohio River and the Mississippi River.
2) To use seines except in the Illinois, Mississippi, Ohio and Wabash Rivers (except seining will not be permitted in Boston Bay and its connected backwaters above the mouth of Boston Bay in Mercer County).
3) To use trammel nets in the Ohio River with less than 4 inch bar mesh netting.
c) Musseling devices used in waters open to commercial musseling shall conform to all regulations as outlined below and in Articles 1 and 15 of 515 ILCS 5.
d) It shall be unlawful to use hand forks except in the Mississippi River.
e) It shall be unlawful to use basket dredges, mechanical devices and hand dredges in the taking of mussels.
f) It shall be unlawful to harvest mussels in the Ohio River except by using crowfoot bars.

DEPARTMENT OF NATURAL RESOURCES

NOTICE OF PROPOSED AMENDMENT(S)

g) It shall be unlawful to tether or hold mussels in any containment device. Mussels must be taken to the boat or released each day.

h) Brail or crowfoot bars must be 20 feet or less in length. Not more than 3 bars may be possessed in each boat.

(Source: Amended at 22 Ill. Reg. _____, effective _____)

Section 830.60 Species

a) The following species of fish may be taken by licensed commercial fishermen:
   '1) Carp
   2) Buffalo
   3) Freshwater drum
   4) Catfishes (includes bullheads)
   5) Paddlefish (only in waters specified in Section 830.30)
   6) Carpsuckers
   7) Suckers (except Longnose Sucker)
   8) Redhorses (except River Redhorse and Greater Redhorse)
   9) Goldeye and Mooneye
   10) Gar (except alligator gar)
   11) Bowfin
   12) American mussel
   13) Shovelnose sturgeon
   14) Gizzard shad
   15) White amur (grass carp)
   16) Minnows
   17) Goldfish
   18) Bighead Carp and Silver Carp

b) The following species of mussels may be taken by licensed commercial musselers:
   1) Washboard (Megalonaias nervosa) (Ohio River Only)
   2) Threeridge (Amblema plicata)
   3) Mapleleaf (Quadrula quadrula)
   4) Pimpleback (Quadrula pustulosa)
   5) Monkeyface (Quadrula metanevra)
   6) Wartyback (Quadrula nodulata)
   7) Pigtoe (Fusconaia flava-forma undata)
   8) Hickory Nut (Obovaria olivaria)
   9) Pink Heelsplitter (Potamilus alatus)
   10) Pocketbook (Lampsilis ovata)
   11) Black Sandshell (Ligumia recta)

(Source: Amended at 22 Ill. Reg. _____, effective _____)

Section 830.70 Size Limit

DEPARTMENT OF NATURAL RESOURCES

NOTICE OF PROPOSED AMENDMENT(S)

a) No channel catfish, blue catfish, flathead catfish or white catfish under 15 inches in length, undressed, or 12 inches in length, dressed, or 10.7 inches when dressed with the first vertebrae (T bone) removed, may be taken except in the Ohio River.

b) There is no size limit on other species listed in Section 830.60(a).

c)' All Washboard mussels shall measure not less than 4.0 inches. All relic (dead) Washboards shall measure not less than 4.0 inches.

d) All Threeridge and maple leaf mussels shall measure not less than 2.75 inches.

e) All Threeridge mussels shall measure not less than 3.0 inches.

f)e+ All other mussels listed in 830.60(b), shall measure not less than 2.5 inches.

(Source: Amended at 22 Ill. Reg. _____, effective _____)

Section 830.90 Revocation and Suspension of Commercial Fishing and Musseling Privileges, Hearings and Appeals and Reporting Requirements

a) In accordance with Section 20-105 of the Fish and Aquatic Life Code [515 ILCS 5/20-105]; failure to comply with the provisions of the Fish and Aquatic Life Code of Illinois pertaining to commercial fishing and/or musseling in Illinois waters, and this part will result in suspension or revocation of the commercial fishing and/or musseling licenses. The procedure by which suspensions and revocations are made, the rights of commercial fishermen and musselers to notice and hearing, and the procedures governing such hearings are set forth in 17 Ill. Adm. Code 2530 (Rules governing Department Formal Hearings Conducted for Rule-Making and Contested Cases).

b) Where waters of the State are open to commercial fishing or musseling by contract, the contract will be revoked upon failure of the contractor to comply with all terms of the contract. Furthermore, any violation of a contract issued by the Director of Conservation or his agents shall be considered a violation of this Administrative Order and subject to the penalties as set forth in Sections 20-35 and 20-105 of the Fish and Aquatic Life Code [515 ILCS 5/20-35, 20-105].

c) Commercial fishermen shall submit an accurate record of the undressed weights of the species of fish harvested to the Department by January 31 of the following year, whether or not any fish were harvested.

d) Commercial fishermen on the Ohio River shall submit to the Department an accurate monthly record of the undressed weights and species of fish harvested by the 10th of each month following harvest, whether or not any fish were harvested.

e)d) Holders of a commercial mussel harvest license shall submit an accurate record of the types and pounds of each species of mussel and/or relic mussel shells harvested or purchased on a monthly basis during the season by the 10th of each month following harvest, whether

DEPARTMENT OF NATURAL RESOURCES

NOTICE OF PROPOSED AMENDMENT(S)

or not any mussels or mussel shells were harvested. Reports must be submitted on official Department of Natural Resources report forms.

f)e) Holders of a commercial mussel dealer's license shall submit an accurate record of the types and pounds of each species of mussel and/or relic mussel shells purchased on a monthly basis during the season by the 10th of each month following purchase, whether or not any mussels or mussel shells were purchased. Reports must be submitted on official Department of Natural Resources report forms.

g)f) Failure of licensed commercial mussel dealers, fishermen or musselors to submit the required reports in a manner and time frame specified by the Department shall be grounds for refusal on the part of the Department to issue said individuals a license application for the following year until all required reports are received by the Department.

(Source: Amended at 22 Ill. Reg. _____, effective _____)

POLLUTION CONTROL BOARD

NOTICE OF PROPOSED AMENDMENTS

1) Heading of the Part: Primary Drinking Water Standards

2) Code Citation: 35 Ill. Adm. Code 611

3) Section Numbers: Proposed Action:
   611.102   Amended
   611.720   Amended

4) Statutory Authority: 415 ILCS 5/7.2, 17.5, and 27

5) A Complete Description of the Subjects and Issues Involved: A more detailed description of this regulation may be found in the Board's opinion and order of December 4, 1997, docketed by the Board as R98-2, which is available from the address specified in number 11 below. The Board is proposing amendments to add 66 additional analytical methods for compliance with current radionuclide drinking water standards and monitoring requirements. The methods are applicable to gross alpha, gross beta, tritium, uranium, radium-226, radium-228, gamma emitters, and radioactive cesium, iodine, and strontium. (The proposed amendments are identical in substance to USEPA rules at 40 CFR 141.25.)

Section 9.1(e) of the Environmental Protection Act (Act) [415 ILCS 5/9.1(e)] provides that Section 5 of the Illinois Administrative Procedure Act (IAPA) [5 ILCS 100/5-35 and 5-40] shall not apply. Because this rulemaking is not subject to Section 5 of the IAPA, it is not subject to first or second notice by JCAR.

6) Will this proposed rule replace an emergency rule currently in effect? No

7) Does this rulemaking contain an automatic repeal date? No

8) Does this proposed rule contain incorporations by reference? Yes, the proposed amendments contain additions to the incorporations by reference located in Section 611.102. The incorporations by reference are amended to reflect the addition of the 66 additional analytical methods that are proposed in Section 611.720.

9) Are there any other proposed amendments pending on this Part? No

10) Statement of Policy Objectives: This rulemaking does not create a State mandate.

11) Time, Place, and Manner in which interested persons may comment on this proposed rulemaking: Written comments concerning this rulemaking should reference R98-2 and be sent to:

Dorothy Gunn

POLLUTION CONTROL BOARD

NOTICE OF PROPOSED AMENDMENTS

Clerk of the Pollution Control Board
100 West Randolph Street
Suite 11-500
Chicago, IL 60601
312/814-6931

Questions regarding this proposal may be directed to Amy Muran Felton at
312-814-7011.

12) Initial Regulatory Flexibility Analysis: This proposal is filed pursuant
to the Environmental Protection Act.

   A) Types of small businesses affected: Any public water system that has
      at least 15 service connections or regularly serves an average of at
      least 25 individuals daily at least 60 days out of the year.

   B) Reporting, bookkeeping, or other procedures required for compliance:
      Sample analysis by certified laboratories.

   C) Types of professional skills necessary for compliance: Sample
      analysis by certified laboratories.

13) Regulatory Agenda on which this rulemaking was summarized: August 1997

The full text of the Proposed Amendments begin on the next page:

POLLUTION CONTROL BOARD

NOTICE OF PROPOSED AMENDMENTS

TITLE 35: ENVIRONMENTAL PROTECTION
SUBTITLE F: PUBLIC WATER SUPPLIES
CHAPTER I: POLLUTION CONTROL BOARD

PART 611
PRIMARY DRINKING WATER STANDARDS

SUBPART A: GENERAL

POLLUTION CONTROL BOARD

NOTICE OF PROPOSED AMENDMENTS

POLLUTION CONTROL BOARD

NOTICE OF PROPOSED AMENDMENTS

POLLUTION CONTROL BOARD

NOTICE OF PROPOSED AMENDMENTS

POLLUTION CONTROL BOARD

NOTICE OF PROPOSED AMENDMENTS

AUTHORITY: Implementing Sections 17 and 17.5 and authorized by Section 27 of
the Environmental Protection Act [415 ILCS 5/17, 17.5 and 27].

SOURCE: Adopted in R88-26 at 14 Ill. Reg. 16517, effective September 20, 1990;
amended in R90-21 at 14 Ill. Reg. 20448, effective December 11, 1990; amended
in R90-13 at 15 Ill. Reg. 1562, effective January 22, 1991; amended in R91-3 at
16 Ill. Reg. 19010, effective December 1, 1992; amended in R92-3 at 17 Ill.
Reg. 7796, effective May 18, 1993; amended in R93-1 at 17 Ill. Reg. 12650,
effective July 23, 1993; amended in R94-4 at 18 Ill. Reg. 12291, effective July
28, 1994; amended in R94-23 at 19 Ill. Reg. 8613, effective June 20, 1995;
amended in R95-17 at 20 Ill. Reg. 14493, effective October 22, 1996; amended in
R98-2 at 22 Ill. Reg. _____, effective _____.

NOTE: In this Part, superscript number or letters are denoted by parentheses;
subscript are denoted by [brackets].

SUBPART A: GENERAL

Section 611.102 Incorporations by Reference

a) Abbreviations and short-name listing of references. The following
    names and abbreviated names, presented in alphabetical order, are used
    in this Part to refer to materials incorporated by reference:

        "Amco-AEPA-1 Polymer" is available from Advanced Polymer Systems.

        "ASTM Method" means a method published by and available from the
        American Society for Testing and Materials (ASTM).

        "Colisure Test" means "Colisure Presence/Absence Test for
        Detection and Identification of Coliform Bacteria and Escherichia
        Coli in Drinking Water", available from Millipore Corporation,
        Technical Services Department.

        "Dioxin and Furan Method 1613" means "Tetra- through
        Octa-Chlorinated Dioxins and Furans by Isotope-Dilution

POLLUTION CONTROL BOARD

NOTICE OF PROPOSED AMENDMENTS

HRGC/HRMS", available from NTIS.

"GLI Method 2" means GLI Method 2, "Turbidity", Nov. 2, 1992, available from Great Lakes Instruments, Inc.

"Guidance Manual for Compliance with the Filtration and Disinfection Requirements for Public Water Systems Using Surface Water Sources", available from USEPA Science and Technology Branch.

"HASL Procedure Manual" means HASL Procedure Manual, HASL 300, available from ERDA Health and Safety Laboratory.

"Maximum Permissible Body Burdens and Maximum Permissible Concentrations of Radionuclides in Air and in Water for Occupational Exposure", NCRP Report Number 22, available from NCRP.

"NCRP" means "National Council on Radiation Protection".

"NTIS" means "National Technical Information Service".

"New Jersey Radium Method" means "Determination of Radium 228 in Drinking Water", available from the New Jersey Department of Environmental Protection.

"New York Radium Method" means "Determination of Ra-226 and Ra-228 (Ra-02)", available from the New York Department of Public Health.

"ONGP-MUG Test" (meaning "minimal medium ortho-nitrophenyl-beta-d-galactopyranoside-4-methyl-umbelliferyl -beta-d-glucuronide test"), also called the "Autoanalysis Colilert System", is method 9223, available in "Standard Methods for the Examination of Water and Wastewater", 18th ed., from American Public Health Association.

"Procedures for Radiochemical Analysis of Nuclear Reactor Aqueous Solutions", available from NTIS.

"Radiochemical Methods" means "Interim Radiochemical Methodology for Drinking Water", available from NTIS.

"Standard Methods", means "Standard Methods for the Examination of Water and Wastewater", available from the American Public Health Association or the American Waterworks Association.

"Technical Bulletin 601" means "Technical Bulletin 601, "Standard

POLLUTION CONTROL BOARD

NOTICE OF PROPOSED AMENDMENTS

Method of Testing for Nitrate in Drinking Water", July, 1994, available from Analytical Technology, Inc.

"Technicon Methods" means "Fluoride in Water and Wastewater", available from Technicon.

"USDOE Manual" means "EML Procedures Manual", available from the United State Department of Energy.

"USEPA Asbestos Methods – 100.1" means Method 100.1, "Analytical Method for Determination of Asbestos Fibers in Water", available from NTIS.

"USEPA Asbestos Methods-100.2" means Method 100.2, "Determination of Asbestos Structures over 10-micron in Length in Drinking Water", available from NTIS.

"USEPA Environmental Inorganics Methods" means "Methods for the Determination of Inorganic Substances in Environmental Samples", available from NTIS.

"USEPA Environmental Metals Methods" means "Methods for the Determination of Metals in Environmental Samples", available from NTIS.

"USEPA Organic Methods" means "Methods for the Determination of Organic Compounds in Drinking Water", July, 1991, for Methods 502.2, .505, 507, 508, 508A, 515.1, and 531.1; "Methods for the Determination of Organic Compounds in Drinking Water--Supplement I", July, 1990, for Methods 506, 547, 550, 550.1, and 551; and "Methods for the Determination of Organic Compounds in Drinking Water--Supplement II", August, 1992, for Methods 515.2, 524.2, 548.1, 549.1, 552.1, and 555, available from NTIS. Methods 504.1, 508.1, and 525.2 are available from EPA EMSL.

"USGS Methods" means "Methods of Analysis by the U.S. Geological Survey National Water Quality Laboratory--Determination of Inorganic and Organic Constituents in Water and Fluvial Sediments", available from NTIS and USGS.

"USEPA Interim Radiochemical Methods" means "Interim Radiochemical Methodology for Drinking Water", EPA 600/4-75-008 (revised), March 1976. Available from NTIS.

"USEPA Radioactivity Methods" means "Prescribed Procedures for Measurement of Radioactivity in Drinking Water", EPA 600/4-80-032, August 1980. Available from NTIS.

POLLUTION CONTROL BOARD

NOTICE OF PROPOSED AMENDMENTS

"USEPA Radiochemical Analyses" means "Radiochemical Analytical Procedures for Analysis of Environmental Samples", March 1979. Available from NTIS.

"USEPA Radiochemistry Methods" means "Radiochemistry Procedures Manual", EPA 520/5-84-006, December 1987. Available from NTIS.

"USEPA Technical Notes" means "Technical Notes on Drinking Water Methods", available from NTIS.

"Waters Method B-1011" means "Waters Test Method for the Determination of Nitrite/Nitrate in Water Using Single Column Ion Chromatography", available from Millipore Corporation, Waters Chromatography Division.

b) The Board incorporates the following publications by reference:

Access Analytical Systems, Inc.. See Environetics, Inc.

Advanced Polymer Systems, 3696 Haven Avenue, Redwood City, CA 94063 415-366-2626:

Amco-AEPA-1 Polymer. See 40 CFR 141.22(a) (1995). Also, as referenced in ASTM D1889.

American Public Health Association, 1015 Fifteenth Street NW, Washington, DC 20005 800-645-5476:

"Standard Methods for the Examination of Water and Wastewater", 17th Edition 1989 (referred to as "Standard Methods, 17th ed.").

"Standard Methods for the Examination of Water and Wastewater", 18th Edition, 1992, including "Supplement to the 18th Edition of Standard Methods for the Examination of Water and Wastewater", 1994 (collectively referred to as "Standard Methods, 18th ed."). See the methods listed separately for the same references under American Water Works Association.

"Standard Methods for the Examination of Water and Wastewater", 19th Edition, 1995 (referred to as "Standard Methods, 19th ed.").

Supplement to the 18th edition of Standard Methods for the Examination of Water and Wastewater, 1994.

American Water Works Association et al., 6666 West Quincy Avenue,

POLLUTION CONTROL BOARD

NOTICE OF PROPOSED AMENDMENTS

Denver, CO 80235 303-794-7711:

Standard Methods for the Examination of Water and Wastewater, 13th Edition, 1971 (referred to as "Standard Methods, 13th ed.").

Method 302, Gross Alpha and Gross Beta Radioactivity in Water (Total, Suspended and Dissolved).

Method 303, Total Radioactive Strontium and Strontium 90 in Water.

Method 304, Radium in Water by Precipitation.

Method 305, Radium 226 by Radon in Water (Soluble, Suspended and Total).

Method 306, Tritium in Water.

Standard Methods for the Examination of Water and Wastewater, 18th Edition, 1992 (referred to as "Standard Methods, 18th ed."):

Method 2130 B, Turbidity, Nephelometric Method.

Method 2320 B, Alkalinity, Titration Method.

Method 2510 B, Conductivity, Laboratory Method.

Method 2550, Temperature, Laboratory and Field Methods.

Method 3111 B, metals by Flame Atomic Absorption Spectrometry, Direct Air-Acetylene Flame Method.

Method 3111 D, Metals by Flame Atomic Absorption Spectrometry, Direct Nitrous Oxide-Acetylene Flame Method.

Method 3112 B, Metals by Cold-Vapor Atomic Absorption Spectrometry, Cold-Vapor Atomic Absorption Spectrometric Method.

Method 3113 B, Metals by Electrothermal Atomic Absorption Spectrometry, Electrothermal Atomic Absorption Spectrometric Method.

Method 3114 B, Metals by Hydride Generation/Atomic

POLLUTION CONTROL BOARD

NOTICE OF PROPOSED AMENDMENTS

Absorption   Spectrometry,   Manual   Hydride
Generation/Atomic Absorption Spectrometric Method.

Method 3120 B, Metals by Plasma Emission Spectroscopy,
Inductively Coupled Plasma (ICP) Method.

Method 3500-Ca D, Calcium, EDTA Titrimetric Method.

Method 4110 B, Determination of Anions by Ion
Chromatography, Ion Chromatography with Chemical
Suppression of Eluent Conductivity.

Method 4500-CN C, Cyanide, Total Cyanide after
Distillation.

Method 4500-CN E, Cyanide, Colorimetric Method.

Method 4500-CN F, Cyanide, Cyanide-Selective Electrode
Method.

Method 4500-CN G, Cyanide, Cyanides Amenable to
Chlorination after Distillation.

Method 4500-Cl D, Chlorine (Residual), Amperometric
Titration Method.

Method 4500-Cl E, Chlorine (Residual), Low-Level
Amperometric Titration Method.

Method 4500-Cl F, Chlorine (Residual), DPD Ferrous
Titrimetric Method.

Method   4500-Cl   G,   Chlorine   (Residual),   DPD
Colorimetric Method.

Method 4500-Cl H, Chlorine (Residual), Syringaldazine
(FACTS) Method.

Method 4500-Cl I, Chlorine (Residual), Iodometric
Electrode Technique.

Method 4500-ClO[2] C, Chlorine Dioxide, Amperometric
Method I.

Method 4500-ClO[2] D, Chlorine Dioxide, DPD Method.

Method 4500-ClO[2] E, Chlorine Dioxide, Amperometric
Method II (Proposed).

POLLUTION CONTROL BOARD

NOTICE OF PROPOSED AMENDMENTS

Method 4500-F B, Fluoride, Preliminary Distillation
Step.

Method 4500-F C, Fluoride, Ion-Selective Electrode
Method.

Method 4500-F D, Fluoride, SPADNS Method.

Method 4500-F E, Fluoride, Complexone Method.

Method 4500-H(+) B, pH Value, Electrometric Method.

Method 4500-NO[2] B, Nitrogen (Nitrite), Colorimetric
Method.

Method 4500-NO[3] D, Nitrogen (Nitrate), Nitrate
Electrode Method.

Method 4500-NO[3] E, Nitrogen (Nitrate), Cadmium
Reduction Method.

Method 4500-NO[3] F, Nitrogen (Nitrate), Automated
Cadmium Reduction Method.

Method 4500-O[3] B, Ozone (Residual) (Proposed),
Indigo Colorimetric Method.

Method 4500-P E, Phosphorus, Ascorbic Acid Method.

Method 4500-P F, Phosphorus, Automated Ascorbic Acid
Reduction Method.

Method 4500-Si D, Silica, Molybdosilicate Method.

Method 4500-Si E, Silica, Heteropoly Blue Method.

Method   4500-Si   F,   Silica,   Automated   Method for
Molybdate-Reactive Silica.

Method 4500-SO[4](2-) C, Sulfate, Gravimetric Method
with Ignition of Residue.

Method 4500-SO[4](2-) D, Sulfate, Gravimetric Method
with Drying of Residue.

Method   4500-SO[4](2-)   F,   Sulfate,   Automated
Methylthymol Blue Method,

POLLUTION CONTROL BOARD

NOTICE OF PROPOSED AMENDMENTS

Method 6651, Glyphosate Herbicide (Proposed).

Method 7110 B, Gross Alpha and Beta Radioactivity
(Total, Suspended, and Dissolved), Evaporation Method
for Gross Alpha-Beta.

Method 7110 C, Gross Alpha and Beta Radioactivity
(Total, Suspended, and Dissolved), Coprecipitation
Method for Gross Alpha Radioactivity in Drinking Water
(Proposed).

Method 7500-Cs B, Radioactive Cesium, Precipitation
Method.

Method 7500-3H, B, Tritium, Liquid Scintillation
Spectrometric Method

Method 7500-I B, Radioactive Iodine, Precipitation
Method.

Method 7500-I C, Radioactive Iodine, Ion-Exchange
Method.

Method 7500-I D, Radioactive Iodine, Distillation
Method.

Method 7500-Ra B, Radium, Precipitation Method.

Method 7500-Ra C, Radium, Emanation Method.

Method 7500-Ra D, Radium, Sequential Precipitation
Method (Proposed).

Method 7500-U B, Uranium, Radiochemical Method
(Proposed).

Method 7500-U C, Uranium, Isotopic Method (Proposed).

Method 9215 B, Heterotrophic Plate Count, Pour Plate
Method.

Method 9221 A, Multiple-Tube Fermentation Technique
for Members of the Coliform Group, Introduction.

Method 9221 B, Multiple-Tube Fermentation Technique
for Members of the Coliform Group, Standard Total
Coliform Fermentation Technique.

POLLUTION CONTROL BOARD

NOTICE OF PROPOSED AMENDMENTS

Method 9221 C, Multiple-Tube Fermentation Technique
for Members of the Coliform Group, Estimation of
Bacterial Density.

Method 9221 D, Multiple-Tube Fermentation Technique
for Members of the Coliform Group, Presence-Absence
(P-A) Coliform Test.

Method 9222 A, Membrane Filter Technique for Members
of the Coliform Group, Introduction.

Method 9222 B, Membrane Filter Technique for Members
of the Coliform Group, Standard Total Coliform
Membrane Filter Procedure.

Method 9222 C, Membrane Filter Technique for Members
of the Coliform Group, Delayed-Incubation Total
Coliform Procedure.

Method 9223, Chromogenic Substrate Coliform Test
(Proposed).

Standard Methods for the Examination of Water and
Wastewater, 18th Edition Supplement, 1994 (Referred to as
"Standard Methods, 18th ed."):

Standard Methods for the Examination of Water and
Wastewater, 19th Edition, 1995 (referred to as "Standard
Methods, 19th ed."):

   Method 7120.

   Method 7500-U C, Uranium, Isotopic Method.

   Method 6610, Carbamate Pesticides.

Analytical Technology, Inc. ATI Orion, 529 Main Street, Boston,
MA 02129:

   Technical Bulletin 601, "Standard Method of Testing for
   Nitrate in Drinking Water", July 1994, PN 221890-001
   (referred to as "Technical Bulletin 601").

ASTM, American Society for Testing and Materials, 1976 Race
Street, Philadelphia, PA 19103 215-299-5585:

   ASTM Method D511-93 A and B, "Standard Test Methods for
   Calcium and Magnesium in Water", "Test Method

POLLUTION CONTROL BOARD

NOTICE OF PROPOSED AMENDMENTS

A--complexometric Titration" & "Test Method B--Atomic Absorption Spectrophotometric", approved 1993.

ASTM Method D515-88 A, "Standard Test Methods for Phosphorus in Water", "Test Method A--Colorimetric Ascorbic Acid Reduction", approved August 19, 1988.

ASTM Method D859-88 A, "Standard Test Method for Silica in Water", approved August 19, 1988.

ASTM Method D1067-92 B, "Standard Test Methods for Acidity or Alkalinity in Water", "Test Method B--Electrometric or Color-Change Titration", approved May 15, 1992.

ASTM Method D1125-91 A, "Standard Test Methods for Electrical Conductivity and Resistivity of Water", "Test Method A--Field and Routine Laboratory Measurement of Static (Non-Flowing) Samples", approved June 15, 1991.

ASTM Method D1179-93 B "Standard Test Methods for Fluouride in Water", "Test Method B--Ion Selective Electrode", approved 1993.

ASTM Method D1293-84 "Standard Test Methods for pH of Water", "Test Method A--Precise Laboratory Measurement" & "Test Method B--Routine or Continuous Measurement", approved October 26, 1984.

ASTM Method D1688-90 A or C, "Standard Test Methods for Copper in Water", "Test Method A--atomic Absorption, Direct" & "Test Method C--Atomic Absorbtion, Graphite Furnace", approved March 15, 1990.

ASTM Method D2036-91 A or B, "Standard Test Methods for Cyanide in Water", "Test Method A--Total Cyanides after Distillation" & "Test Method B--Cyanides Amenable to Chlorination by Difference", approved September 15, 1991.

ASTM Method D2459-72, "Standard Test Method for Gamma Spectrometry in Water", approved July 28, 1972, discontinued in 1988.

ASTM Method D2460-90, "Standard Test Method for Radionuclides of Radium in Water", approved 1990.

ASTM Method D2907-91, "Standard Test Methods for Microquantities of Uranium in Water by Fluorometry", "Test Method A--Direct Fluorometric" & "Test Method

POLLUTION CONTROL BOARD

NOTICE OF PROPOSED AMENDMENTS

B--Extraction", approved June 15, 1991.

ASTM Method D2972-93 B or C, "Standard Test Methods for Arsenic in Water", "Test Method B--Atomic Absorption, Hydride Generation" & "Test Method C--Atomic Absorption, Graphite Furnace", approved 1993.

ASTM Method D3223-91, "Standard Test Method for Total Mercury in Water", approved September 23, 1991.

ASTM Method D3454-91, "Standard Test Method for Radium-226 in Water", approved 1991.

ASTM Method D3559-90 D, "Standard Test Methods for Lead in Water", "Test Method D--Atomic Absorption, Graphite Furnace", approved August 6, 1990.

ASTM Method D3645-93 B, "Standard Test Methods for Beryllium in Water", "Method B--Atomic Absorption, Graphite Furnace", approved 1993.

ASTM Method D3649-91, "Standard Test Method for High-Resolution Gamma-Ray Spectrometry of Water", approved 1991.

ASTM Method D3697-92, "Standard Test Method for Antimony in Water", approved June 15, 1992.

ASTM Method D3859-93 A, "Standard Test Methods for Selenium in Water", "Method A--Atomic Absorption, Hydride Method", approved 1993.

ASTM Method D3867-90 A and B, "Standard Test Methods for Nitrite-Nitrate in Water", "Test Method A--Automated Cadmium Reduction" & "Test Method B--Manual Cadmium Reduction", approved January 10, 1990.

ASTM Method D3972-90, "Standard Test Method for Isotopic Uranium in Water by Radiochemistry", approved 1990.

ASTM Method D4107-91, "Standard Test Method for Tritium in Drinking Water", approved 1991.

ASTM Method D4327-91, "Standard Test Method for Anions in Water by Ion Chromatography", approved October 15, 1991.

Method 6610, Carbamate Pesticides.

POLLUTION CONTROL BOARD

NOTICE OF PROPOSED AMENDMENTS

ASTM Method D4785-88, "Standard Test Method for Low-Level Iodine-131 in Water", approved 1988.

ASTM Method D5174-91, "Standard Test Method for Trace Uranium in Water by Pulsed-Laser Phosphorimetry", approved 1991.

ERDA Health and Safety Laboratory, New York, NY:

HASL Procedure Manual, HASL 300, 1973. See 40 CFR 141.25(b)(2) (1995).

Great Lakes Instruments, Inc., 8855 North 55th Street, Milwaukee, WI 53223:

GLI Method 2, "Turbidity", Nov. 2, 1992.

Millipore Corporation, Technical Services Department, 80 Ashby Road, Milford, MA 01730 800-654-5476:

Colisure Presence/Absence Test for Detection and Identification of Coliform Bacteria and Escherichia Coli in Drinking Water, February 28, 1994 (referred to as "Colisure Test").

Millipore Corporation, Waters Chromatography Division, 34 Maple St., Milford, MA 01757 800-252-4752:

Waters Test Method for the Determination of Nitrite/Nitrate in Water Using Single Column Ion Chromatography, Method B-1011 (referred to as "Waters Method B-1011").

NCRP. National Council on Radiation Protection, 7910 Woodmont Ave., Bethesda, MD 301-657-2652:

"Maximum Permissible Body Burdens and Maximum Permissible Concentrations of Radionuclides in Air and in Water for Occupational Exposure", NCRP Report Number 22, June 5, 1959.

NTIS. National Technical Information Service, U.S. Department of Commerce, 5285 Port Royal Road, Springfield, VA 22161 (703) 487-4650 or (800) 553-6847:

"Interim Radiochemical Methodology for Drinking Water", EPA 600/4-75-008 (revised), March 1976 (referred to as "USEPA Interim Radiochemical Methods"). (Pages 1, 4, 6, 9, 13, 16, 24, 29, 34)

POLLUTION CONTROL BOARD

NOTICE OF PROPOSED AMENDMENTS

Method 100.1, "Analytical Method for Determination of Asbestos Fibers in Water", EPA-600/4-83-043, September, 1983, Doc. No. PB83-160471 (referred to as "USEPA Asbestos Methods-100.1").

Method 100.2, "Determination of Asbestos Structures over 10-micron in Length in Drinking Water", EPA-600/4-83-043, June, 1994, Doc. No. PB94-201902 (Referred to as "USEPA Asbestos Methods-100.2").

"Methods for Chemical Analysis of Water and Wastes", March, 1983, Doc. No. PB84-128677 (referred to as "USEPA Inorganic Methods"). (Methods 150.1, 150.2, and 245.2, which formerly appeared in this reference, are available from USEPA EMSL.)

"Methods for the Determination of Metals in Environmental Samples", June, 1991, Doc. No. PB91-231498 (referred to as "USEPA Environmental Metals Methods").

"Methods for the Determination of Organic Compounds in Drinking Water", December, 1988, revised July, 1991, EPA-600/4-88/039 (referred to as "USEPA Organic Methods"). (For methods 502.2, 505, 507, 508, 508A, 515.1 and 531.1.)

"Methods for the Determination of Organic Compounds in Finished Drinking Water--Supplement I", July, 1990, EPA-600-4-90-020 (referred to as "USEPA Organic Methods"). (For methods 506, 547, 550, 550.1, and 551.)

"Methods for the Determination of Organic Compounds in Finished Drinking Water--Supplement II", August, 1992, EPA-600/R-92-129 (referred to as "USEPA Organic Methods"). (For methods 515.2, 524.2, 548.1, 549.1, 552.1 and 555.)

"Prescribed Procedures for Measurement of Radioactivity in Drinking Water", EPA 600/4-80-032, August 1980 (referred to as "USEPA Radioactivity Methods"). (Methods 900, 901, 901.1, 902, 903, 903.1, 904, 905, 906, 908, 908.1)

"Procedures for Radiochemical Analysis of Nuclear Reactor Aqueous Solutions", H.L. Krieger and S. Gold, EPA-R4-73-014, May, 1973. Doc. No. PB222-154/7BA.

"Radiochemical Analytical Procedures for Analysis of Environmental Samples", March 1979, Doc. No., EMSLLV 053917 (referred to as "USEPA Radiochemical Analyses"). (Pages 1, 19, 33, 65, 87, 92)

POLLUTION CONTROL BOARD

NOTICE OF PROPOSED AMENDMENTS

"Radiochemistry Procedures Manual",   EPA-520/5-84-006,
December 1987, Doc. No. PB-84-215581 (referred to as "USEPA
Radiochemistry Methods"). (Methods 00-01, 00-02, 00-07,
N-02, Ra-03, Ra-04, Ra-05, Sr-04)

"Technical   Notes   on   Drinking   Water·   Methods",
EPA-600/R-94-173,   October,   1994,   Doc.   No.   PB-104766
(referred to as "USEPA Technical Notes").
BOARD NOTE: USEPA made the following assertion with regard
to this reference at 40 CFR 141.23(k)(1) and 141.24(e) and
(h)(11) (1995): This document contains other analytical
test procedures and approved analytical methods that remain
available for compliance monitoring until July 1, 1996.

"Tetra- through Octa-Chlorinated Dioxins and Furans by
Isotope Dilution HRGC/HRMS", October, 1994, EPA-821-B-94-005
(referred to as "Dioxin and Furan Method 1613").

New Jersey Department of Environment, Division of Environmental
Quality, Bureau of Radiation and Inorganic Analytical Services, 9
Ewing Street, Trenton, NJ 08625:

"Determination of Radium 228 in Drinking Water", August
1980.

New York Department of Health, Radiological Sciences Institute,
Center for Laboratories and Research, Empire State Plaza, Albany,
NY 12201:

"Determination of Ra-226 and Ra-228 (Ra-02)", January 1980,
revised June 1982.

Technicon Industrial Systems, Tarrytown, NY 10591:

"Fluoride in Water and Wastewater", Industrial Method
#129-71W, December, 1972 (referred to as "Technicon Methods:
Method #129-71W").   See 40 CFR 141.23(f)(10), footnotes 6
and 7 (1995).

"Fluoride in Water and Wastewater", #380-75WE, February,
1976 (referred   to   as   "Technicon Methods: Method
#380-75WE").   See 40 CFR 141.23(f)(10), footnotes 6 and 7
(1995).

United States Department of Energy, available at the
Environmental Measurements Laboratory, U.S. Department of Energy,
376 Hudson Street, New York, NY 10014-3621:

POLLUTION CONTROL BOARD

NOTICE OF PROPOSED AMENDMENTS

"EML Procedures Manual", 27th Edition, Volume 1, 1990.

United States Environmental Protection Agency, EMSL, Cincinnati,
OH 45268 513-569-7586:

"Interim Radiochemical Methodology for Drinking Water",
EPA-600/4-75-008 (referred to as "Radiochemical Methods").
(Revised) March, 1976.

"Methods for the Determination. of Organic Compounds in
Finished Drinking Water and Raw Source Water" (referred to
as "USEPA Organic Methods"). (For methods 504.1, 508.1, and
525.2 only.) See NTIS.

"Procedures for Radiochemical Analysis of Nuclear Reactor
Aqueous Solutions". See NTIS.

U.S. EPA, Science and Technology Branch, Criteria and Standards
Division, Office of Drinking Water, Washington D.C. 20460:

"Guidance Manual for Compliance with the Filtration and
Disinfection Requirements for Public Water Systems using
Surface Water Sources", October, 1989.

USGS, Books and Open-File Reports Section. United States
Geological Survey, Federal Center, Box 25425, Denver, CO
8025-0425:

Methods available upon request by method number from
"Methods of Analysis by the U.S. Geological Survey National
Water Quality Laboratory--Determination of Inorganic and
Organic Constituents in Water and Fluvial Sediments", Open
File Report 93-125 or Book 5, Chapter A-1, "Methods for
Determination of Inorganic Substances in Water and Fluvial
Sediments", 3d ed., Open-File Report 85-495, 1989, as
appropriate (referred to as "USGS Methods").

I-1030-85

I-1062-85

I-1601-85

I-1700-85

I-2598-85

I-2601-90

POLLUTION CONTROL BOARD

NOTICE OF PROPOSED AMENDMENTS

I-2700-85

I-3300-85

Methods available upon request by method number from "Methods for Determination of Radioactive Substances in Water and Fluvial Sediments", Chapter A5 in Book 5 of "Techniques of Water-Resources Investigation of the United States Geological Survey", 1997.

R-1110-76

R-1111-76

R-1120-76

R-1140-76

R-1141-76

R-1142-76

R-1160-76

R-1171-76

R-1180-76

R-1181-76

R-1182-76

c) The Board incorporates the following federal regulations by reference: 40 CFR 136, Appendix B and C (1995).
d) This Part incorporates no later amendments or editions.

(Source: Amended at 22 Ill. Reg. _____, effective _____)

SUBPART Q: RADIOLOGICAL MONITORING AND ANALYTICAL REQUIREMENTS

Section 611.720 Analytical Methods

a) The methods specified below, incorporated by reference in Section 611.102, are to be used to determine compliance with Sections 611.330 and 611.331, except in cases where alternative methods have been approved in accordance with Section 611.480.
1) Radiochemical Methods:

POLLUTION CONTROL BOARD

NOTICE OF PROPOSED AMENDMENTS

2) Standard Methods, 13th Edition:
A) Gross Alpha and Beta: Method 302;
B) Total Radium: Method 304;
C) Radium-226: Method 305;
D) Strontium-89,90: Method 303;
E) Tritium: Method 306;
3) ASTM Methods:
A) Cesium-134: ASTM D-2459;
B) Uranium: ASTM D-2907;
1) Gross Alpha and Beta:
A) ASTM Method 302;
B) Standard Method:
i) Method 302; or
ii) Method 7110 B;
C) USEPA Interim Radiochemical Methods: page 1;
D) USEPA Radioactivity Methods: Method 900;
E) USEPA Radiochemical Analyses: page 1;
F) USEPA Radiochemistry Methods: Method 00-01; or
G) USGS Methods: Method R-1120-76.
2) Gross Alpha:
A) Standard Methods: Method 7110 C; or
B) USEPA Radiochemistry Methods: Method 00-02.
3) Radium 226:
A) ASTM Methods:
i) Method D 2460-90; or
ii) Method D 3454-91;
B) New York Radium Method;
C) Standard Methods:
i) Method 304;
ii) Method 305;
iii) Method 7500-Ra B; or
iv) Method 7500-Ra C;
D) USDOE Methods: Method Ra-05;
E) USEPA Interim Radiochemical Methods: page 13, page 14;
F) USEPA Radioactivity Methods: Method 903, 903.1;
G) USEPA Radiochemical Analyses: page 19;
H) USEPA Radiochemistry Methods: Method Ra-03, Ra-04; or
I) USGS Methods:
i) Method R-1140-76; or
ii) Method R-1141-76.
4) Radium 228:
A) Standards Methods:
i) Method 304; or
ii) Method 7500-Ra D;
B) New York Radium Method;
C) USEPA Interim Radiochemical Methods: page 24;
D) USEPA Radioactivity Methods: Method 904;
E) USEPA Radiochemical Analyses: page 19;

POLLUTION CONTROL BOARD

NOTICE OF PROPOSED AMENDMENTS

F) USEPA Radiochemistry Methods: Method Ra-05; or
G) USGS Methods: Method R-1142-76.
5) Uranium:
  A) ASTM Methods:
    i) Method D 2907;
    ii) Method D 2907-91;
    iii) Method D 3972-90; or
    iv) Method D 5174-91;
  B) New Jersey Radium Method;
  C) USEPA Radioactivity Methods: Method 908, 908.1;
  D) USEPA Radiochemical Analyses: page 33;
  E) USEPA Radiochemistry Methods: Method 00-07; or
  F) USGS Methods:
    i) Method R-1180-76;
    ii) Method R-1181-76; or
    iii) Method R-1182-76.
6) Cesium:
  A) ASTM Methods:
    i) Method D 2459-72; or
    ii) Method D 3649-91;
  B) Standard Methods:
    i) Method 7120 (19th ed.); or
    ii) Method 7500-Cs B;
  C) USDOE Methods: Method 4.5.2.3;
  D) USEPA Interim Radiochemical Methods: page 4;
  E) USEPA Radioactivity Methods: Methods 901, 901.1;
  F) USEPA Radiochemical Analyses: page 92; or
  G) USGS Methods:
    i) Method R-1110-76; or
    ii) Method R-1111-76.
7) Iodine:
  A) ASTM Methods:
    i) D 3649-91; or
    ii) D 4785-88;
  B) Standard Methods:
    i) Method 7120 (19th ed.);
    ii) Method 7500-I B;
    iii) Method 7500-I C; or
    iv) Method 7500-I D;
  C) USDOE Methods: Method 4.5.2.3;
  D) USEPA Interim Radiochemical Methods: pages 6, 9;
  E) USEPA Radioactivity Methods: Methods 901.1, 902; or
  F) USEPA Radiochemical Analyses: page 92.
8) Strontium-89 & 90:
  A) Standard Methods:
    i) Method 303; or
    ii) Method 7500-Sr B;
  B) USDOE Methods:

POLLUTION CONTROL BOARD

NOTICE OF PROPOSED AMENDMENTS

    i) Method Sr-01; or
    ii) Method Sr-02;
  C) USEPA Interim Radiochemical Methods: page 29;
  D) USEPA Radioactivity Methods: Method 905;
  E) USEPA Radiochemical Analyses: page 65;
  F) USEPA Radiochemistry Methods: Method Sr-04; or
  G) USGS Methods: Method R-1160-76.
9) Tritium:
  A) ASTM Methods: Method D.4107-91;
  B) Standard Methods:
    i) Method 306; or
    ii) Method 7500-3H B;
  C) USEPA Interim Radiochemical Methods: page 34;
  D) USEPA Radioactivity Methods: Method 906;
  E) USEPA Radiochemical Analyses: page 87;
  F) USEPA Radiochemistry Methods: Method H-02; or
  G) USGS Methods: Method R-1171-76.
10) Gamma Emitters:
  A) ASTM Methods:
    i) Method D 3649-91; or
    ii) Method D 4785-88;
  B) Standard Methods:
    i) Method 7120 (19th ed.);
    ii) Method 7500-Cs B; or
    iii) Method 7500-I B;
  C) USDOE Method: Method 4.5.2.3;
  D) USEPA Radioactivity Methods: Methods 901, 901.1, 902;
  E) USEPA Radiochemical Analyses: page 92; or
  F) USGS Methods: Method R-1110-76.
b) When the identification and measurement of radionuclides other than those listed in subsection (a) are required, the following methods, incorporated by reference in Section 611.101, are to be used, except in cases where alternative methods have been approved in accordance with Section 611.480:
  1) "Procedures for Radiochemical Analysis of Nuclear Reactor Aqueous Solutions", available from NTIS.
  2) HASL Procedure Manual, HASL 300.
c) For the purpose of monitoring radioactivity concentrations in drinking water, the required sensitivity of the radioanalysis is defined in terms of a detection limit. The detection limit must be that concentration which can be counted with a precision of plus or minus 100 percent at the 95 percent confidence level (1.96 sigma where sigma is the standard deviation of the net counting rate of the sample).
  1) To determine compliance with Section 611.330(a) the detection limit must not exceed 1 pCi/L. To determine compliance with Section 611.330(b) the detection limit must not exceed 3 pCi/L.
  2) To determine compliance with Section 611.331 the detection limits must not exceed the concentrations listed in that Section.

POLLUTION CONTROL BOARD

NOTICE OF PROPOSED AMENDMENTS

d)   To judge compliance with the MCLs listed in Sections 611.330 and
     611.331, averages of data must be used and must be rounded to the same
     number of significant figures as the MCL for the substance in
     question.
     BOARD NOTE: Derived from 40 CFR 141.25 (1995).

(Source: Amended at   22   Ill.   Reg.   _____,   effective
_____)

POLLUTION CONTROL BOARD

NOTICE OF PROPOSED AMENDMENTS

1)   Heading of the Part: Tiered Approach to Corrective Action Objectives

2)   Code Citation: 35 Ill. Adm. Code 742

3)   Section Numbers: Proposed Action:
     742.210   Amended
     742.310   Amended
     742.415   Amended
     742.510   Amended
     742.900   Amended
     742.Appendix A.Table H   Amended
     742.Appendix B.Table C   Amended
     742.Appendix B.Table D   Amended
     742.Appendix C.Table I   Amended

4)   Statutory Authority: 415 ILCS 5/27, 28 and 58.11(c)

5)   Complete Description of the Subjects and Issues Involved: This rulemaking
     concerns amendments to 35 Ill. Adm. Code 742, Dockets (A) and (B), adopted
     by the Board on June 5, 1997, and December 4, 1997, respectively. Docket
     (A) was published in the Illinois Register on June 27, 1997, at 21 Ill.
     Reg. 7942. Docket (B) was published in the Illinois Register on December
     19, 1997, at 21 Ill. Reg. 16391. Specifically, the amendments revise
     Appendix A.Table H entitled "Chemicals Whose Tier I Class I Groundwater
     Remediation Objective Exceed the 1 in 1,000,000 Cancer Risk
     Concentration". As a consequence of changes to Appendix A.Table H,
     Appendix B.Tables C and D have been amended.

     The remaining proposed amendments revise certain Sections in Part 742 in
     order to make non-substantive grammatical, typographical, and mechanical
     changes that were identified after the adoption of Dockets (A) and (B).

     This proposal for rulemaking is being filed with the Pollution Control
     Board by the Illinois Environmental Protection Agency (Agency) in response
     to the directive of the legislature in P.A. 89-431, effective December 15,
     1995, and amended by P.A. 89-443, effective July 1, 1996. P.A. 89-431 and
     P.A. 89-443 established a Title XVII in the Environmental Protection Act
     (Act), entitled "Site Remediation Program". As a result of this proposal
     the Agency, among other things, established procedures for the development
     of risk-based remediation objectives for remediation sites (also known as
     TACO). The TACO rules were adopted on June 5, 1997 and became effective
     on July 1, 1997.

     A Tier 1 analysis requires the remediation applicant to compare
     contamination levels of constituents of concern at the remediation site to
     pre-determined remediation objectives. If any of the contaminants of
     concern exceed the pre-determined levels, the remediation applicant can
     remediate until the objectives are achieved or it can perform a Tier 2 or

POLLUTION CONTROL BOARD

NOTICE OF PROPOSED AMENDMENTS

Tier 3 remediation.

A Tier 2 analysis uses equations (Soil Screening level and Risk Based Corrective Action) set forth in the rules to develop alternative remediation objectives for constituents of concern, using site-specific information. If any contaminants of concern are found to exceed the remediation objectives using the Tier 2 equations, the remediation applicant can either remediate until the objectives are achieved or develop alternative objectives using a Tier 3 analysis.

A Tier 3 analysis allows the remediation applicant to develop remediation objectives using alternative parameters (so long as the remediation applicant provides a mathematical justification for the use of the modified or alternative parameters) not found in Tier 1 or Tier 2. If any of the contaminants of concern are found to exceed the Tier 3 remediation objectives, the remediation applicant would be required to remediate until it achieves those objectives.

6) Will this Proposed Rule Replace an Emergency Rule Currently in Effect? No

7) Does this Rulemaking Contain an Automatic Repeal Date? No

8) Does this Proposed Rule (amendment, repealer) Contain Incorporations by Reference? Yes

9) Are there any other Proposed Amendments on this Part? No

10) Statement of Policy Objectives: These proposed rules are required by P.A. 89-431 and P.A. 89-443, and do not create or enlarge a State mandate, as defined in Section 3(b) of the State Mandate Act [30 ILCS 805/3(b)].

11) Time, Place, and Manner in which Interested Person may Comment on this Proposed Rulemaking: Written comments concerning this rulemaking should reference R97-12(C), and should be sent to:

    Dorothy Gunn
    Clerk of the Pollution Control Board
    100 West Randolph Street
    Suite 11-500
    Chicago, IL 60601
    (312) 814-3620

    and

    Kimberly Robinson
    Assistant Counsel
    Illinois Environmental Protection Agency
    Division of Legal Counsel

POLLUTION CONTROL BOARD

NOTICE OF PROPOSED AMENDMENTS

    P.O. Box 19276
    Springfield, IL 62794-9276
    (217) 782-5544

Questions regarding this proposal may be addressed to: Amy Muran Felton, Staff Attorney, Illinois Pollution Control Board, 100 West Randolph Street, Suite 11-500, Chicago, IL 60601, (312)814-7011.

12) Initial Regulatory Flexibility Analysis: This proposal is mandated by Section 58.11(c) of the Environmental Protection Act [415 ILCS 5/58.11(c)], as added by P.A. 89-431, as amended by P.A. 89-443.

    A) Types of small businesses affected: The proposed tiered approach to establishing corrective action objectives would be applicable to any small business conducting remedial actions pursuant to any remediation programs under the Environmental Protection Act, including, but not limited to, the Site Remediation Program (35 Ill. Adm. Code 740), the Underground Storage Tank Program (35 Ill. Adm. Code 732) and the Resource Conservation and Recovery Program (35 Ill. Adm. Code 729.)

    B) Reporting, bookkeeping or other procedures required for compliance: None

    C) Types of professional skills necessary for compliance: None

13) Regulatory Agenda on which this Rulemaking was Summarized: This rule was not included on either of the 2 most recent agendas because: It was not anticipated at the time the 2 most recent agendas were prepared.

The Full Text of the Proposed Amendments Begin on the Next Page:

POLLUTION CONTROL BOARD

NOTICE OF PROPOSED AMENDMENTS

TITLE 35: ENVIRONMENTAL PROTECTION
SUBTITLE G: WASTE DISPOSAL
CHAPTER I: POLLUTION CONTROL BOARD
SUBCHAPTER f: RISK BASED CLEANUP OBJECTIVES

PART 742
TIERED APPROACH TO CORRECTIVE ACTION OBJECTIVES

SUBPART A: INTRODUCTION

POLLUTION CONTROL BOARD

NOTICE OF PROPOSED AMENDMENTS

POLLUTION CONTROL BOARD

NOTICE OF PROPOSED AMENDMENTS

SUBPART K: ENGINEERED BARRIERS

Section
742.1100   Engineered Barriers
742.1105   Engineered Barrier Requirements

APPENDIX A   General
ILLUSTRATION A   Developing Soil Remediation Objectives Under the Tiered Approach
ILLUSTRATION B   Developing Groundwater Remediation Objectives Under the Tiered Approach
TABLE A   Soil Saturation Limits ($C[sat]$) for Chemicals Whose Melting Point is Less Than 30°C
TABLE B   Tolerance Factor (K)
TABLE C   Coefficients {A[N-I+1]} for W Test of Normality, for N=2(1)50
TABLE D   Percentage Points of the W Test for N=3(1)50
TABLE E   Similar-Acting Noncarcinogenic Chemicals
TABLE F   Similar-Acting Carcinogenic Chemicals
TABLE G   Concentrations of Inorganic Chemicals in Background Soils
TABLE H   Chemicals Whose Tier 1 Class I Groundwater Remediation Objective Exceeds the 1 in 1,000,000 Cancer Risk Concentration
APPENDIX B   Tier 1 Tables and Illustrations
ILLUSTRATION A   Tier 1 Evaluation
TABLE A   Tier 1 Soil Remediation Objectives for Residential Properties
TABLE B   Tier 1 Soil Remediation Objectives for Industrial/Commercial Properties
TABLE C   pH Specific Soil Remediation Objectives for Inorganics and Ionizing Organics for the Soil Component of the Groundwater Ingestion Route (Class I Groundwater)
TABLE D   pH Specific Soil Remediation Objectives for Inorganics and Ionizing Organics for the Soil Component of the Groundwater Ingestion Route (Class II Groundwater)
TABLE E   Tier 1 Groundwater Remediation Objectives for the Groundwater Component of the Groundwater Ingestion Route
TABLE F   Values Used to Calculate the Tier 1 Soil Remediation Objectives for the Soil Component of the Groundwater Ingestion Route
APPENDIX C   Tier 2 Tables and Illustrations
ILLUSTRATION A   Tier 2 Evaluation for Soil
ILLUSTRATION B   Tier 2 Evaluation for Groundwater
ILLUSTRATION C   US Department of Agriculture Soil Texture Classification
TABLE A   SSL Equations
TABLE B   SSL Parameters
TABLE C   RBCA Equations
TABLE D   RBCA Parameters
TABLE E   Default Physical and Chemical Parameters
TABLE F   Methods for Determining Physical Soil Parameters
TABLE G   Error Function (erf)
TABLE H   Q/C Values by Source Area

POLLUTION CONTROL BOARD

NOTICE OF PROPOSED AMENDMENTS

TABLE I   K[oc] Values for Ionizing Organics as a Function of pH (cm(3)/g or L/kg)
TABLE J   Values to be Substituted for k[a] When Evaluating Inorganics as a Function of pH (cm(3)[water]/g[soil])
TABLE K   Parameter Estimates for Calculating Water-Filled Soil Porosity (Omega[w])

AUTHORITY: Implementing Sections 22.4, 22.12, Title XVI, and Title XVII and authorized by Sections 27, 57.14, and 58.5 of the Environmental Protection Act (415 ILCS 5/22.4, 22.12, 27, 57.14 and 58.5 and Title XVI and Title XVII].

SOURCE: Adopted in R97-12(A) at 21 Ill. Reg. 7942, effective July 1, 1997; amended in R97-12(B) at 21 Ill. Reg. 16391, effective December 8, 1997; amended in R97-12(C) at 22 Ill. Reg. _____, effective _____.

Note: In this Part, superscript numbers or letters are denoted by parentheses; subscript are denoted by brackets; SUM means the summation series or sigma function as used in mathematics; and the English words Alpha, Lambda and Omega are substituted for the Greek symbols because of computer program limitations.

SUBPART B: GENERAL

Section 742.210 Incorporations by Reference

a) The Board incorporates the following material by reference:

ASTM. American Society for Testing and Materials, 1916 Race Street, Philadelphia, PA 19103, (215) 299-5400

ASTM D 2974-87, Standard Test Method for Moisture, Ash and Organic Matter of Peat and Other Organic Soils, approved May 29, 1987 (reapproved 1995).

ASTM D 2488-93, Standard Practice for Description and Identification of Soils (Visual-Manual Procedure), approved September 15, 1993.

ASTM D 1556-90, Standard Test Method for Density and Unit Weight of Soil in Place by the Sand-Cone Method, approved June 29, 1990.

ASTM D 2167-94, Standard Test Method for Density and Unit Weight of Soil in Place by the Rubber Balloon Method, approved March 15, 1994.

ASTM D 2922-91, Standard Test Methods for Density of Soil and Soil-Aggregate in Place by Nuclear Methods (Shallow Depth), approved December 23, 1991.

POLLUTION CONTROL BOARD

NOTICE OF PROPOSED AMENDMENTS

ASTM D 2937-94, Standard Test Method for Density of Soil in Place by the Drive-Cylinder Method, approved June 15, 1994.

ASTM D 854-92, Standard Test Method for Specific Gravity of Soils, approved November 15, 1992.

ASTM D 2216-92, Standard Method for Laboratory Determination of Water (Moisture) Content of Soil and Rock, approved June 15, 1992.

ASTM D 4959-89, Standard Test Method for Determination of Water (Moisture) Content of Soil by Direct Heating Method, approved June 30, 1989 (reapproved 1994).

ASTM D 4643-93, Standard Test Method for Determination of Water (Moisture) Content of Soil by the Microwave Oven Method, approved July 15, 1993.

ASTM D 5084-90, Standard Test Method for Measurement of Hydraulic Conductivity of Saturated Porous Materials Using a Flexible Wall Permeameter, approved June 29, 1990.

ASTM D 422-63, Standard Test Method for Particle-Size Analysis of Soils, approved November 21, 1963 (reapproved 1990).

ASTM D 1140-92, Standard Test Method for Amount of Material in Soils Finer than the No. 200 (75 um) Sieve, approved November 15, 1992.

ASTM D 3017-88, Standard Test Method for Water Content of Soil and Rock in Place by Nuclear Methods (Shallow Depth), approved May 27, 1988.

ASTM D 4525-90, Standard Test Method for Permeability of Rocks by Flowing Air, approved May 25, 1990.

ASTM D 2487-93, Standard Test Method for Classification of Soils for Engineering Purposes, approved September 15, 1993.

ASTM E 1527-93, Standard Practice for Environmental Site Assessments: Phase I Environmental Site Assessment Process, approved March 15, 1993. Vol. 11.04.

ASTM E 1739-95, Standard Guide for Risk-Based Corrective Action Applied at Petroleum Release Sites, approved September 10, 1995.

Barnes, Donald G. and Dourson, Michael. (1988). Reference Dose (RfD): Description and Use in Health Risk Assessments. Regulatory

POLLUTION CONTROL BOARD

NOTICE OF PROPOSED AMENDMENTS

Toxicology and Pharmacology. 8, 471-486.

GPO. Superintendent of Documents, U.S. Government Printing Office, Washington, DC 20401, (202) 783-3238.

USEPA Guidelines for Carcinogenic Risk Assessment, 51 Fed. Reg. 33992-34003 (September 24, 1986).

"Test Methods for Evaluating Solid Waste, Physical/Chemical Methods", USEPA Publication number SW-846 (Third Edition, November 1986), as amended by Updates I and IIA (Document No. 955-001-00000-1)(contact USEPA, Office of Solid Waste, for Update IIA).

"Methods for the Determination of Organic Compounds in Drinking Water", EPA Publication No. EPA/600/4-88/039 (December 1988 (Revised July 1991)).

"Methods for the Determination of Organic Compounds in Drinking Water, Supplement II", EPA Publication No. EPA/600/R-92/129 (August 1992).

"Methods for the Determination of Organic Compounds in Drinking Water, Supplement III", EPA Publication No. EPA/600/R-95/131 (August 1995).

IRIS. Integrated Risk Information System, National Center for Environmental Assessment, U.S. Environmental Protection Agency, 26 West Martin Luther King Drive, MS-190, Cincinnati, OH 45268, (513) 569-7254.

"Reference Dose (RfD): Description and Use in Health Risk Assessments", Background Document 1A (March 15, 1993).

"EPA Approach for Assessing the Risks Associated with Chronic Exposures to Carcinogens", Background Document 2 (January 17, 1992).

Nelson, D.W., and L.E. Sommers. 1982. Total carbon, organic carbon, and organic matter. In: A.L. Page (ed.), Methods of Soil Analysis. Part 2. Chemical and Microbiological Properties. 2nd Edition, pp. 539-579, American Society of Agronomy. Madison, WI.

NTIS. National Technical Information Service, 5285 Port Royal Road, Springfield, WA 22161, (703) 487-4600.

"Dermal Exposure Assessment: Principles and Applications", EPA Publication No. EPA/600/8-91/011B (January 1992).

POLLUTION CONTROL BOARD

NOTICE OF PROPOSED AMENDMENTS

"Exposure Factors Handbook", EPA Publication No. EPA/600/8-89/043 (July 1989).

"Risk Assessment Guidance for Superfund, Vol. I; Human Health Evaluation Manual, Supplemental Guidance: Standard Default Exposure Factors", OSWER Directive 9285.6-03 (March 1991).

"Rapid Assessment of Exposure to Particulate Emissions from Surface Contamination Sites", EPA Publication No. EPA/600/8-85/002 (February 1985), PB 85-192219.

"Risk Assessment Guidance for Superfund, Volume I; Human Health Evaluation Manual (Part A)", Interim Final, EPA Publication No. EPA/540/1-89/002 (December 1989).

"Risk Assessment Guidance for Superfund, Volume I; Human Health Evaluation Manual, Supplemental Guidance, Dermal Risk Assessment Interim Guidance", Draft (August 18, 1992).

"Soil Screening Guidance: Technical Background Document", EPA Publication No. EPA/540/R-95/128, PB96-963502 (May 1996).

"Soil Screening Guidance: User's Guide", EPA Publication No. EPA/540/R-96/018, PB96-963505 (April 1996).

Superfund Exposure Assessment Manual", EPA Publication No. EPA/540/1-88/001 (April 1988).

RCRA Facility Investigation Guidance, Interim Final, developed by USEPA (EPA 530/SW-89-031), 4 volumes, May 1989.

b) CFR (Code of Federal Regulations). Available from the Superintendent of Documents, U.S. Government Printing Office, Washington, D.C. 20402, (202)783-3238:

     40 CFR 761.120 (1993).

c) This Section incorporates no later editions or amendments.

(Source: Amended at 22 Ill. Reg. _____, effective _____)

Section 742.310 Inhalation Exposure Route

The inhalation exposure route may be excluded from consideration if:
a) The requirements of Sections 742.300 and 742.305 are met; and
b) An institutional control, in accordance with Subpart J, is in place that meets the following requirements:
    1) Either:
       A) The concentration of any contaminant of concern _within ten_

POLLUTION CONTROL BOARD

NOTICE OF PROPOSED AMENDMENTS

feet of the land surface or _within_ "_un feet of_ any man-made pathway shall not exceed the Tier 1 remediation objective under Subpart E for the inhalation exposure route; or
     B) An engineered barrier, as set forth in Subpart K and approved by the Agency, is in place; and
    2) Requires safety precautions for the construction worker if the Tier 1 construction worker remediation objectives are exceeded.

(Source: Amended at 22 Ill. Reg. _____, effective _____)

SUBPART D: DETERMINING AREA BACKGROUND

Section 742.415 Use of Area Background Concentrations

a) A person may request that area background concentration ~~concentrations~~ determined pursuant to Sections 742.405 and 742.410 be used according to the provisions of subsection (b) of this Section. Such request shall address the following:
    1) The natural or man-made pathways of any suspected off-site contamination reaching the site;
    2) Physical and chemical properties of suspected off-site contaminants of concern reaching the site; and
    3) The location and justification of all background sampling points.
b) Except as specified in subsections (c) and (d) of this Section, an area background concentration may be used as follows:
    1) To support a request to exclude a chemical as a contaminant of concern from further consideration for remediation at a site due to its presence as a result of background conditions; or
    2) As a remediation objective for a contaminant of concern at a site in lieu of objectives developed pursuant to the other procedures of this Part.
c) An area background concentration shall not be used _in the_ event that _the Agency has determined in writing_ that _the background level for a regulated substance poses an acute_ threat _to human health or the environment at the site when considering the post-remedial action land use._ (Section 58.5(b)(3) of the Act)
d) _In the event that the concentration of a regulated substance of concern on the site exceeds a remediation objective adopted by the Board for residential land use, the property may not be converted to residential use unless such remediation objective or an alternative risk-based remediation objective for that regulated substance of concern is first achieved._ If the land use is restricted, there shall be an institutional control in place in accordance with Subpart J. (Section 58.5(b)(2) of the Act)

(Source: Amended at 22 Ill. Reg. _____, effective _____)

POLLUTION CONTROL BOARD

NOTICE OF PROPOSED AMENDMENTS

SUBPART E: TIER 1 EVALUATION

Section 742.510 Tier 1 Remediation Objectives Tables

a) Soil remediation objectives are listed in Appendix B, Tables A, B, C and D.
   1) Appendix B, Table A is based upon residential property use.
      A) The first column to the right of the chemical name lists soil remediation objectives for the soil ingestion exposure route.
      B) The second column lists the soil remediation objectives for the inhalation exposure route.
      C) The third and fourth columns list soil remediation objectives for the soil component of the groundwater ingestion exposure route for the respective classes of groundwater:
         i) Class I groundwater; and
         ii) Class II groundwater.
      D) The final column lists the Acceptable Detection Limit (ADL), only where applicable.
   2) Appendix B, Table B is based upon industrial/commercial property use.
      A) The first and third columns to the right of the chemical name list the soil remediation objectives for the soil ingestion exposure route based on two receptor populations:
         i) Industrial/commercial; and
         ii) Construction worker.
      B) The second and fourth columns to the right of the chemical name list the soil remediation objectives for the inhalation exposure route based on two receptor populations:
         i) Industrial/commercial; and
         ii) Construction worker.
      C) The fifth and sixth columns to the right of the chemical name list the soil remediation objectives for the soil component of the groundwater ingestion exposure route for two classes of groundwater:
         i) Class I groundwater; and
         ii) Class II groundwater.
   3) Appendix B, Tables C and D set forth pH specific soil remediation objectives for inorganic and ionizing organic chemicals for the soil component of the groundwater ingestion route.
      A) Table C sets forth remediation objectives based on Class I groundwater and Table D sets forth remediation objectives based on Class II groundwater.
      B) The first column in Tables C and D lists the chemical names.
      C) The second through ninth columns to the right of the chemical names list the pH based soil remediation objectives.

POLLUTION CONTROL BOARD

NOTICE OF PROPOSED AMENDMENTS

   4) For the inorganic chemicals listed in Appendix B, Tables A and B, the soil component of the groundwater ingestion exposure route shall be evaluated using TCLP (SW-846 Method 1311) or SPLP (SW-846 Method 1312), incorporated by reference at Section 742.210 unless a person chooses to evaluate the soil component on the basis of the total amount of contaminant in a soil sample result in accordance with subsection (a)(5) of this Section.
   5) For those inorganic and ionizing organic chemicals listed in Appendix B, Tables C and D, if a person elects to evaluate the soil component of the groundwater ingestion exposure route based on the total amount of contaminant in a soil sample result (rather than TCLP or SPLP analysis), the person shall determine the soil pH at the site and then select the appropriate soil remediation objectives based on Class I and Class II groundwaters from Tables C and D, respectively. If the soil pH is less than 4.5 or greater than 8.0, then Tables C and D cannot be used.
   6) Unless one or more exposure routes are excluded from consideration under Subpart C, the most stringent soil remediation objective of the exposure routes (i.e., soil ingestion exposure route, inhalation exposure route, and soil component of the groundwater ingestion exposure route) shall be compared to the concentrations of soil contaminants of concern measured at the site. When using Appendix B, Table B to select soil remediation objectives for the ingestion exposure route and inhalation exposure route, the remediation objective shall be the more stringent soil remediation objective of the industrial/commercial populations and construction worker populations.
   7) Confirmation sample results may be averaged or soil samples may be composited in accordance with Section 742.325.
   8) If a soil remediation objective for a chemical is less than the ADL, the ADL shall serve as the soil remediation objective.
b) Groundwater remediation objectives for the groundwater component of the groundwater ingestion exposure route are listed in Appendix B, Table E. However, Appendix B, Table E must be corrected for the cumulative effect of mixtures of similar-acting noncarcinogenic chemicals as set forth in Section 742.505(b)(3).
   1) The first column to the right of the chemical name lists groundwater remediation objectives for Class I groundwater, and the second column lists the groundwater remediation objectives for Class II groundwater.
   2) To use Appendix B, Table E of this Part, the 35 Ill. Adm. Code 620 classification for groundwater at the site shall be determined. The concentrations of groundwater contaminants of concern at the site are compared to the applicable Tier 1 groundwater remediation objectives for the groundwater component of the groundwater ingestion exposure route in Appendix B, Table E.

POLLUTION CONTROL BOARD

NOTICE OF PROPOSED AMENDMENTS

c) For contaminants of concern not listed in Appendix B, Tables A, B and
    E, a person may request site-specific remediation objectives from the
    Agency or propose site-specific remediation objectives in accordance
    with 35 Ill. Adm. Code 620, Subpart I of this Part, or both.

(Source: Amended at   22   Ill. Reg. _____,   effective
_____)

SUBPART I: TIER 3 EVALUATION

Section 742.900 Tier 3 Evaluation Overview

a) Tier 3 sets forth a flexible framework to develop remediation
    objectives outside of the requirements of Tiers 1 and 2. Although
    Tier 1 and Tier 2 evaluations are not prerequisites to conduct Tier 3
    evaluations, data from Tier 1 and Tier 2 can assist in developing
    remediation objectives under a Tier 3 evaluation.
b) The level of detail required to adequately characterize a site depends
    on the particular use of Tier 3. Tier 3 can require additional
    investigative efforts beyond those described in Tier 2 to characterize
    the physical setting of the site. However, in situations where
    remedial efforts have simply reached a physical obstruction additional
    investigation may not be necessary for a Tier 3 submittal.
c) Situations that can be considered for a Tier 3 evaluation include, but
    are not limited to:
    1) Modification of parameters not allowed under Tier 2;
    2) Use of models different from those used in Tier 2;
    3) Use of additional site data to improve or confirm predictions of
        exposed receptors to contaminants of concern;
    4) Analysis of site-specific risks using formal risk assessment,
        probabilistic data analysis, and sophisticated fate and transport
        models (e.g., requesting a target hazard quotient greater than 1
        or a target cancer risk greater than 1 in 1,000,000);
    5) Requests for site-specific remediation objectives because an
        assessment indicates further remediation is not practical;
    6) Incomplete human exposure pathway(s) not excluded under Subpart
        C;
    7) Use of toxicological-specific information not available from the
        sources listed in Tier 2;
    8) Land uses which are substantially different from the assumed
        residential or industrial/commercial property uses of a site
        (e.g., a sm site will be used for recreation in the future and
        cannot be evaluated in Tiers 1 or 2); and .
    9) Requests for site-specific remediation objectives which exceed
        Tier 1 groundwater remediation objectives so long as   the
        following is demonstrated:
        A) *To the extent practical, the exceedance of the groundwater
            quality standard has been minimized and beneficial use*

POLLUTION CONTROL BOARD

NOTICE OF PROPOSED AMENDMENTS

            *appropriate to the groundwater that was impacted has been
            returned; and*
        B) *Any threat to human health or the environment has been
            minimized.* [Section 58.5(D)(4)(A) of the Act)
d) 'For requests of a target cancer risk ranging between 1 in 1,000,000
    and 1 in 10,000 at the point of human exposure or a target hazard
    quotient greater than 1 at the point of human exposure, the
    requirements of Section 742.915 shall be followed. Requests for a
    target cancer risk exceeding 1 in 10,000 at the point of human
    exposure are not allowed.
e) Requests for approval of a Tier 3 evaluation must be submitted to the
    Agency for review under the specific program under which remediation
    is performed. When reviewing a submittal under Tier 3, the Agency
    shall consider *whether the interpretations and conclusions reached are
    supported by the information gathered.* [Section 58.7(e)(1) of the
    Act] *The agency shall approve a Tier 3 evaluation if the person
    submits the information required under this Part and establishes
    through such information that public health is protected and that
    specified risks to human health and the environment have been
    minimized.*

(Source: Amended at   22   Ill.   Reg. _____,   effective
_____)

Section 742.APPENDIX A General

Section 742.TABLE H Chemicals Whose Tier 1 Class I Groundwater Remediation
Objective Exceeds the 1 in 1,000,000 Cancer Risk Concentration

Chemical	Class I Groundwater Remediation Objective (mg/l)	1 in 1,000,000 Cancer Risk Concentration (mg/l)	ADL (mg/l)
Aldrin	0.00004	0.0000052	0.00004
Benzo(a)pyrene	0.0002	0.00000125	0.00023
Bis(2-chloroethyl)ether	0.01	0.0000778	0.01
Bis(2-ethylhexyl)phthalate	0.006	0.00618	0.0027
Carbon Tetrachloride	0.005	0.000669	0.00003
Chlordane	0.002	0.0000668	0.00014
Dibenzo(a,h)anthracene	0.0003	0.00001205	0.0003
1,2-Dibromo-3-chloropropane	0.0002	0.000061B	0.0002
1,2-Dibromoethane	0.00005	0.0000010B4	0.00005
3,3'-Dichlorobenzidine	0.02	0.000180B	0.02
1,2-Dichloroethane	0.005	0.000944	0.00003
Dieldrin	0.00002	0.0000053B	0.00002
Heptachlor	0.0004	0.0000196B	0.00003
Heptachlor epoxide	0.0002	0.00000944	0.00032
Hexachlorobenzene	0.00002	0.000053B	0.00006
alpha-HCH	0.00003	0.0000146B	0.00003
Tetrachloroethylene	0.005	0.00169B	0.00001
Toxaphene	0.003	0.0000778	0.00086
Vinyl chloride	0.002	0.00004545	0.00006

Ionizable Organics

N-Nitrosodiphenylamine	0.01	0.0178B	0.01
N-Nitrosodi-n-propylamine	0.01	0.00001205	0.01
Pentachlorophenol	0.001	0.000713	0.001
2,4,6-Trichlorophenol	0.0064	0.00077B	0.0064

Inorganics

Arsenic	0.05	0.0000527B	0.001
Beryllium	0.004	0.0000288B3	0.004

    (Source: Amended   at   22   Ill.   Reg. _____, effective

Section 742.APPENDIX B Tier 1 Tables and Illustrations

Section 742.TABLE C pH Specific Soil Remediation Objectives for Inorganics and
Ionizing Organics for the Soil Component of the Groundwater Ingestion Route
(Class I Groundwater)

POLLUTION CONTROL BOARD

NOTICE OF PROPOSED AMENDMENTS

POLLUTION CONTROL BOARD

NOTICE OF PROPOSED AMENDMENTS

(Source: Amended   at   22   Ill.   Req.   __
_____).

Chemical (totals) (mg/kg)	pH 4.5 to 4.74	pH 4.75 to 5.24	pH 5.25 to 5.74	pH 5.75 to 6.24	pH 6.25 to 6.64	pH 6.65 to 6.89	pH 6.9 to 7.24	pH 7.25 to 7.74	pH 7.75 to 8.0
Thallium	1.6	1.8	2.0	2.4	2.6	2.8	3.0	3.4	3.8
Vanadium	980	980	980	980	980	980	980	980	980
Zinc	1,000	1,800	2,600	3,600	5,100	6,200	7,500	16,000	53,000
Organics									
Benzoic Acid	440	420	410	400	400	400	400	400	400
2-Chlorophenol	4.0	4.0	4.0	4.0	3.9	3.9	3.9	3.6	3.1
2,4-Dichlorophenol	1.0	1.0	1.0	1.0	1.0	1.0	1.0	0.86	0.69
Dinoseb	8.4	4.5	1.9	0.82	0.43	0.34	0.31	0.27	0.25
Pentachlorophenol	0.54	0.32	0.15	0.07	0.04	0.03	0.02	0.02	0.02
2,4,5-TP (Silvex)	26	16	12	11	11	11	11	11	11
2,4,5-Trichlorophenol	400	390	390	370	320	270	230	130	64
2,4,6-Trichlorophenol	0.37	0.36	0.34	0.262	0.20	0.15	0.13	0.09	0.07

POLLUTION CONTROL BOARD

NOTICE OF PROPOSED AMENDMENTS

Section 742.TABLE D pH Specific Soil Remediation Objectives for Inorganics and Ionizing Organics for the Soil Component of the Groundwater Ingestion Route (Class II Groundwater)

Chemical (totals) (mg/kg)	pH 4.5 to 4.74	pH 4.75 to 5.24	pH 5.25 to 5.74	pH 5.75 to 6.24	pH 6.25 to 6.64	pH 6.65 to 6.89	pH 6.9 to 7.24	pH 7.25 to 7.74	pH 7.75 to 8.0
Inorganics									
Antimony	20	20	20	20	20	20	20	20	20
Arsenic	100	100	100	110	110	120	120	120	120
Barium	260	490	850	1,200	1,500	1,600	1,700	1,800	2,100
Beryllium	140	260	420	820	2,800	7,900	17,000	130,000	1,000,000
Cadmium	10	17	27	37	52	75	110	590	4,300
Chromium (+6)	No Data	No Data	No Data	No Data	No Data	No Data	No Data	No Data	No Data
Copper	330	580	2,100	11,000	59,000	130,000	200,000	330,000	330,000
Cyanide	120	120	120	120	120	120	120	120	120
Mercury	0.05	0.06	0.14	0.75	4.4	10	16	32	40
Nickel	400	730	1,100	1,500	2,000	2,600	3,500	14,000	76,000
Selenium	24	17	12	8.8	6.3	5.2	4.5	3.3	2.4
Thallium	16	18	20	24	26	28	30	34	38
Zinc	2,000	3,600	5,200	7,200	10,000	12,000	15,000	32,000	110,000

POLLUTION CONTROL BOARD

NOTICE OF PROPOSED AMENDMENTS

mical (totals) /kg	pH 4.5 to 4.74	pH 4.75 to 5.24	pH 5.25 to 5.74	pH 5.75 to 6.24	pH 6.25 to 6.64	pH 6.65 to 6.89	pH 6.9 to 7.24	pH 7.25 to 7.74	pH 7.75 to 8.0
ganics									
zoic Acid	440	420	410	400	400	400	400	400	400
hlorophenol	20	20	20	20	20	20	19	3.6	3.1
-hlorophenol	1.0	1.0	1.0	1.0	1.0	1.0	1.0	0.86	0.69
1oseb	84	45	19	8.2	4.3	3.4	3.1	2.7	2.5
tachlorophenol	2.7	1.6	0.75	0.33	0.18	0.15	0.12	0.11	0.10
,5-TP (Silvex)	130	79	62	57	55	55	55	55	55
,5-ichlorophenol	2,000	2,000	1,900	1,800	1,600	1,400	1,200	640	64
1,6-ichlorophenol	0.37 0.36 0.34 0.36 0.20 0.15 1.9 1.8 1.7 1.4 1.0 0.72						0.13	0.09	0.07

97

TION CONTROL BOARD

F PROPOSED AMENDMENTS

2   Ill.   Reg.   _____,   effective

POLLUTION CONTROL BOARD

NOTICE OF PROPOSED AMENDMENTS

Section 742.APPENDIX C Tier 2 Tables and Illustrations

Section 742.TABLE I K[oc] Values for Ionizing Organics as a Function of pH (cm(3)/g or L/kg)

pH	Benzoic Acid	2-Chloro-phenol	2,4-Dichloro-phenol	Pentachloro-phenol	2,4,5-Trichloro-phenol	2,4,6-Trichloro-phenol	Dinoseb	2,3,5-TP (Silvex)
4.5	1.07E+01	3.98E+02	1.59E+02	1.34E+04	2.37E+03	1.06E+03	3.00E+04	1.29E+04
4.6	9.16E+00	3.98E+02	1.59E+02	1.24E+04	2.37E+03	1.05E+03	2.77E+04	1.13E+04
4.7	7.79E+00	3.98E+02	1.59E+02	1.13E+04	2.37E+03	1.05E+03	2.41E+04	1.01E+04
4.8	6.58E+00	3.98E+02	1.59E+02	1.02E+04	2.37E+03	1.05E+03	2.12E+04	9.16E+03
4.9	5.54E+00	3.98E+02	1.59E+02	9.05E+03	2.37E+03	1.04E+03	1.85E+04	8.40E+03
5.0	4.64E+00	3.98E+02	1.59E+02	7.96E+03	2.36E+03	1.03E+03	1.59E+04	7.76E+03
5.1	3.88E+00	3.98E+02	1.59E+02	6.93E+03	2.36E+03	1.03E+03	1.36E+04	7.30E+03
5.2	3.25E+00	3.98E+02	1.59E+02	5.97E+03	2.35E+03	1.01E+03	1.15E+04	6.91E+03
5.3	2.72E+00	3.98E+02	1.59E+02	5.10E+03	2.34E+03	9.99E+02	9.66E+03	6.60E+03
5.4	2.29E+00	3.98E+02	1.58E+02	4.32E+03	2.33E+03	9.82E+02	8.10E+03	6.36E+03
5.5	1.94E+00	3.97E+02	1.58E+02	3.63E+03	2.32E+03	9.62E+02	6.77E+03	6.18E+03
5.6	1.65E+00	3.97E+02	1.58E+02	3.05E+03	2.31E+03	9.39E+02	5.65E+03	6.00E+03
5.7	1.43E+00	3.97E+02	1.58E+02	2.58E+03	2.29E+03	9.10E+02	4.73E+03	5.88E+03
5.8	1.24E+00	3.97E+02	1.58E+02	2.18E+03	2.27E+03	8.77E+02	3.97E+03	5.78E+03
5.9	1.09E+00	3.97E+02	1.57E+02	1.84E+03	2.24E+03	8.39E+02	3.35E+03	5.70E+03

POLLUTION CONTROL BOARD

NOTICE OF PROPOSED AMENDMENTS

pH	Benzoic Acid	2-Chloro-phenol	2,4-Dichloro-phenol	Pentachloro-phenol	2,4,5-Trichloro-phenol	2,4,6-Trichloro-phenol	Dinoseb	2,3,5-TP (Silvex)
6.0	9.69E-01	3.96E+02	1.57E+02	1.56E+03	2.21E+03	7.96E+02	2.84E+03	5.64E+03
6.1	8.73E-01	3.96E+02	1.57E+02	1.33E+03	2.17E+03	7.48E+02	2.43E+03	5.59E+03
6.2	7.59E-01	3.96E+02	1.56E+02	1.15E+03	2.12E+03	6.91E+02	2.10E+03	5.55E+03
6.3	7.36E-01	3.95E+02	1.55E+02	9.98E+02	2.06E+03	6.44E+02	1.83E+03	5.53E+03
6.4	6.89E-01	3.94E+02	1.54E+02	8.77E+02	1.99E+03	5.99E+02	1.63E+03	5.50E+03
6.5	6.51E-01	3.93E+02	1.53E+02	7.81E+02	1.91E+03	5.33E+02	1.45E+03	5.48E+03
6.6	6.20E-01	3.93E+02	1.52E+02	7.03E+02	1.82E+03	4.80E+02	1.32E+03	5.46E+03
6.7	5.95E-01	3.90E+02	1.50E+02	6.40E+02	1.71E+03	4.29E+02	1.21E+03	5.45E+03
6.8	5.76E-01	3.88E+02	1.47E+02	5.93E+02	1.60E+03	3.81E+02	1.13E+03	5.44E+03
6.9	5.60E-01	3.86E+02	1.45E+02	5.52E+02	1.47E+03	3.38E+02	1.05E+03	5.43E+03
7.0	5.47E-01	3.83E+02	1.41E+02	5.21E+02	1.34E+03	3.00E+02	9.96E+02	5.43E+03
7.1	5.38E-01	3.79E+02	1.38E+02	4.96E+02	1.21E+03	2.67E+02	9.52E+02	5.42E+03
7.2	5.32E-01	3.75E+02	1.33E+02	4.76E+02	1.07E+03	3.39E+02	9.18E+02	5.42E+03
7.3	5.25E-01	3.69E+02	1.28E+02	4.61E+02	9.43E+02	2.15E+02	8.90E+02	5.42E+03
7.4	5.19E-01	3.62E+02	1.21E+02	4.43E+02	8.19E+02	1.95E+02	8.68E+02	5.41E+03
7.5	5.16E-01	3.54E+02	1.34E+02	4.37E+02	7.03E+02	1.78E+02	8.50E+02	5.41E+03
7.6	5.13E-01	3.44E+02	1.07E+02	4.29E+02	2.99E+02	1.64E+02	8.36E+02	5.41E+03

POLLUTION CONTROL BOARD

NOTICE OF PROPOSED AMENDMENTS

H	Benzoic Acid	2-Chloro-phenol	2,4-Dichloro-phenol	Pentachloro-phenol	2,4,5-Trichloro-phenol	2,4,6-Trichloro-phenol	Dinoseb	2,3,5-TP (Silvex)
.7	5.09E-01	3.33E+02	9.84E+01	4.23E+02	5.07E+02	1.53E+02	8.25E+02	5.41E+03
.8	5.06E-01	3.19E+02	8.97E+01	4.18E+02	4.26E+02	1.44E+02	8.17E+02	5.41E+03
.9	5.06E-01	3.04E+02	8.07E+01	4.14E+02	3.57E+02	1.37E+02	8.10E+02	5.41E+03
.0	5.06E-01	2.86E+02	7.17E+01	4.10E+02	2.98E+02	1.31E+02	8.04E+02	5.41E+03

POLLUTION CONTROL BOARD

NOTICE OF PROPOSED AMENDMENTS

(Source: Amended at 22 Ill. Reg. _____, effective
_____)

ILLINOIS RACING BOARD

NOTICE OF PROPOSED AMENDMENTS

1) Heading of the Part: Pari-Mutuels

2) Code Citation: 11 Ill. Adm. Code 300

3) Section Numbers: Proposed Action:
   300.100   Amendment

4) Statutory Authority: 230 ILCS 5/9(b)

5) A Complete Description of the Subjects and Issues Involved: This
   rulemaking requires the licensees to provide complaint forms at all
   information windows.

6) Will these proposed amendments replace emergency amendments currently in
   effect? No

7) Does this rulemaking contain an automatic repeal date? No

8) Do these proposed amendments contain incorporation by reference? No

9) Are there any other proposed amendments pending in this Part? No

10) Statement of Statewide Policy Objectives: No local governmental units
    will be required to increase expenditures.

11) Time, Place and Manner in which interested persons may comment on this
    proposed rulemaking: Written comments should be submitted, within 45 days
    after this notice, to:

        Gina DiCaro
        Illinois Racing Board
        Legal Department
        100 West Randolph, Ste. 11-100
        Chicago, IL 60601
        (312) 814-5070

12) Initial Regulatory Flexibility Analysis:

    A) Types of small business affected: None

    B) Reporting, bookkeeping or other procedures required for compliance:
       None

    C) Types of professional skills necessary for compliance: None

13) Regulatory Agenda which this rulemaking was summarized: This rulemaking
    was not included on either of the 2 most recent agendas because: This
    rulemaking was not anticipated by the Board.

ILLINOIS RACING BOARD

NOTICE OF PROPOSED AMENDMENTS

The full text of the proposed amendment begins on the next page:

ILLINOIS RACING BOARD

NOTICE OF PROPOSED AMENDMENTS

TITLE 11: ALCOHOL, HORSE RACING, AND LOTTERY
SUBTITLE B: HORSE RACING
CHAPTER I: ILLINOIS RACING BOARD
SUBCHAPTER a: GENERAL RULES

PART 300
PARI-MUTUELS

Section
300.10   General
300.20   Records
300.30   Pari-Mutuel Tickets
300.40   Pari-Mutuel Wagers
300.50   Pari-Mutuel Races
300.60   Advanced Wagering
300.70   Scratches or Non-Starter
300.80   Pools Dependent Upon Betting Interests
300.90   Minimum Payoff
300.100   Pari-Mutuel Complaints

AUTHORITY: Implementing and authorized by Section 9(b) of the Illinois Horse
Racing Act of 1975 [230 ILCS 5/9(b)].

SOURCE: Adopted at 19 Ill. Reg. 13935, effective October 1, 1995; emergency
amendment at 20 Ill. Reg. 12522, effective September 1, 1996, for a maximum of
150 days; amended at 21 Ill. Reg. 955, effective January 7, 1997; amended at 22
Ill. Reg. _____, effective _____.

Section 300.100 Pari-Mutuel Complaints

a) Illinois Racing Board complaint forms shall be made available to the public
by all licensees at the information window. Upon receiving any such complaint
form, the licensee shall submit a copy to the Board with a statement of the
action taken, if any, or proposed action to be taken by the licensee.
b) All licensees shall submit every complaint report to the State
Director of Mutuels within 48 hours after the complaint is made.

(Source: Amended at 22 Ill. Reg. _____, effective

ILLINOIS RACING BOARD

NOTICE OF PROPOSED AMENDMENTS

1) Heading of the Part: Programs

2) Code Citation: 11 Ill. Adm. Code 415

3) Section Numbers: Proposed Action:
   415.10   Amendments

4) Statutory Authority: 230 ILCS 5/9(b)

5) A Complete Description of the Subjects and Issues Involved: This rulemaking requires licensees to notify patrons, in the official program, that complaint forms are available at the information window. Also, this rulemaking removes the provision requiring information on the Special Purse and Reward Fund to be contained in the official program.

6) Will these proposed amendments replace emergency amendments currently in effect? No

7) Does this rulemaking contain an automatic repeal date? No

8) Do these proposed amendments contain incorporation by reference? No

9) Are there any other proposed amendments pending in this Part? No

10) Statement of Statewide Policy Objectives: No local governmental units will be required to increase expenditures.

11) Time, Place and Manner in which interested persons may comment on this proposed rulemaking: Written comments should be submitted, within 45 days after this notice, to:

    Gina DiCaro
    Illinois Racing Board
    Legal Department
    100 West Randolph, Ste. 11-100
    Chicago, IL 60601
    (312) 814-5070

12) Initial Regulatory Flexibility Analysis:

    A) Types of small business affected: None

    B) Reporting, bookkeeping or other procedures required for compliance: None

    C) Types of professional skills necessary for compliance: None

13) Regulatory Agenda which this rulemaking was summarized: This rulemaking

ILLINOIS RACING BOARD

NOTICE OF PROPOSED AMENDMENTS

was not included on either of the 2 most recent agendas because: This rulemaking was not anticipated by the Board.

The full text of the proposed amendment begins on the next page:

ILLINOIS RACING BOARD

NOTICE OF PROPOSED AMENDMENTS

TITLE 11: ALCOHOL, HORSE RACING, AND LOTTERY
SUBTITLE B: HORSE RACING
CHAPTER I: ILLINOIS RACING BOARD
SUBCHAPTER b: RULES APPLICABLE TO ORGANIZATION LICENSEES

PART 415
PROGRAMS

Section
415.10   Required Information
415.20   Supply Information for Patrons (Repealed)
415.30   Thoroughbred Programs
415.40   Harness Programs
415.50   Quarterhorse Programs
415.60   Availability of Programs
415.70   Distribution of Programs

AUTHORITY: Implementing and authorized by Section 9(b) of the Illinois Horse
Racing Act of 1975 [230 ILCS 5/9(b)].

SOURCE: Adopted at 4 Ill. Reg. 43, effective October 20, 1980; codified at 5
Ill. Reg. 10900; emergency amendment at 7 Ill. Reg. 16201, effective November
28, 1983, for a maximum of 150 days; amended at 8 Ill. Reg. 5698, effective
April 16, 1984; amended at 14 Ill. Reg. 11314, effective July 3, 1990; amended
at 16 Ill. Reg. 7486, effective April 24, 1992; amended at 18 Ill. Reg. 17756,
effective November 28, 1994; amended at 19 Ill. Reg. 12691, effective September
1, 1995; amended at 21 Ill. Reg. 12208, effective September 1, 1997; amended at
22 Ill. Reg. _____, effective _____.

Section 415.10 Required Information

Programs shall contain the following information:
    a) A statement that the race meeting is conducted pursuant to a license
        issued by the Board and pursuant to the rules and regulations of the
        Board.
    b) The address and telephone number of the central office of the Board.
    c) The names of the Board members, the officers and directors of the
        organization licensee, and Board and track racing officials.
    d) The post time of the first pari-mutuel race of each program.
    e) The--information--specified--in--Section--415.60-regarding-the-Special
        Purse-and-Reward-Fund.
    e)f) A symbol identifying the horses that have been administered
        furosemide prior to each race and, where applicable, a different
        symbol identifying horses that have been administered furosemide for
        the first time.
    f)g) A notice specifying the exact location of information and/or
        complaint window or windows for the convenience of the patrons.
    g)h) A clear, conspicuous statement of the racing organization's election

ILLINOIS RACING BOARD

NOTICE OF PROPOSED AMENDMENTS

        to impose a surcharge under Section 26.3 of the Horse Racing Act of
        1975.
    h)i) A brief description of the pari-mutuel wagering system.
    i)j) A statement that wagers are to be made by program number and not by
        post position or handicap rating number.
    j)k) A statement that pay-offs are not permitted until the stewards have
        notified the pari-mutuel department of the official order of finish.
    k)l) A statement that tickets should be retained until the official
        results have been posted.
    l)m) A statement that the Illinois Racing Board rules and complaint forms
        are available for--public--inspection at the information and/or
        complaint window and at the office of the Illinois Racing Board.

(Source: Amended   at   22   Ill.   Reg.   _____,   effective
_____.)

TEACHERS' RETIREMENT SYSTEM OF THE STATE OF ILLINOIS

NOTICE OF PROPOSED AMENDMENTS

1) **Heading of the Part:** The Administration and Operation of the Teachers' Retirement System

2) **Code Citation:** 80 Ill. Adm. Code 1650

3) **Section Numbers:**   **Proposed Action:**
   1650.290   Amendment
   1650.346   New Section
   1650.350   Amendment
   1650.360   Amendment
   1650.480   New Section
   1650.575   New Section
   1650.595   New Section
   1650.1000   Amendment
   1650.1010   Amendment
   1650.1030   Amendment
   1650.1040   Amendment
   1650.1050   Amendment

4) **Statutory Authority:** Implementing and authorized by Article 16 of the Illinois Pension Code [40 ILCS 5/Art. 16]; Freedom of Information Act [5 ILCS 140]; Internal Revenue Code [26 U.S.C. 1 et seq.]; Section 5-15 of the Illinois Administrative Procedure Act [5 ILCS 100/5-15].

5) **A Complete Description of the Subjects and Issues Involved:** Section 1650.290 is being amended to remove those portions of the rule dealing with the collection of member overpayments, which will be covered in new Section 1650.595.

Section 1650.346 defines terms used in 40 ILCS 5/16-127(b)(5)(iv), which was added by P.A. 90-32 and which gives teachers who left teaching prior to 1983 to adopt an infant under age three the right to purchase optional service credit.

Section 1650.350 is being amended to allow members to receive a bonus based upon unused sick days if the bonus is paid post-retirement and is not included in the members' final average salary calculation.

Section 1650.360 is being amended to inform employers and employees exactly what is needed in settlement agreements and judgment orders to have salary reported to and receive service credit from the System.

Section 1650.480 is a new rule explaining under what circumstances the System will allow funds to be "rolled over" into the System to purchase optional service or to repay prior refunds.

Section 1650.575 defines the term "full-time student" used in 40 ILCS 5/16-140(4), which was added by P.A. 90-448 and which provides increased

TEACHERS' RETIREMENT SYSTEM OF THE STATE OF ILLINOIS

NOTICE OF PROPOSED AMENDMENTS

survivor benefits to dependent children ages 18 to 27 who are full-time students.

Section 1650.595 establishes the collection parameters for receivables of the System from members, annuitants or beneficiaries who received benefits in excess of the amount due them. The collection parameters are in harmony with the recently adopted rules of the Debt Collection Board and the authorizing language of 30 ILCS 210/5 and recognize the somewhat unique nature of those receivables.

Sections 1650.1000, 1650.1010, 1650.1030, 1650.1040, and 1650.1050 are being amended to shorten the candidate petition circulation period to 180 days prior to election; adopt an envelope-within-an-envelope vote by mail system; and to accommodate voting for a possible annuitant trustee position.

6) **Will this proposed amendment replace an emergency amendment currently in effect?** Yes

7) **Does this rulemaking contain an automatic repeal date?** No

8) **Does this proposed amendment contain incorporations by reference?** No

9) **Are there any other proposed amendments pending on this Part?** No

10) **Statement of Statewide Policy Objectives:** Not Applicable

11) **Time, Place, and Manner in which interested persons may comment on this proposed rulemaking:** Comments on the proposed amendment may be submitted in writing for a period of 45 days following publication of this Notice to:

   Carl Mowery, General Counsel
   Erin Smith, Legal Assistant
   Teachers' Retirement System
   2815 West Washington, P. O. Box 19253
   Springfield, Illinois 62794-9253
   (217) 753-0961

12) **Initial Regulatory Flexibility Analysis:** These rules will not affect small businesses.

   A) **Types of small businesses, small municipalities and not for profit corporations affected:** None

   B) **Reporting, bookkeeping or other procedures required for compliance:** None

TEACHERS' RETIREMENT SYSTEM OF THE STATE OF ILLINOIS

NOTICE OF PROPOSED AMENDMENTS

C) Types of professional skills necessary for compliance: None

13) Regulatory Agenda on which this rulemaking was summarized: July 1997

The full text of the Proposed Amendments begin on the next page:

TEACHERS' RETIREMENT SYSTEM OF THE STATE OF ILLINOIS

NOTICE OF PROPOSED AMENDMENTS

TITLE 80: PUBLIC OFFICIALS AND EMPLOYEES
SUBTITLE D: RETIREMENT SYSTEMS
CHAPTER III: TEACHERS' RETIREMENT SYSTEM OF
THE STATE OF ILLINOIS

PART 1650
THE ADMINISTRATION AND OPERATION OF THE
TEACHERS' RETIREMENT SYSTEM

SUBPART A: REPORTS BY BOARD OF TRUSTEES

TEACHERS' RETIREMENT SYSTEM OF THE STATE OF ILLINOIS

NOTICE OF PROPOSED AMENDMENTS

TEACHERS' RETIREMENT SYSTEM OF THE STATE OF ILLINOIS

NOTICE OF PROPOSED AMENDMENTS

TEACHERS' RETIREMENT SYSTEM OF THE STATE OF ILLINOIS

NOTICE OF PROPOSED AMENDMENTS

SUBPART M: RETIREMENT BENEFITS

Section
1650.2900 Excess Benefit Arrangement

AUTHORITY: Implementing and authorized by Article 16 of the Illinois Pension Code [40 ILCS 5/Art. 16]; Freedom of Information Act [5 ILCS 140]; Internal Revenue Code [26 U.S.C. 1 et seq.)]; Section 5-15 of the Illinois Administrative Procedure Act [5 ILCS 100/5-15].

SOURCE: Filed June 20, 1958; emergency rules adopted at 2 Ill. Reg. 49, p. 249, effective November 29, 1978, for a maximum of 150 days; adopted at 3 Ill. Reg. 9, p. 1, effective March 3, 1979; codified at 8 Ill. Reg. 16350; amended at 9 Ill. Reg. 20885, effective December 17, 1985; amended at 12 Ill. Reg. 16896, effective October 3, 1988; amended at 14 Ill. Reg. 18305, effective October 29, 1990; amended at 15 Ill. Reg. 16731, effective November 5, 1991; amended at 17 Ill. Reg. 1631, effective January 22, 1993; amended at 18 Ill. Reg. 6349, effective April 15, 1994; emergency amendment at 18 Ill. Reg. 8949, effective May 24, 1994, for a maximum of 150 days; emergency modified at 18 Ill. Reg. 12880; amended at 18 Ill. Reg. 15154, effective September 27, 1994; amended at 20 Ill. Reg. 3118, effective February 5, 1996; emergency amendment at 21 Ill. Reg. 483, effective January 1, 1997, for a maximum of 150 days; amended at 21 Ill. Reg. 2422, effective January 31, 1997; amended at 21 Ill. Reg. 4844, effective March 27, 1997; emergency amendment at 21 Ill. Reg. _____, effective December 5, 1997, for a maximum of 150 days; amended at 22 Ill. Reg. _____, effective _____.

SUBPART C: FILING OF CLAIMS

Section 1650.290 Offsets

a) Benefits received by a member under the Workers' Compensation Act [820 ILCS 305] or the Workers' Occupational Diseases Act [820 ILCS 310] with respect to a disability shall be applied as an offset against any occupational disability benefit provided by the System with respect to the same accident, illness or disease.

1) If the amount of compensation received is less than the monthly benefit provided under the Illinois Pension Code, only the amount of the excess of such monthly benefit over the amount of such compensation shall be payable by the System. If the amount of compensation received equals or exceeds the monthly benefit provided under the Illinois Pension Code, no benefit shall be payable by the System during the period compensation is paid under the Workers' Compensation Act or Workers' Occupational Diseases Act.

2) If the compensation for disability or death is received in a commuted lump sum or partly in a commuted lump sum and partly in monthly or weekly sums, the System shall, for offset purposes,

TEACHERS' RETIREMENT SYSTEM OF THE STATE OF ILLINOIS

NOTICE OF PROPOSED AMENDMENTS

consider the compensation as if it had been paid at a weekly rate as prescribed under the Workers' Compensation Act or Workers' Occupational Diseases Act.

3) In the event the whole or any part of the benefits received under the Workers' Compensation Act or Workers' Occupational Diseases Act is commuted into one sum, the aggregate sum of the benefits so commuted and not the commuted value thereof shall be used for purposes of ascertaining the amount of offset.

4) The amount considered for offset purposes shall not be reduced by any legal expenses granted from the award to the member.

5) An offset shall not be applied to medical expenses paid on behalf of or to the claimant.

b) Whenever--the--System--determines--benefits--except--for--an--impermissible refund-as-defined-in-Section-1650.240,-have-been-paid--erroneously--or in--an--excess-amount-greater-than-$50.00,-the-System-shall-record-such overpayment-as-an-accounts-receivable-and-notify-the--payee--or--other person-from-whom-repayment-is-expected-of-the-amount-due.

c) Interest--shall--accrue--at--the-statutory-rate-beginning-on-the-first-day of--the--month--following-30-days-from-the-date-of-notification-by-the System-with-the-exception-of:

1) Those-balances-owed-for--overpayment--of--disability--retirement annuity--resulting--from-excess-earned-income-which-are-recovered in-full--in--the--calendar--year--in--which--the--overpayment--is determined;-and

2) Any-overpayments-with-a-beginning-balance-of-less-than-$1,000.

d) The--overpayment--will--be--collected-in-accordance-with-the-following criteria:

1) Overpayment-to-benefit-recipient.--The-amount-owed-must-be-repaid to-the-System--in--a--lump--sum--or--by--offset--against--monthly benefits;--however,--the--payment-schedule-shall-not-exceed-sixty months.--Minimum-monthly-payments-will-be-set--according--to--the following-scale-based-on-monthly-benefit-level:

A) If--the--benefit-recipient's-gross-monthly-benefit-is-$1,000 or-less,-the-minimum-monthly-payment-by-offset-is--equal--to 5%-of-the-gross;

B) If--the--benefit-recipient's-gross-monthly-benefit-is-more than-$1,000--but--less--than--$2,501,--the--minimum--monthly payment-by-offset-is-equal-to-7.5%-of-the-gross;

C) If--the--benefit-recipient's-gross-monthly-payment-by-offset or-more,-the-minimum-monthly-payment-by-offset-is--equal--to 10%-of-the-gross;

2) Overpayment--to--current--contributing--or--inactive-member.--The amount-owed-must-be-repaid-in-a-lump-sum;-in-monthly-payments--by check--or--money--order;--or--by--offset--against--future-benefits payable-to-the-overpaid-individual--unless--the--overpayment--is required--to-be-collected-from-the-individual's-beneficiaries-in which-case--it--will--be--collected--according--to--the--terms--of subsection--(d)(3)--below).---If--by--offset-against-the-overpaid

TEACHERS' RETIREMENT SYSTEM OF THE STATE OF ILLINOIS

NOTICE OF PROPOSED AMENDMENTS

individual's-future-benefits,-at-the--time--the--benefits--become
payable-the-minimum-monthly-payments-will-be-determined-according
to--the--scale--and--schedule--set-forth-in-subsection--(d)(1)(A)
through-(d)(1)(C)-above.

3) Overpayment-to-benefit-recipient-now-deceased,--to--be--collected
    from-beneficiaries.

    A) If-the-beneficiary-is-the-recipient-of-monthly-benefits,-the
        amount-owed-must-be-repaid-in-the-same-manner,-involving-the
        same--payment--options,--as--the--schedule-of-repayments-for
        overpaid-contributing-or--inactive--members,--set--forth--in
        subsection--(d)(1)-above,-provided,-however,-that-no-payment
        schedule-may--exceed--the--projected--life--of--the--benefit
        entitlements,--For--example,--if-the-beneficiary-is-a-minor
        child,--the--repayment--must--be--completed--before--the
        beneficiary-reaches-majority.

    B) If--the--beneficiary--is-the-recipient-of-a-lump-sum-benefit
        only,-the-System-will--impose--a--full--offset--up--to--and
        including--if--necessary--the--full-amount-of-the-lump-sum
        benefit.

4) The-System-will-pursue-collection-through--any--available--means
    including--seeking--the--assistance--of-the-Attorney-General,-the
    Debt-Collection-Board,-or-private-collection-agencies,

5) In-any-cases-in-which-fraud-is-suspected-in--connection--with--an
    overpayment,--the--System--will--enlist--the--aid-of-the-Attorney
    General-or-such--law--enforcement--agency--or--prosecutor--having
    appropriate--jurisdiction--for--a--determination-whether-fraud-has
    occurred,--and,--if--it--has,--for--further--official--action--as
    necessary-and-appropriate,

(Source: Amended at 22   Ill.   Reg. _____,   effective
_____)

SUBPART D: MEMBERSHIP AND SERVICE CREDITS

Section 1650.346 Service Credit for Periods Away From Teaching Due to Adoption

a) Service credit of up to three years shall be granted for periods
    beginning prior to July 1, 1983, during which a teacher ceased covered
    employment for the purpose of adopting an infant under three years of
    age or caring for a newly adopted infant under three years of age.

b) For purposes of determining eligibility to receive optional service
    credit under the provisions of 40 ILCS 5/16-127(b)(5)(iv), the
    following definitions shall apply:

    1) "Ceased covered employment" shall mean the submission of a
        resignation that terminated employment in a position requiring
        membership contributions to the System as a condition of
        employment.

    2) "For the purpose of adopting an infant under three years of age"

TEACHERS' RETIREMENT SYSTEM OF THE STATE OF ILLINOIS

NOTICE OF PROPOSED AMENDMENTS

        shall mean the termination of covered employment:

        A) to meet the requirements of an adoption agency or similar
            entity resulting in the adoption of an infant who is under
            the age of three at the time the member terminates covered
            employment; or

        B) to formally commence judicial or administrative proceedings
            to adopt an infant who is under the age of three at the time
            the adoption proceedings were initiated; or

        C) to care for an infant under the age of three while an
            adoption proceeding is ongoing which results in the adoption
            of the infant.

    3) "Caring for a newly adopted infant under three years of age"
        shall mean providing care to an adopted infant of less than three
        years of age when the interruption of service begins within 180
        days of the court order declaring the member the adoptive parent
        of such an infant.

    4) "Teaching service creditable under this System or the State
        Universities Retirement System" means employment in a position
        requiring membership contributions to the System or the State
        Universities Retirement System as a condition of employment.

c) The documents necessary to establish service credit under this Section
    shall include:

    1) Employment records;

    2) Birth certificates;

    3) Court records;

    4) Adoption agency records;

    5) Governmental records; and/or

    6) Other documentation, such as corroborating affidavits, that are
        based upon actual knowledge and are sufficiently specific as to
        times, dates, places and surrounding circumstances so that the
        proof of service submitted to the System reliably documents the
        service credit to be established while eliminating the
        possibility of mistake or fraud.

d) For purposes of granting service credit for periods away from teaching
    due to adoption, the statutory return-to-teaching requirement is met
    when the member returns to teaching service creditable under this
    System or the State Universities Retirement System for the period the
    member was away from teaching due to adoption or one year, whichever
    is less.

(Source: Added at 22 Ill. Reg. _____,   effective
_____)

Section 1650.350 Service Credit for Unused Accumulated Sick Leave Upon
Retirement

a) To be creditable for retirement purposes, sick leave days must
    actually be available for use by a member in the event of illness.

TEACHERS' RETIREMENT SYSTEM OF THE STATE OF ILLINOIS

NOTICE OF PROPOSED AMENDMENTS

Service credit is not available and shall not be computed for sick leave days added to the record of a member for the purpose of increasing a member's retirement service credit. To determine if any sick leave days granted by an employer in excess of the member's normal annual sick leave allotment during a member's final years of employment are actually available for use and reportable to the System as service credit, the System shall apply the following formula:

1) from the date upon which the sick leave days were granted, the number of days remaining in the school term or the member's employment agreement, whichever is greater, until termination shall be determined;

2) from the resulting number of days the System shall subtract the number of sick leave days previously accrued by the member; and

3) the difference is the maximum number of sick leave days that may be reported in addition to those days previously accrued, provided that the employer will allow the member to use such days in the event of illness prior to termination.

b) Unused and uncompensated sick leave days are not eligible for service credit at retirement when the member receives direct compensation for such days. Direct compensation means payment of salary, wages, fringe benefits, contributions, bonuses and lump sum payments before or after retirement. Notwithstanding the foregoing provisions of this subsection (b), a member is not deemed compensated if his or her employer maintains or establishes a reward system (based upon daily attendance of employees) which pays additional benefits to a member (including but not limited to salary) and which does not reduce the accumulated sick leave days available for use and credited to the member by the employer. Effective July 1, 1998, if a member receives payment of ~~any kind~~ for accumulated sick leave days that is also reportable to the System as creditable earnings ~~before or after termination~~, no service credit shall be available for the days so compensated.

c) For purposes of calculating a retirement annuity, the System shall not grant service credit for accumulated sick leave days withdrawn by the member from a sick leave bank in excess of the days deposited therein and unused by the member.

d) Accumulated personal leave days are governed by the same standards set forth in subsections (a) and (h) above for sick leave days, but only if they were actually available for use by a member in the event of illness.

e) Accumulated, unused vacation days are not creditable with the System.

(Source: Amended at 22 Ill. Reg. _____, effective _____)

Section 1650.360 Settlement Agreements and Judgments ~~Service and Earnings Credit Obtained Pursuant to Labor Contract Litigation~~

TEACHERS' RETIREMENT SYSTEM OF THE STATE OF ILLINOIS

NOTICE OF PROPOSED AMENDMENTS

a) In the event a member and employer enter into a settlement agreement to resolve employment issues which affect service and earnings credit, the following provisions shall govern the computation of creditable service and the reporting of creditable earnings. ~~When a member loses service credit and creditable earnings as a result of a disputed dismissal or suspension and a judgment or agreement is entered resulting in an award or agreed amount of settlement to the member to compensate the member for lost salary during the period of the dismissal or suspension, service and earnings credit shall be granted provided:~~

~~1) the award or settlement agreement identifies the time period for which the member should have received service credit and the amount of salary allocable under the award or agreement to each school term; and~~

~~2) the required contributions are paid within one year after the award or agreement; otherwise interest shall be charged at the applicable statutory rate from the date of the award or agreement as specified in Section 16-113 of the Act.~~

b) To ensure the reportability of service and earnings credit in settlement agreements covering a retroactive time period, the settlement agreement must contain the following: ~~Provided, however if the cash award or settlement amount is either more or less than what the member's salary rate would have been for the time period in question, the contributions shall be assessed against that which the member would have earned had the dispute not occurred.~~

1) the time period for which the member would have received salary or service credit;

2) a statement the settlement is an award of back salary; and

3) the amount of salary the member would have been paid during the period covered by the settlement agreement had the employment issue not arisen.

c) Contributions on retroactive settlement agreements are based upon the salary a member would have otherwise earned but for the employment issue.

d) All required contributions due on retroactive settlement agreements must be paid within one year after the date of the settlement agreement; otherwise interest shall be charged at the applicable statutory rate from the date of the settlement agreement.

e) To ensure the reportability of service and earnings credit in settlement agreements covering a prospective time period, the settlement agreement must contain the following:

1) the time period for which the member is to receive service credit, not to exceed one year;

2) a statement confirming the member is to be employed as a teacher;

3) a statement that the member will continue to receive the same salary on regular pay dates and fringe benefits to which he or she would be entitled.

4) If a resignation date is contained in the settlement agreement,

TEACHERS' RETIREMENT SYSTEM OF THE STATE OF ILLINOIS

NOTICE OF PROPOSED AMENDMENTS

it must not be prior to the end of the time period covered by the settlement agreement.

f) Service credit is not presumed available nor salary presumed reportable for prospective settlement agreements covering in excess of one year.

g) To ensure the reportability of service and earnings credit awarded pursuant to a judgment of a court of competent jurisdiction, the judgment order must contain:
   1) the time period for which the court determines the member should have received salary or service credit.
   2) a statement the judgment is an award of salary.
   3) the amount of salary the member would have received during the period covered by the judgment.

h) Contributions on judgments are based upon the salary a member would have otherwise earned but for the issue being litigated.

(Source: Amended   at   22   Ill.   Reg.   _____,   effective
_____)

SUBPART E: CONTRIBUTION CREDITS AND PAYMENTS

Section 1650.480 Rollovers to the System

a) The System may accept a rollover initiated by a member as payment for optional service credit, to repay a refund, or to pay the member contribution required to retire without discount. For a rollover to be accepted by the System, the following conditions must be met:
   1) the member must establish an account receivable with the System prior to initiating the rollover;
   2) the rollover must be from an "eligible retirement plan" as defined in subsection (b) below and not jeopardize the System's tax exempt status or create adverse consequences for the System;
   3) the rollover must be an "eligible rollover distribution" described in section 402(c) of the Internal Revenue Code (26 U.S.C. Section 402(c)) and the Treasury Regulations promulgated thereunder;
   4) the rollover funds must belong solely to the member, and not to any other person including, without limitation, a spouse, unless the member obtains the funds as the result of a Qualified Domestic Relations Order (QDRO);
   5) the amount of the rollover does not exceed the amount due the System; and
   6) the member has provided the System with a rollover certification, confirming that the rollover does not contain any deductible member contributions.

b) For purposes of this Section, the term "eligible retirement plan" shall mean any tax qualified plan under Code Section 401(a) and 403(a) (26 U.S.C. Sections 401(a), 403(a)) or a conduit individual

TEACHERS' RETIREMENT SYSTEM OF THE STATE OF ILLINOIS

NOTICE OF PROPOSED AMENDMENTS

retirement account/annuity as provided in Code Section 408 (26 U.S.C. Section 408).

c) Prior to accepting any transfers to which this Section applies, the System may require the member to establish that the amounts to be transferred to the System meet the requirements of this Section and may also require the member to provide an opinion of counsel satisfactory to the System that the amounts to be transferred meet the requirements of this Section.

d) The acceptance of a rollover shall be subject to any Regulations, Procedures, or other guidance issued by the Internal Revenue Service.

e) A member's rights with respect to the rollover contributions shall be 100 percent vested and nonforfeitable.

(Source: Added   at   22   Ill.   Reg.   _____,   effective
_____)

SUBPART F: RULES GOVERNING ANNUITANTS AND BENEFICIARIES

Section 1650.575 Full-time Student - Receipt of Survivors Benefits Until Age 22

a) For purposes of 40 ILCS 5/16-140(4), a full-time student shall be one who is enrolled in a course of study in an accredited educational institution (other than a program of study by correspondence), and who is carrying a full-time workload as determined by the educational institution during the regular school year for the course of study the student is pursuing.

b) Accredited educational institutions include schools, colleges, universities, and post-secondary vocational institutions whose courses of study are approved by appropriate state or federal educational accreditation authorities.

c) A regular school year is the eight to nine months which includes two semester terms or three quarter terms (or their equivalent), excluding the summer term. Terms that begin after April 15 and before September 16 are considered summer terms.

d) Survivors benefits shall be payable during the period between regular school years if the benefit recipient was a full-time student the preceding semester term or quarter term (or their equivalent).

e) To verify that an eligible child is a full-time student, the System must receive a certification signed by an official of the educational institution confirming that the student is a full-time student as provided in subsection (a) above.

(Source: Added   at   22   Ill.   Reg.   _____,   effective
_____)

Section 1650.595 Overpayments

TEACHERS' RETIREMENT SYSTEM OF THE STATE OF ILLINOIS

NOTICE OF PROPOSED AMENDMENTS

a) When the System determines benefits, except for an impermissible
    refund as defined in Section 1650.240, have been paid erroneously in
    an amount greater than $50 to a member, annuitant or beneficiary
    (recipient), the System shall record such overpayment as an accounts
    receivable and make demand upon the recipient for the amount due.
b) Interest shall accrue on overpayments at the rate of 0.83% per month
    beginning on the first day of the month following 30 days from the
    date of notification to the recipient of the overpayment.
c) The System shall use its best efforts to ensure repayment of
    overpayments within 36 months of such overpayment.
d) If the recipient of an overpayment fails to repay the amount due plus
    any applicable interest within 36 months, the System will collect any
    amount plus applicable interest outstanding at the time the recipient
    next receives a benefit from the System by withholding 10% of the
    recipient's gross payment, if a periodic payment, including any
    reciprocal system payments, or 100% if a lump sum payment.
e) The System shall retain the option to refer any debt due the System to
    the Attorney General, the Debt Collection Board, the Comptroller's
    Offset System, or private collection agencies at any time it deems
    appropriate.

(Source: Added   at   22   Ill.   Reg. _____,   effective
_____)

SUBPART L: BOARD ELECTION PROCEDURES

Section 1650.1000 Nomination of Candidates

a) Any candidate for a vacant teacher position on the System's Board of
    Trustees shall be nominated by a written petition signed by no fewer
    than 500 individuals who, as of the date of signing, were teachers as
    defined in Section 16-106 of the Illinois Pension Code [40 ILCS
    5/16-106].
b) Any candidate for a vacant annuitant position on the System's Board of
    Trustees shall be nominated by a written petition signed by no fewer
    than 500 individuals who, as of the date of signing, were teachers as
    defined in Section 16-111.1 of the Illinois Pension Code [40 ILCS
    5/16-111.1].
c) Petitions may be circulated for signatures by any individual or entity
    for a period of time commencing the November 1 immediately preceding
    the election date and ending with at-any-time-during-the--school--term
    in--which--the--election-is-held-and-prior-to the time for filing such
    petition with the Board's secretary as provided in subsection (b)(5)
    of Section 1650.1010.
d) An individual eligible to sign a petition nominating a candidate for a
    vacant teacher position on the Board may sign petitions for as many
    candidates as desired.
e) An individual eligible to sign a petition nominating a candidate for a

TEACHERS' RETIREMENT SYSTEM OF THE STATE OF ILLINOIS

NOTICE OF PROPOSED AMENDMENTS

    vacant annuitant position on the Board may sign petitions for as many
    candidates as desired.

(Source: Amended   at   22   Ill.   Reg. _____,   effective
_____)

Section 1650.1010 Petitions

a) All petitions shall be in the form adopted by the System. Petition
    forms may be obtained from the System, upon request of any individual
    or entity.
b) A valid petition nominating a candidate for a vacant teacher position
    or a vacant annuitant position on the System's Board of Trustees shall
    meet the following requirements:
    1) The-petition-must-be-in-writing;
    1)2) The petition must bear the requisite number of original
        signatures of individuals eligible to nominate the candidate
        pursuant to subsection (a) or (b) of Section 1650.1000. A valid
        petition may consist of multiple pages and may contain blank
        signature lines; however, all valid signatures thereon must be
        original signatures;
    2)3) Each signature of an eligible voter must be accompanied by the
        signing person's name, and printing the person's full name,
        street address, city, and state;
    3)4) The petition shall bear the notarized signature of the
        individual who circulated the petition for signatures, verifying
        that the signatures contained thereon were signed in that
        individual's presence, are genuine, and that to the best of the
        circulating individual's knowledge, the persons who signed the
        petition were eligible to do so as provided in subsection (a) or
        (b) of Section 1650.1000;
    4)5) Petitions shall be filed with the Board's secretary not less
        than 90 nor more than 120 days prior to the election day;
    5)6) Petitions filed less than 90 days prior to the election day are
        invalid and will be returned to the party submitting such
        petition for filing; and
    6)7) Petitions filed more than 120 days prior to the election day
        will not be accepted and will be returned to the party submitting
        such petition for filing. Nothing in this subsection precludes
        the timely re-filing of petitions filed more than 120 days prior
        to the election day.
c) The Board's secretary shall determine the validity of all petitions
    not less than 75 days prior to the election day.
d) Any individual may, upon reasonable notice to the System, examine the
    petitions which have been filed with the System with respect to the
    election to take place that year; provided, however, that in order to
    protect the signing teachers' and annuitants' rights to privacy and
    confidentiality as to their names, addresses, and social security

TEACHERS' RETIREMENT SYSTEM OF THE STATE OF ILLINOIS

NOTICE OF PROPOSED AMENDMENTS

numbers, such examination shall only take place subject to the following limitations:

1) Petitions may only be examined at the System's offices after the validity of the petitions has been verified by the Board's secretary as provided above in subsection (c) of this Section;

2) Petitions may not be removed from the System's offices, copied, or duplicated by any means; and

3) Petitions, including any information thereon, shall not be subject to production or disclosure under the provisions of the Illinois Freedom of Information Act (FOIA) [5 ILCS 140].

(Source: Amended at 22 Ill. Reg. _____, effective _____)

Section 1650.1030 Election Materials

a) At least 10 days prior to the election day, the System shall mail to the eligible voter's latest address known to the System the following election materials:

1) A preprinted, perforated ballot/signature card listing, in alphabetical order, either the teacher candidates or the annuitant candidates, depending on the basis for the individual's eligible voter status as provided in Section 1650.1020(a) or (b); and

2) A preprinted, return envelope addressed to the System's Board; and ~perforated~with~one~section~marked~"For~Ballot~~Only,"~~and the~other~section~marked~"For~Signature~Card~Only."

3) A preprinted envelope marked "For Ballot Only."

b) If an eligible voter has not received any or all of the election materials specified in subsection (a) of this Section prior to the election day, the eligible voter may request that the System send election materials to him or her. Upon~such~request,~the~System~shall verify~that~the~requesting~individual~is~an~eligible~voter~as~provided in~Section~1650.1020,~~and~upon~such~verification~shall~send~the eligible~voter~a~written~certification~of~nonreceipt~in~the~form prescribed~by~the~System.~~The~eligible~voter~shall~complete~the certification~attesting~to~nonreceipt~of~election~materials~and~return it~to~the~System.

1) Upon such request, the System shall verify that the requesting individual is an eligible voter as provided in Section 1650.1020, and upon such verification shall send the eligible voter a written certification of nonreceipt in the form prescribed by the System and the election materials via first class U.S. mail, or if the election is less than one week away, via priority U.S. mail.

2) The eligible voter shall complete the certification attesting to nonreceipt of election materials and attach it to the signature card.

TEACHERS' RETIREMENT SYSTEM OF THE STATE OF ILLINOIS

NOTICE OF PROPOSED AMENDMENTS

c)~~Upon~~receipt~~of~~the~~certification~~of~nonreceipt~provided~above~in subsection~(b)~~of~~this~~Section,~~the~~System~~shall~~mail~~election materials~~to~the~requesting~eligible~voter~via~first~class~U.S.~mail, or~if~the~election~is~less~than~one~week~away,~via~priority~U.S.~mail. All~requirements~imposed~by~Section~~1650.1040~~regarding~~marking~~of ballots~~and~~by~~Section~~1650.1050~regarding~return~of~ballots~shall remain~applicable.

c) If previously mailed election materials are returned to the System undelivered at least one week prior to the election day and a forwarding address has been provided, the System shall mail election materials to the forwarding address via first class U.S. mail.

(Source: Amended at 22 Ill. Reg. _____, effective _____)

Section 1650.1040 Marking of Ballots

A valid ballot must conform to the following requirements:

a) All choices of candidates must be indicated by a cross mark consisting of two lines which intersect inside the square immediately before the name of the selected candidate. If two lines do not intersect inside the square, the mark is invalid and will not be counted;

b) Each eligible voter is entitled to only one vote for any particular candidate;

c) With respect to a ballot where there are two trustees to be elected, each eligible voter may vote for only one candidate for each position to be elected containing~the~names~of~candidates~for~a~vacant~teacher position~on~the~board,~no~more~than~two~candidates~~may~~be~~selected. If more than two candidates are selected, the ballot is invalid and will not be counted. If only one candidate is selected, the selection will count as only one vote; and

d)~~With~respect~to~a~ballot~containing~the~names~of~candidates~for~a vacant~annuitant~position~on~the~board,~no~more~than~one~candidate~may be~selected.~~~~If~more~than~one~candidate~is~selected,~the~ballot~is invalid~and~will~not~be~counted;~and

d) Handwritten entries of candidates are invalid and will not be counted.

(Source: Amended at 22 Ill. Reg. _____, effective _____)

Section 1650.1050 Return of Ballots

a) Upon receipt of the election materials specified above in Section 1650.1030, the eligible voter shall:

1) Mark his or her ballot in accordance with Section 1650.1040;

2) Write his or her signature, and address, and social security number on the signature card;

TEACHERS' RETIREMENT SYSTEM OF THE STATE OF ILLINOIS

NOTICE OF PROPOSED AMENDMENTS

3) Detach the completed ballot and signature card along the perforated lines;

4) Place the completed ballot into the perforated section of the return envelope marked "For Ballot Only", without separating the sections of the envelope;

5) Place the completed signature card and the ballot envelope into the perforated section of the return envelope marked "For Signature Card Only", without separating the sections of the envelope; and

6) Attach postage, seal and mail via U.S. mail or express delivery service the unseparated return envelope consisting of both the "For Ballot Only" and the "For Signature Card Only" sections, so as to ensure that it will reach the System at or prior to 10:00 a.m. on the election day.

b) Ballots must be received at the System via U.S. mail or express delivery service at or prior to 10:00 a.m. on the election day. Ballots received after 10:00 a.m. on the election day are invalid and will not be counted.

c) All eligible voters must return their ballots to the System individually, either via U.S. mail or express delivery service. Ballots returned to the System in bulk, via hand delivery, or delivery other than as specified in this subsection, are invalid and will not be counted.

d) Ballots not returned in the "For Ballot Only" "For Signature Card Only" section of the perforated envelope are invalid and will not be counted.

e) Ballots returned with an unsigned signature card, or without a signature card, are invalid and will not be counted.

f) Ballots returned in any envelope other than the return perforated envelope provided by the System are invalid and will not be counted.

g) The perforated return envelope must not be separated into sections. If the return envelope is separated prior to the System's receipt, the ballot contained therein is invalid and will not be counted.

(Source: Amended at 22 Ill. Reg. _____, effective _____)

DEPARTMENT OF AGRICULTURE

NOTICE OF ADOPTED AMENDMENT(S)

1) Heading of the Part: Animal Diagnostic Laboratory Act

2) Code Citation: 8 Ill. Adm. Code 110

3) Section Numbers: Adopted Action:
   110.10   Amended
   110.90   Amended

4) Statutory Authority: Animal Disease Laboratory Act [510 ILCS 10]

5) Effective Date of amendments: January 1, 1998

6) Does this rulemaking contain an automatic repeal date? No

7) Does this proposed amendment contain incorporations by reference? No

8) Date Filed in Agency's Principal Office: January 1, 1998

9) Notices of Proposal Published in Illinois Register:
   September 5, 1997, 21 Ill. Reg. 11990

10) Has JCAR issued a Statement of Objections to these rules? No

11) Differences between proposal and final version: None

12) Have all the changes agreed upon by the agency and JCAR been made as indicated in the agreement letter issued by JCAR? N/A

13) Will this amendment replace an emergency amendment in effect? No

14) Are there any amendments pending on this Part? No

15) Summary and Purpose of amendments: An amendment to the Animal Disease Laboratory Act (P.A. 90-403, effective January 1, 1998) requires the Department to define the term (non-agricultural samples). The fees for testing non-agricultural samples will be deposited into the Illiois Department of Agriculture Laboratory Services Revolving Fund. Testing fees are already established in this Part. A fee is being established for the CELISA test for equine infectious anemia. This test is a special one-hour test that is being offered as an alternative test and will have to be requested by the submitting veterinarian. The Johne?s ELISA test is added to the Animal Disease Laboratory in Centralia as a result of the new Johne?s Herd Certification Program. The laboratory will be certified to conduct the test by January 1, 1998.

16) Information and questions regarding this adopted amendment shall be directed to:

DEPARTMENT OF AGRICULTURE

NOTICE OF ADOPTED AMENDMENT(S)

Debbie Wakefield
Illinois Department of Agriculture
State Fairgrounds
Springfield, Illinois 62794-9281
217/785-5713
Facsimile: 217/785-4505

The full text of Adopted Amendments begins on the next page:

DEPARTMENT OF AGRICULTURE

NOTICE OF ADOPTED AMENDMENT(S)

TITLE 8: AGRICULTURE AND ANIMALS
CHAPTER I: DEPARTMENT OF AGRICULTURE
SUBCHAPTER b: ANIMALS AND ANIMAL PRODUCTS
(EXCEPT MEAT AND POULTRY INSPECTION ACT REGULATIONS)

PART 110
ANIMAL DIAGNOSTIC LABORATORY ACT

Section
110.10   Definitions
110.20   Submitting Specimens
110.30   Payment For Laboratory Services
110.40   Tests Not Covered By Fee Schedule
110.50   Minimum Fees
110.60   Euthanasia Fees
110.70   Clinical Pathology Fees
110.80   Histopathology Fees
110.90   Microbiology Fees
110.100   Parasitology Fees
110.110   Toxicology Fees
110.120   Miscellaneous Fees
110.130   Meats Chemistry Fees
110.140   Liquor Control Commission Fees

AUTHORITY: Implementing and authorized by the Animal Disease Laboratory Act [510 ILCS 10].

SOURCE: Adopted and codified at 8 Ill. Reg. 9047, effective July 1, 1984; amended at 9 Ill. Reg. 4471, effective March 22, 1985; amended at 9 Ill. Reg. 19638, effective January 1, 1985; amended at 10 Ill. Reg. 9733, effective May 21, 1986; amended at 11 Ill. Reg. 10163, effective May 15, 1987; amended at 12 Ill. Reg. 3379, effective January 25, 1988; amended at 13 Ill. Reg. 3617, effective April 15, 1989; amended at 14 Ill. Reg. 1907, effective January 19, 1990; amended at 14 Ill. Reg. 3416, effective March. 1, 1990; amended at 14 Ill. Reg. 15304, effective September 10, 1990; amended at 16 Ill. Reg. 11416, effective July 1, 1992; amended at 18 Ill. Reg. 1825, effective February 1, 1994; amended at 18 Ill. Reg. 17433, effective December 1, 1994; amended at 20 Ill. Reg. 255, effective January 1, 1996; amended at 20 Ill. Reg. 16176, effective January 1, 1997; amended at 21 Ill. Reg. _____, effective

JAN 0 1 1998

Section 110.10 Definitions

"Accession" is one animal or group of animals or samples from the same location, representative of a single disease or disease problem, and received at the laboratory on the same day.

"C" indicates the test is performed at the Animal Disease

DEPARTMENT OF AGRICULTURE

NOTICE OF ADOPTED AMENDMENT(S)

Laboratory--Centralia.

"G" indicates the test is performed at the Animal Disease Laboratory--Galesburg.

"Non-agricultural samples" include all samples of municipal and private water submitted for potability testing and/or chemical or bacteriological screening; all samples from members of the canine or feline species for any type of procedure or testing; all samples submitted for Meats chemistry analysis, other than those submitted by Illinois Department of Agriculture personnel; and all environmental samples (soil, water or vegetation) not involved with production of a cash or feed crop.

"S" indicates the test is performed at the State-Federal Serology Laboratory, Springfield.

"Specimen" is any animal or plant tissue or substance to which a test or procedure is applied.

(Source: Amended at 21 Ill. Reg. ⁙⁙, effective JAN 21 1947)

Section 110.90 Microbiology Fees

The following are the fees for microbiology:
a) Bacteriology, Mycoplasma and Fungi
    1) Aerobic or anaerobic culture without
        sensitivity testing............................. 10.00 C, G
    2) Aerobic culture with sensitivity testing......... 15.00 C, G
    3) Clostridium perfringens serotyping............... 5.00 G
    4) Milk samples for mastitis evaluation
        1-4 specimens................................... 15.00 C, G
        (additional specimens, each at)................. 2.00 C, G
        Wisconsin mastitis test
        1-10 specimens, each............................ 2.00 C
        (additional specimens, each at)................. 1.00 C
    5) Leptospirosis--6 serotypes
        Microtiter test-per specimen.................... 2.00 C, G
    6) Canine brucellosis--per specimen................. 5.00 C, G, S
    7) Fluorescent Antibody Test (FA)................... 10.00 C, G
    8) Escherichia coli serotyping...................... 3.00 C
    9) Campylobacter (culture)......................... 4.00 C, G
    10)
        Salmonella isolation using enrichment media..... 6.00 C, G
    11) Hemophilus (culture)............................ 3.00 C, G
    12) Nasal Swabs--Bordetella......................... 2.00 C, G
    13) Listeria (culture).............................. 4.00 C, G

DEPARTMENT OF AGRICULTURE

NOTICE OF ADOPTED AMENDMENT(S)

    14) Haemophilus equigenitalis (CEM)................. 4.00 C, G
    15) Spirochetes (swine dysentery--Treponema sp.).... 3.00 C, G
    16) Johne's Bacillus (first specimen).............. 7.00 C, G
        (each additional specimen)...................... 4.00 C, G
    17) Prepare and Supply Transport Media (per tube)... 1.00 C, G
    18) Return culture for bacterin production
        per organism.................................... 2.00 C, G
    19) Mycology Testing................................ 6.00 C, G
    20) Microscopic examination......................... 3.00 C
    21) Mycoplasma Testing.............................. 6.00 C, G
    22) E. Coli or Metritis (1-4 specimens)............. 15.00 C, G
        (each additional specimen)...................... 2.00 C, G
    23) Trichomonas transport media.................... 4.00 C, G
b) Virology
    1) Electron Microscopy--fecal...................... 15.00 G
    2) Pseudorabies Serology (positive or negative).....no charge C, G
        Pseudorabies Serology Out-of-State.............. 3.00 C, G
        Pseudorabies Serology (positive or
        negative) and end titer......................... 3.00 C, G
        Pseudorabies Serology (request for screen
        at dilution of 1:2)............................. 3.00 C, G
    3) Fluorescent Antibody Test (each disease)........ 10.00 C, G
    4) Rabies.. 5.00 C, G
    5) Virus Isolation in Cell Culture
        (1 specimen).................................... 15.00 C, G
        Each additional specimen........................ 10.00 C, G
    6) Viral Serology (each disease)
        (1-5 specimens, each)........................... 3.00 C, G
        (Each additional specimen)...................... 1.00 C, G
    7) Feline Leukemia Virus........................... 10.00 C
    8) Feline Infectious Peritonitis (F.I.P.).......... 5.00 C
    9) Canine parvo-virus (ELISA) fecal............... 5.00 C, G
    10) Canine parvo-virus serum........................ 5.00 C
    11) Canine distemper on serum....................... 5.00 C
    12) Rota-virus on fecal............................. 10.00 C
    13) Semen testing (export)......................... 10.00 C
    14) Swine enterovirus (8 serotypes)................ 12.00 C
    15) FeLV-FeLT....................................... 15.00 C
    16) Porcine fetal fluid IgG......................... 3.00 G
    17) Feline lentivirus (FeLT)........................ 10.00 C
    18) Encephalomyocarditis
        (1-5 specimens, each)........................... 3.00 C, G
        (Each additional specimen)...................... 1.00 C, G
    19) PRRS (screening 1:20).......................... 2.00 G
        PRRS end titer.................................. 4.00 C, G
c) Chlamydia Isolation in Cell Culture................. 15.00 C, G
d) Miscellaneous serology
    1) Toxoplasmosis (first sample).................... 5.00 C

DEPARTMENT OF AGRICULTURE

NOTICE OF ADOPTED AMENDMENT(S)

(Each additional sample)............................	2.50	C
2) EIA-AGID...	2.50	S
EIA-CELISA.....................................	10.00	S
3) Mare Immunological Pregnancy Test		
(35-60 days post-service)...........................	15.00	C
4) Aleutian Disease-Mink (immunoelectrophoresis).......	.20	S
5) Out-of-State brucellosis serology..................	.50	C, G, S
6) Brucellosis testing other than bovine,		
porcine and canine................................	.50	C, G, S
7) Bluetongue (1-5 specimens, each)....................	3.00	C
(Each additional specimen).........................	2.00	C
8) Bovine leukosis (BLV-AGID) (1-5 specimens, each).....	3.00	C, S
(Each additional specimen).........................	1.00	C, S
9) Vesicular stomatitis		
(1-5 samples each).................................	3.00	C
(Each additional sample)...........................	2.00	C
10) Complement Fixation Serology		
(1-5 specimens, each)..............................	3.00	C
(Each additional specimen).........................	1.00	C
Note: The Complement Fixation Serology tests include		
testing for anaplasmosis, and chlamydia.		
11) Johne's ELISA 1-3 specimens, each....................	20.00	C
4-12 Specimens, each...............................	10.00	C
13 or more specimens, each.........................	5.00	C

(Source: Amended at 21 Ill. Reg. _____, effective
JAN 01 1998)

DEPARTMENT OF AGRICULTURE(S)

NOTICE OF ADOPTED AMENDMENT(S)

1) Heading of the Part: Bovine Brucellosis

2) Code Citation: 8 Ill. Adm. Code 75

3)
Section Numbers:	Adopted Action:
75.5	Amended
75.10	Amended
75.60	Amended
75.80	Amended
75.90	Amended
75.120	Amended
75.150	Amended
75.180	Amended
75.190	Amended
75.200	Amended
75.220	Amended

4) Statutory Authority: Illinois Bovine Brucellosis Eradication Act [510 ILCS 30].

5) Effective Date of amendments: January 1, 1998

6) Does this rulemaking contain an automatic repeal date? No

7) Does this proposed amendment contain incorporations by reference? Yes

8) Date Filed in Agency's Principal Office: January 1, 1998

9) Notices of Proposal Published in Illinois Register: September 5, 1997, 21 Ill. Reg. 11996

10) Has JCAR issued a Statement of Objections to these rules? No

11) Differences between proposal and final version: None

12) Have all the changes agreed upon by the agency and JCAR been made as indicated in the agreement letter issued by JCAR? N/A

13) Will this amendment replace an emergency amendment in effect? No

14) Are there any amendments pending on this Part? None

15) Summary and Purpose of amendments: This Part is being amended to include bison in accordance with P.A. 90-192, effective 7/24/97. The current edition of the Code of Federal Regulations is being adopted. Sections 75.180 and 75.220 are amended to reflect the fact that Illinois does not recognize brucellosis state classification for bison. In Sections 75.80 and 75.200, the location of the required "S" brand for suspect animals is

DEPARTMENT OF AGRICULTURE(S)

NOTICE OF ADOPTED AMENDMENT(S)

moved from the jaw to the hip as required by the U.S. Department of
Agriculture.

16) Information and questions regarding this adopted amendment shall be
directed to:

    Debbie Wakefield
    Illinois Department of Agriculture
    State Fairgrounds
    Springfield, IL 62794-9281
    217/782-2172
    Facsimile: 217/785-4505

The full text of Adopted Amendments begins on the next page:

DEPARTMENT OF AGRICULTURE(S)

NOTICE OF ADOPTED AMENDMENT(S)

TITLE 8: AGRICULTURE AND ANIMALS
CHAPTER I: DEPARTMENT OF AGRICULTURE
SUBCHAPTER b: ANIMALS AND ANIMAL PRODUCTS
(EXCEPT MEAT AND POULTRY INSPECTION ACT REGULATIONS)

PART 75
BOVINE BRUCELLOSIS

AUTHORITY: Implementing and authorized by the Illinois Bovine Brucellosis
Eradication Act [510 ILCS 30].

SOURCE: Regulations Relating to Bovine Brucellosis, filed January 17, 1972,
effective January 27, 1972; filed May 3, 1972, effective May 13, 1972; filed
December 6, 1972, effective December 16, 1972; filed June 20, 1973, effective
June 20, 1973; filed December 14, 1973, effective December 24, 1973; filed

DEPARTMENT OF AGRICULTURE(S)

NOTICE OF ADOPTED AMENDMENT(S)

August 19, 1975, effective August 29, 1975; filed March 12, 1976, effective March 22, 1976; filed June 21, 1976, effective July 1, 1976; filed December 29, 1976, effective January 8, 1977; amended at 2 Ill. Reg. 24, p. 55, effective June 15, 1978; amended at 3 Ill. Reg. 34, p. 96, effective August 24, 1979; amended at 5 Ill. Reg. 720, effective January 2, 1981; codified at 5 Ill. Reg. 10453; amended at 7 Ill. Reg. 1737, effective January 28, 1983; amended at 7 Ill. Reg. 1733, effective February 2, 1983; amended at 8 Ill. Reg. 5891, effective April 23, 1984; amended at 9 Ill. Reg. 4483, effective March 22, 1985; amended at 9 Ill. Reg. 19647, effective January 1, 1986; amended at 10 Ill. Reg. 9741, effective May 21, 1986; amended at 11 Ill. Reg. 10169, effective May 15, 1987; amended at 12 Ill. Reg. 3386, effective January 22, 1988; amended at 13 Ill. Reg. 3636, effective March 13, 1989; amended at 14 Ill. Reg. 1911, effective January 19, 1990; amended at 18 Ill. Reg. 1833, effective January 24, 1994; amended at 20 Ill. Reg. 1509, effective January 12, 1996; amended at 20 Ill. Reg. 16181, effective January 1, 1997; amended at 21 Ill. Reg. _ _ _ _ _ _ _, effective _ _ _ JAN 01 1998_ _ _.

Section 75.5 Definitions

The definitions for the rules of this Part shall be as stated in 8 Ill. Adm. Code 20.1. The following definition shall also apply:

"Act" means the Illinois Bovine Brucellosis Eradication Act [510 ILCS 30].

"Registered animal" means an animal for which individual records of ancestry are recorded and maintained by a breed association whose purpose is the improvement of the bovine species, and for which individual registration certificates are issued and recorded by such breed association. The breed associations recognized by the Department are those recognized by the United States Department of Agriculture (9 CFR 51.1, (1997 1996).

(Source: Amended at 21 Ill. Reg. _ _ _ _ _, effective _ _ _ _ _ _ _)

Section 75.10 Official Classification of the Results of the Brucellosis Blood Test

a) The official tests and classification of results for the brucellosis blood and milk tests shall be as prescribed in the Brucellosis Eradication Uniform Methods and Rules as approved by the United States Animal Health Association (P.O. Box K227, Suite 114, 1610 Forest Avenue, Richmond, Virginia 23228, May 6, 1992 as amended February 2, 1993 and June 18, 1994) and the United States Department of Agriculture and/or 9 CFR 78.1 (1997 1996).

b) The card (Buffered Brucella Antigen) test and or Buffered Acidified Plate Antigen (BAPA) test shall be the official tests used at licensed

DEPARTMENT OF AGRICULTURE(S)

NOTICE OF ADOPTED AMENDMENT(S)

livestock auction markets in the State. The CITE (Registered) test shall be used as an optional a supplemental test whenever the card test is used.

c) The official brucellosis test for cattle or bison imported into Illinois shall be one conducted at an approved laboratory.

(Source: Amended at 21 Ill. Reg. _ _ _ _ _ _ _, effective _ _ JAN 01 1998 _ _)

Section 75.60 Identification of Cattle or Bison

a) All purebred or crossbred cattle or bison subject to registration vaccinated with brucella abortus vaccine shall be identified on the report of vaccination by their registration number. or dam's registration number, or record association approved individual tattoo or microchip. All grade or not permanently identified cattle or bison so vaccinated shall be ear tagged in the right ear with an official identification tag. In addition to the above identification, all animals shall be identified at the time of vaccination by a tattoo in the right ear. When using a Strain 19 vaccine, the tattoo shall show the quarter and year of vaccination and the letter "V" in the Federal shield. The number of the quarter shall precede the letter "V" in the shield and the last figure of the year shall follow the letter "V" in the shield, as for example, 4V7--"4" means the last quarter (Oct., Nov., Dec.) of the year, "V" means vaccinated, and "7" means the year (example 1997 1997). When using a RB-51 vaccine (cattle only), the tattoo shall show the letter "R", then the Federal shield followed by the last number of the year the animal was vaccinated (example, RV6 would be an animal vaccinated with the RB-51 vaccine in 1996).

b) All cattle or bison, except permanently identified purebred or crossbred animals, tested for brucellosis in the State of the Illinois shall be identified by an official ear tag placed in the right ear, which tag shall bear a prefix number or letter followed by the number on the face of the tag, and on the reverse side shall bear the word "Illinois."

c) Purebred or crossbred registered cattle or bison may be identified for test or vaccination by the purebred or crossbred registration number or individual registration breed tattoo or microchip.

(Source: Amended at 21 Ill. Reg. _ _ _ _ _, effective _ _ _ _ _ _ _)

Section 75.80 Sale of Suspects and Negative Animals From Quarantined Herds

Suspects or negative exposed animals from herds under quarantine may be shipped by the owner direct to a recognized slaughtering establishment, a public stockyards or to a licensed livestock auction market, accompanied by Federal Form VS 1-27 to be sold for slaughter only and shipment reported to the

DEPARTMENT OF AGRICULTURE(S)

NOTICE OF ADOPTED AMENDMENT(S)

Department. Suspects shall not be diverted from the destination listed on the VS Form 1-27, and any other shipping forms must accompany the cattle or bison to their destination. The buyer of such animals must also ensure that the VS Form 1-27 and any other shipping forms are given to the driver transporting the animals to their destination. Such cattle or bison are to be identified by an ear tag supplied by the Department and by branding with a hot iron the letter "S" on the left hip jaw in letters not less than 2 nor more than 3 inches in height, before the animals leave the premises where they are quarantined, except that cattle or bison for slaughter shall be exempt from the "S" branding requirements of this regulation when moved direct from a feedlot on the quarantined premises to a recognized slaughtering establishment in a vehicle which has been sealed by a Department employee, or a person designated by the Department.

(Source: Amended at 21 Ill. Reg. _____, effective
JAN 0 1 1998)

Section 75.90 Release of Herds or Cattle or Bison Under Quarantine

a) Herds which disclose reactors shall be quarantined until depopulated or official tests indicate brucellosis infection no longer exists in the herd.

b) An additional official test of all test-eligible cattle or bison in the herd is required not less than 6 months after release of the herd quarantine or not less than 10 months after removal of the last reactor. For the purpose of this Section, "test-eligible" cattle or bison means all cattle or bison 6 months of age or over except steers, spayed heifers, and official brucellosis calfhood vaccinates under 24 months of age for beef breeds or bison and 20 months of age for dairy breeds.

c) Such herd retests shall be conducted at State-Federal expense; provided, funds are available. The blood samples shall be submitted for diagnosis to an approved laboratory.

(Source: Amended at 21 Ill. Reg. _____, effective
JAN 0 1 1998)

Section 75.120 Requirements for Establishing and Maintaining Certified Brucellosis-Free Herds of Cattle or Bison

Certified brucellosis-free herds shall be established and maintained in accordance with the Brucellosis Eradication Uniform Methods and Rules as approved by the United States Animal Health Association (P.O. Box K227, Suite 114, 1610 Forest Avenue, Richmond, Virginia 23228; May 6, 1992 as amended February 2, 1993 and June 16, 1994) and the United States Department of Agriculture and/or 9 CFR 78.1 (1997 1996).

(Source: Amended at 21 Ill. Reg. _____, effective

DEPARTMENT OF AGRICULTURE(S)

NOTICE OF ADOPTED AMENDMENT(S)

JAN 0 1 1998

Section 75.150 Cattle or Bison for Immediate Slaughter

Cattle or bison for immediate slaughter accompanied by a consignment and consigned to a recognized slaughtering establishment or markets identified under Section 17a of the Act may be shipped into Illinois without brucellosis test or official interstate health certificate. Such cattle or bison shall not be diverted en route and shall be held in quarantine until slaughtered within 10 days of entry.

(Source: Amended at 21 Ill. Reg. _____, effective
JAN 0 1 1998)

Section 75.180 Dairy or Breeding Cattle or Bison

All dairy or breeding cattle or bison transported or moved into the State of Illinois, unless said cattle or bison are consigned direct to and delivered by the transportation company within the confines of a public stockyards, livestock auction market or marketing center, shall be accompanied by an official certificate of health showing:

a) All such cattle or bison over 6 months of age are negative to brucellosis blood test within 30 days prior to shipment, OR

b) All cattle originated from a certified brucellosis-free herd, Class Free State or country, or bison from a certified brucellosis-free herd. State status is not recognized for bison. Certified herd number shall be given and the cattle or bison shall be identified by ear tag number, registration name and number, dam's registration number, or record association approved individual tattoo, OR

c) Cattle are official brucellosis calfhood vaccinates under 24 months of age for beef breeds or bison and 20 months of age for dairy breeds.

All unvaccinated dairy or breeding heifers or bison over 6 months of age or bulls more than 18 months of age moving through an out-of-state auction market or marketing center must be accompanied by an official health certificate showing a negative test for brucellosis within 30 days prior to entry, regardless of state or herd status. Official brucellosis calfhood vaccinates do not need to be tested until they are 24 months of age for beef breeds and bison and 20 months of age for dairy breeds.

(Source: Amended at 21 Ill. Reg. _____, effective
JAN 0 1 1998)

Section 75.190 Additional Requirements on Cattle and Bison from States Designated as Class B and Class C States

a) In addition to other entry requirements, a prior permit must be obtained for dairy, feeding or breeding cattle or bison, except those consigned direct to slaughter or calves under 6 months of age except

DEPARTMENT OF AGRICULTURE(S)

NOTICE OF ADOPTED AMENDMENT(S)

as further provided for in this Section, entering Illinois from states designated by the U.S. Department of Agriculture as Class B and Class C under provisions of the Brucellosis Eradication Uniform Methods and Rules as recommended and approved by the United States Animal Health Association (P. O. Box K227, Suite 114, 1610 Forest Avenue, Richmond, Virginia 23228) and by the U.S. Department of Agriculture (May 6, 1992, as amended February 2, 1993 and June 16, 1994). Such prior permits shall be obtained by contacting the Bureau of Animal Health, Illinois Department of Agriculture, State Fairgrounds, P.O. Box 19281, Springfield, Illinois 62794-9281, telephone 217/782-4944. Information regarding the origin, destination and description of the cattle along with the number of animals in the shipment is necessary for obtaining a permit.

b) Breeding cattle or bison 12 months of age or over from such states shall be placed under quarantine and in isolation until retested and negative to an official test for brucellosis conducted not less than 45 days nor more than 120 days after entering Illinois. Breeding cattle or bison originating from certified brucellosis-free herds are exempt from this provision.

c) All female cattle or bison born after July 1, 1985, if more than 4 months of age, except spayed heifers (female cattle or bison may be spayed after entry into Illinois with prior approval from the Department which will be given upon receipt of the name of the veterinarian who will be performing the operation) or those consigned directly to slaughter, entering Illinois from Class B or Class C states must be official calfhood vaccinates and vaccination status shall be recorded on the official interstate health certificate. In lieu of calfhood vaccination, cattle from Class B states entering Illinois for feeding purposes only may be identified with a hot iron brand on either or both jaws or either hip using the letter F of not less than three inches in height.

d) Female cattle or bison, except those consigned directly to slaughter, entering Illinois from Class C states shall, in addition to present entry requirements now on file, either originate from a certified brucellosis-free herd or be spayed and be officially identified by a hot iron brand on either or both jaws or on either hip using an open spade design (e.g., as used in playing cards) of not less than three inches in height. Certification of spaying by an accredited veterinarian is to be shown on the official interstate health certificate. Female cattle or bison may be spayed after entry into Illinois with prior approval from the Department which will be given upon receipt of the name of the veterinarian who will be performing the operation.

e) Calves under two months of age not accompanied by their dams may be imported from Class C states if they meet the following requirements:

1) An entry permit shall be obtained on all shipments. All such calves shall be quarantined until shipped to slaughter or neutered (spayed or castrated).

DEPARTMENT OF AGRICULTURE(S)

NOTICE OF ADOPTED AMENDMENT(S)

2) All calves shall be accompanied by the Certificate of Veterinary Inspection (i.e., health certificate) and shall be individually identified by official eartags. The eartag numbers shall be recorded on the Certificate.

(Source: Amended at 21 Ill. Reg. _____, effective JAN 01 1998)

Section 75.200 Slaughter Cattle and Bison from Class B or Class C States

a) Prior to movement for slaughter, all test-eligible cattle or bison of unknown status originating in Class B or Class C states in accordance with the Brucellosis Eradication Uniform Methods and Rules (May 6, 1992, as amended February 2, 1993 and June 16, 1994; as recommended and approved by the United States Animal Health Association (P.O. Box K227, Suite 114, 1610 Forest Avenue, Richmond, Virginia 23228) and by the United States Department of Agriculture) shall:

1) Be subjected to an official test for brucellosis within 60 days prior to movement from the farm of origin, OR

2) Be subjected to an official test for brucellosis at the market or stockyards (first point testing), OR

3) Be permanently identified with a hot iron "S" brand on the left hip jaw and be accompanied to slaughter by USDA Form VS 1-27, OR

4) Be accompanied by USDA Form VS 1-27 and moved direct to slaughter in sealed trucks and/or compartments, with no intermediate stops.

b) For the purpose of this Section, "test-eligible" cattle or bison means all cattle 18 months of age or over, except steers, spayed heifers, and official brucellosis calfhood vaccinates under 24 months of age for beef breeds and bison and 20 months of age for dairy breeds. Finished fat heifers moving in marketing channels direct to slaughter will not be considered as test-eligible cattle or bison.

(Source: Amended at 21 Ill. Reg. _____, effective JAN 01 1998)

Section 75.220 Recognition of Brucellosis State Status

If there are multiple brucellosis classifications within a state, the lowest classification shall be recognized by this Department as the classification for that entire state. State status is not recognized for bison.

(Source: Amended at 21 Ill. Reg. _____, effective JAN 01 1998)

DEPARTMENT OF AGRICULTURE

NOTICE OF ADOPTED AMENDMENT(S)

1) Heading of the Part: Diseased Animals

2) Code Citation: 8 Ill. Adm. Code 85

3) Section Numbers: Adopted Action:
   85.10   Amended
   85.12   New Section
   85.15   Amended
   85.50   Amended
   85.75   Amended
   85.85   Amended
   85.90   Amended
   85.115   Amended
   85.120   Amended
   85.130   Amended
   85.135   New Section

4) Statutory Authority: Implementing and authorized by the Illinois Diseased
   Animals Act [510 ILCS 50]; Section 6 of the Illinois Bovine Brucellosis
   Eradication Act [510 ILCS 30/6]; Livestock Auction Market Law [225 ILCS
   640]; and Equine Infectious Anemia Control Act [510 ILCS 65].

5) Effective Date of amendments: January 1, 1998

6) Does this rulemaking contain an automatic repeal date? No

7) Does this proposed amendment contain incorporations by reference? Yes

8) Date Filed in Agency's Principal Office: January 1, 1998

9) Notices of Proposal Published in Illinois Register: September 5, 1997, 21
   Ill. Reg. 12005

10) Has JCAR issued a Statement of Objections to these rules? No

11) Differences between proposal and final version: In Section 85.12(b),
    "ruminants" is added after "peste des petits", and "avian" is added after
    "paramyxovirus infection". In Section 85.85(d), "recently" was added
    before "exposed" in the first sentence. In Section 85.120(a), a "PCFIA
    test" is added after "card test". In Section 85.135(a)(1), "on the basis
    of its using USDA approved methods" is added after "Director". In Section
    85.135(d)(7)(C), "(born into)" is added after "natural additions to". In
    Section 85.135(i)(2), "based on epidemiological evidence provided by a
    state or federal veterinarian" is added after "Director". Non-substantive
    editorial corrections are also made.

12) Have all the changes agreed upon by the agency and JCAR been made as
    indicated in the agreement letter issued by JCAR? Yes

DEPARTMENT OF AGRICULTURE

NOTICE OF ADOPTED AMENDMENT(S)

13) Will this amendment replace an emergency amendment in effect? No

14) Are there any amendments pending on this Part? No

15) Summary and Purpose of amendments: P.A. 90-385, effective August 15,
    1997, amended the Illinois Diseased Animals Act. This legislation was
    initiated by the livestock industry and affects how livestock can be sold
    and moved within Illinois. This legislation mandates the Department to
    establish a list of contagious and infectious diseases. Livestock
    originating from herds where these diseases or conditions exist will not
    be able to be sold within the State. In Section 85.12, the Department has
    developed criteria for determining when to designate a disease as
    contagious or infectious as well as a list of contagious and infectious
    diseases. In addition, the reportable disease list and other conditions
    that are considered health hazards to the Illinois livestock industry have
    also been added to the list.

    Q fever, transmissible spongiform encephalopathy, and trichinellosis are
    being added to the reportable disease list.

    All references to the Code of Federal Regulations (CFR) are being updated.

    The regulations for establishing and maintaining accredited
    tuberculosis-free goat herds and tuberculosis testing of cervidae entering
    Illinois are being deleted from this Part and are being moved to the
    Illinois Bovine Tuberculosis Eradication Act regulations.

    Language is being added to preclude persons from altering other types of
    information on health certificates or other official documents
    accompanying livestock.

    Illinois is adopting the USDA program for establishing and maintaining
    certified brucellosis-free cervid herds.

    Upon the request of the cattle and dairy goat industry in Illinois,
    guidelines for establishing and maintaining a herd or flock under the
    Voluntary Paratuberculosis (Johne's disease) certification program as well
    as the national program are being adopted.

16) Information and questions regarding this adopted amendment shall be
    directed to:

        Debbie Wakefield
        Illinois Department of Agriculture
        State Fairgrounds
        Springfield, Illinois 62794-9281
        217/785-5713
        Facsimile: 217/785-4505

DEPARTMENT OF AGRICULTURE

NOTICE OF ADOPTED AMENDMENT(S)

The full text of Adopted Amendments begins on the next page:

DEPARTMENT OF AGRICULTURE

NOTICE OF ADOPTED AMENDMENT(S)

TITLE 8: AGRICULTURE AND ANIMALS
CHAPTER I: DEPARTMENT OF AGRICULTURE
SUBCHAPTER b: ANIMALS AND ANIMAL PRODUCTS
(EXCEPT MEAT AND POULTRY INSPECTION ACT REGULATIONS)

PART 85
DISEASED ANIMALS

AUTHORITY: Implementing and authorized by the Illinois Diseased Animals Act
[510 ILCS 50]; Section 6 of the Illinois Bovine Brucellosis Eradication Act
[510 ILCS 30/6]; Livestock Auction Market Law [225 ILCS 640]; and Equine
Infectious Anemia Control Act [510 ILCS 65].

SOURCE: Regulations Relating to Diseased Animals, filed January 17, 1972,

DEPARTMENT OF AGRICULTURE

NOTICE OF ADOPTED AMENDMENT(S)

effective January 27, 1972; filed August 19, 1975, effective August 29, 1975; filed December 29, 1976, effective January 8, 1977; amended at 2 Ill. Reg. 24, p. 12, effective June 15, 1978; amended at 3 Ill. Reg. 33, p. 337, effective August 17, 1979; amended at 5 Ill. Reg. 724, effective January 2, 1981; codified at 5 Ill. Reg. 10456; amended at 7 Ill. Reg. 1746, effective January 28, 1983; amended at 8 Ill. Reg. 5925, effective April 23, 1984; amended at 9 Ill. Reg. 4489, effective March 22, 1985; amended at 9 Ill. Reg. 18411, effective November 19, 1985; amended at 10 Ill. Reg. 20464, effective January 1, 1987; amended at 12 Ill. Reg. 8283, effective May 2, 1988; amended at 13 Ill. Reg. 3642, effective March 13, 1989; amended at 14 Ill. Reg. 1919, effective January 19, 1990; amended at 14 Ill. Reg. 15313, effective September 10, 1990; amended at 16 Ill. Reg. 11756, effective July 8, 1992; emergency amendment at 17 Ill. Reg. 14052, effective August 16, 1993, for a maximum of 150 days; amended at 18 Ill. Reg. 1850, effective January 24, 1994; emergency amendment at 19 Ill. Reg. 10734, effective July 10, 1995, for a maximum of 150 days; emergency expired December 17, 1995; amended at 20 Ill. Reg. 276, effective January 1, 1996; emergency amendment at 20 Ill. Reg. 6581, effective April 30, 1996, for a maximum of 150 days; amended at 20 Ill. Reg. 13039, effective September 25, 1996; amended at 21 Ill. Reg. ____, effective ___ JAN 3 1998 ___.

Section 85.10 Reportable Diseases

a) Suspected cases of the following diseases shall be reported immediately to the Department:
anthrax
avian influenza
bluetongue
brucellosis -- bovine, swine, equine, and caprine
contagious equine metritis (CEM)
equine infectious anemia (EIA)
equine viral encephalitides
fowl typhoid
hog cholera
infectious encephalomyelitis -- avian
infectious laryngotracheitis
Mycoplasma gallisepticum -- turkeys
Mycoplasma synoviae -- turkeys
Newcastle disease
paramyxovirus infection
paratuberculosis - (Johne's disease)
piroplasmosis
pseudorabies -- (Aujeszky's disease)
psittacosis - (ornithosis)
pullorum disease
Q fever
rabies
salmonella enteritidis -- poultry

DEPARTMENT OF AGRICULTURE

NOTICE OF ADOPTED AMENDMENT(S)

salmonella typhimurium -- poultry
scabies -- cattle and sheep
scrapie
transmissible spongiform encephalopathy (TSE)
trichinellosis
tuberculosis -- bovine
vesicular conditions of any type
any contagious or infectious disease presently considered as "exotic", i.e., not known to exist in the United States

b) Any herd owner, flock owner, veterinarian or other person having knowledge of the disease, failing to report a suspect case of any of the above diseases immediately after discovery, or who is responsible for the spread of the disease, shall be subject to penalty as provided by law.

c) Reports of any of the above diseases shall be made to the Department, telephone 217/782-4944.

(Source: Amended at 21 Ill. Reg. _____, effective ___ JAN 01 1998 ___)

Section 85.12 Contagious or Infectious Diseases

a) The Department will designate a disease as contagious or infectious when it is determined that the disease is a threat to the animal industry. A disease will be considered a threat to the animal industry for any of the following reasons:
1) is of unknown cause or previously not a recognized disease;
2) can cause interstate or international trade restrictions;
3) is highly communicable to other animals or species;
4) has the potential to produce uncontrollable death loss; or
5) is not endemic in the animal industry.

b) The following diseases are considered to be contagious or infectious:
African horse sickness
African swine fever
akabane
anthrax
avian influenza
bluetongue
Borna disease
bovine petechial fever
brucellosis
contagious bovine pleuropneumonia
contagious equine metritis (CEM)
dourine
ephemeral fever
equine infectious anemia (EIA)
equine viral encephalitides
epizootic lymphangitis

DEPARTMENT OF AGRICULTURE

NOTICE OF ADOPTED AMENDMENT(S)

foot and mouth disease
fowl typhoid
glanders
heartwater
hemorrhagic septicemia
hog cholera
horse pox
infectious encephalomyelitis--avian
infectious laryngotracheitis
Japanese B encephalitis
Jembrana disease
louping-ill
lumpy skin disease
Mycoplasma gallisepticum--turkeys
Mycoplasma synovise--turkeys
Nairobi sheep disease
Newcastle disease
peste des petits--ruminants
paramyxovirus infection--avian
paratuberculosis (Johne's disease)
piroplasmosis
pseudorabies (Aujesky's disease)
psittacosis (ornithosis)
pullorum disease
Q fever
rabies
Rift Valley fever
rinderpest
salmonella enteritidis--poultry
salmonella typhimurium--poultry
scabies--cattle and sheep
scrapie
sheep and goat pox
swine vesicular disease
transmissible spongiform encephalopathy (TSE)
trichinellosis
tuberculosis
vesicular conditions of any type
vesicular exanthema of swine
Wesselsbron disease

(Source: Added   at   21   Ill.   Reg. _____, effective

Section 85.15 Truck Cleaning and Disinfection

Any truck or other conveyance in which diseased livestock is transported shall
be cleaned and disinfected immediately after the diseased livestock is unloaded

DEPARTMENT OF AGRICULTURE

NOTICE OF ADOPTED AMENDMENT(S)

as prescribed in the Code of Federal Regulations (9 CFR 71.7, 71.10 - 71.13;
1997 +996).

(Source: Amended   at   21   Ill.   Reg. _____,   effective
_____JAN 9 1 1998_____)

Section 85.50 . Goats

a) Part—A---Brucellosis in Goats
    1) When a serologic test for brucellosis in goats discloses one or
        more reactors, the entire herd shall be placed under 'quarantine
        and the reactor(s) immediately isolated from the remainder of the
        herd, reactor tagged and branded, and slaughtered. After removal
        of the reactor(s), the entire herd shall be retested at time
        intervals and the number of times as requested by the Department.
        The length of the quarantine period shall be determined by the
        Department.
    2) All brucellosis agglutination blood tests of goats shall be made
        at an approved laboratory.
b) Part—B---Requirements for. Establishing and Maintaining Certified
    Brucellosis-Free Herds of Goats
    1) General Requirements
        A) Certified brucellosis-free herd certificates, which shall be
            valid for one year, unless revoked in accordance with the
            procedures as adopted by the United States Animal Health
            Association (P.O. Box X227, Suite 114, 1610 Forest Avenue.
            Richmond, Virginia 23228) and as outlined for cattle
            certificate revocation in the Brucellosis Eradication
            Uniform Methods and Rules, effective May 6, 1992, amended
            February 2, 1993, and June 18, 1994, published by the United
            States Department of Agriculture, Animal and Plant Health
            Inspection Service, shall be issued by the Department.
        B) Certificates shall be extended for a period of one year upon
            evidence of a negative herd retest and compliance with all
            requirements for maintenance of a certified brucellosis-free
            herd.
        C) A "herd" shall be considered as including all animals 6
            months of age and over and shall consist of at least 5
            animals.
        D) All animals in the herd shall be identified by registration
            number, individual tattoo, or ear tag.
        E) All official blood tests of goats shall be conducted at an
            approved laboratory. ·
    2) To Qualify for Certification .
        A) Herds shall be certified upon completion of 2 consecutive
            negative complete herd tests not less than 10 nor more than
            14 months apart.
        B) Animals classified as suspects, in herds that are otherwise

DEPARTMENT OF AGRICULTURE

NOTICE OF ADOPTED AMENDMENT(S)

negative, must be retested at 30-day intervals until their status has been determined. If the suspects are sold or otherwise disposed of before their status has been determined, the entire herd must be retested to achieve a negative herd status. If the suspects are classified as reactors upon retest, the herd is considered to be infected. Diseased goats may only be consigned directly to a slaughtering facility and must be accompanied by a "Permit for Movement, VS Form 1-27".

C) If on the initial herd test, or as a result of any retests of animals in the herd, one or more reactors are disclosed, the entire herd shall be placed under quarantine and the reactor(s) immediately isolated from the remainder of the herd, reactor tagged and branded, and slaughtered. After removal of the reactor(s), the entire herd shall be retested at time intervals and the number of times as requested by the Department. The length of the quarantine period shall be determined by the Department.

3) To Qualify for Recertification

A) A negative herd test conducted within 60 days prior to the anniversary date is required for continuous certification. Upon receipt of a negative herd test, the Department shall extend certification for 12 months from the anniversary date.

B) If the annual test for recertification is conducted within 60 days following the anniversary date and all the animals are negative, certification will be restored and the certification period will be 12 months from the anniversary date.

C) If the annual test for recertification is not conducted within 60 days following the anniversary date, certification is cancelled and recertification requirements are then the same as for initial certification.

D) If suspects or reactors are disclosed on a recertification test, their disposition and herd retest requirements shall be the same as specified in subsection Section 85.50 (b)(2)(B) and (C) of this Section.

E) All official blood tests of goats shall be conducted at an approved laboratory.

4) Additions to Certified Brucellosis-Free Herds

A) Animals originating from other certified herds may be added without tests.

B) Animals originating from herds not certified may be added; provided, they are negative to an official brucellosis test within 60 days prior to addition, are held in isolation from other members of the certified herd for a minimum period of 30 days and are retested and negative at the end of this isolation period.

DEPARTMENT OF AGRICULTURE

NOTICE OF ADOPTED AMENDMENT(S)

C) Purchased additions shall not receive new herd status for sale or exhibition purposes until they have been members of the herd for at least 30 days and are included in a complete herd retest.

e) Part C   Requirements for Establishing and Maintaining Accredited Tuberculosis-Free Herds of Goats

1) General Requirements

A) Accredited tuberculosis-free herd certificates which shall be valid for one year unless revoked in accordance with the procedures outlined in the Bovine Tuberculosis Eradication Uniform Methods and Rules, effective February 3, 1989, Part III B, Accredited Herd Plan for Dairy Goats, shall be issued by the Department (9 CFR 77.1 1996).

B) Certificates may be extended for a period of one year upon evidence of a negative herd retest and compliance with all requirements for maintenance of an accredited tuberculosis-free herd.

C) A "herd" shall be considered as including all animals 12 months of age and over and shall consist of at least 5 animals.

D) All animals in the herd shall be identified by registration number, individual tattoo or ear tag.

E) All official tuberculin tests shall be conducted by an accredited veterinarian or a veterinarian in the employ of the Illinois Department of Agriculture or the United States Department of Agriculture.

2) To Qualify for Accreditation

A) Herds shall be accredited upon completion of 2 consecutive negative complete herd tests not less than 10 nor more than 14 months apart.

B) If a reaction to the tuberculin test is disclosed, the veterinarian reading the test shall, within 24 hours, notify the Department by collect telephone call and make arrangements for a veterinarian trained in conducting the comparative cervical test to retest the animal within 10 days of the original injection. If the animal is identified as a reactor as a result of the comparative cervical test, personnel from either the Illinois Department of Agriculture or the United States Department of Agriculture will issue a quarantine, supervise disposition of animals and conduct additional tests on members of the herd.

3) To Qualify for Reaccreditation

A) A negative herd test conducted within 60 days prior to the anniversary date is required for continuous accreditation. Upon receipt of a negative herd test, the Department shall extend accreditation for 12 months from the anniversary date.

B) If the annual test for reaccreditation is conducted within

DEPARTMENT OF AGRICULTURE

NOTICE OF ADOPTED AMENDMENT(S)

60--days--following--the--anniversary--date;--certification--will
be--restored--and--the--accreditation--period--will--be--12--months
from--the--anniversary--date.

e) If--the--annual--test--for--reaccreditation--is--not--conducted
within--60--days--following--the--anniversary--date;--accreditation
is--cancelled--and--reaccreditation--requirements--are--then--the
same--as--for--initial--accreditation;

b) If--a--reaction--to--the--tuberculin--test--is--disclosed--at--the
time--of--the--reaccreditation--test;--the--procedure--outlined--in
Section--85.50(b)(2)(B)--shall--be--followed.

4) Additions--to--Accredited--Tuberculosis-Free--Herds

A) Animals--originating--from--other--accredited--herds--may--be--added
without--tests.

B) Animals--originating--from--herds--not--accredited--may--be--added;
provided;--they--are--negative--to--an--official--test--for
tuberculosis--within--60--days--prior--to--addition--and--are
retested--and--negative--to--an--official--tuberculin--test--not
sooner--than--60--days--from--the--date--the--previous--test--was
conducted.

C) Purchased--additions--shall--not--receive--new--herd--status--for
sale--or--exhibition--purposes--until--they--have--been--members--of
the--herd--for--at--least--60--days--and--are--included--in--a--complete
herd--retest.

gd) Part--D--. Other Contagious Diseases. All goats, including dairy goats,
will not be allowed to be exhibited in Illinois and must be removed
immediately from the exhibition area if showing signs of any of the
following conditions:
1) Lesions of contagious ecthyma (sore mouth).
2) Active lesions of ringworm with resulting loss of hair.
3) Caseous lymphadenitis as evidenced by draining abscesses.

(Source: Amended at 21 Ill. Reg. _____, effective
JAN 01 1998)

Section 85.75 Cattle Scabies — Additional Requirements on Cattle from Certain
Designated Areas

a) A prior permit must be obtained from the Department before cattle,
except those consigned direct to slaughter, may enter Illinois from
certain designated areas determined to have high incidence of cattle
scabies. The Director of the Department shall have authority to
specify the designated areas from which movement of cattle into
Illinois will be restricted.

b) Cattle from such areas, except those consigned to a recognized
exhibition and moved from Illinois following exhibition (county and
State fairs, other State-supported exhibitions, and breed registry
exhibitions); dairy cattle; or those consigned direct to slaughter,
shall be dipped for cattle scabies within 10 days prior to entry or

DEPARTMENT OF AGRICULTURE

NOTICE OF ADOPTED AMENDMENT(S)

treated in accordance with the procedures as set forth in 9 CFR 73.17
(1997 1996).

c) Each such animal shall be treated with a solution of approved
acaricide and water or other method of treatment approved by the
United States Department of Agriculture (9 CFR 73.10 and 73.17; 1997
1996).

(Source: Amended at 21 Ill. Reg. _____, effective
JAN 01 1998)

Section 85.85 Diseased Animals

a) Any animal affected with or recently exposed to any infectious,
contagious, or communicable disease shall not be shipped or
transported in any manner, or moved into the State of Illinois, except
as permitted by the laws and rules of the State of Illinois.

b) Officials of the United States Department of Agriculture may approve
interstate shipment of some such animals for consignment direct to a
recognized slaughtering center for immediate slaughter.

c) Animals with active lesions of ringworm with resulting loss of hair or
multiple warts visible visable without close examination will not be
permitted to be exhibited in the State and must be removed immediately
from the exhibition area.

d) Any animal infected with or recently exposed to any contagious or
infectious disease cannot be moved into or within Illinois except to
slaughter or to a location for medical examination or treatment. Any
animal infected with or exposed to any contagious or infectious
disease moving through an auction market, marketing center, stockyard
or sale can be sold only through slaughter only sales and must be kept
separated and apart from any breeding or feeding animals on the
premises.

e) Any animal that has died as a result of any contagious, infectious, or
reportable disease can be moved from the premises as long as it is
being disposed of under the provisions of the Illinois Dead Animal
Disposal Act [225 ILCS 610].

(Source: Amended at 21 Ill. Reg. _____, effective
JAN 01 1998)

Section 85.90 Copy of Health Certificate Shall be Furnished

a) A copy of the certificate of health under which livestock is brought
into the State of Illinois, bearing the approval or, if not approved,
the disapproval of the Animal Health Official of the state of origin,
shall be furnished the Department.

b) No person shall change the names, numbers, words, or phrases , or
other information upon an official health certificate, or permit, or
other official document to evade the provisions of the law.

DEPARTMENT OF AGRICULTURE

NOTICE OF ADOPTED AMENDMENT(S)

c) All official brucellosis tests of animals which are intended for
    interstate movement shall be made at an approved laboratory.

(Source: Amended at   21   Ill.   Reg.   _____,   effective
_____ JAN 01 1998 ____)

Section 85.115 Salmonella enteritidis serotype enteritidis

a) The United States Department of Agriculture has declared Salmonella
    enteritidis serotype enteritidis as a communicable disease in poultry.
    The rules pertaining to Salmonella enteritidis serotype enteritidis
    located at 9 CFR 82.30-82.36 (1997 1996) are hereby adopted for the
    State of Illinois. The flocks affected by these regulations are those
    identified in 9 CFR 82.31.

b) All flocks found to be infected with Salmonella enteritidis serotype
    enteritidis shall be quarantined. The quarantine shall remain in
    effect until the flock has been depopulated and premises disinfected
    as prescribed in 9 CFR 82.32(c) or the entire flock is tested negative
    for Salmonella enteritidis serotype enteritidis in accordance with the
    provisions of 9 CFR 82.32(e).

c) Interstate movement of poultry, eggs, equipment and manure from
    infected or test flocks shall be as specified in 9 CFR 82.33.
    Intrastate movement requirements shall be the same as interstate
    movement requirements.

d) If a flock is determined to be an infected flock as defined in 9 CFR
    82.32(c), the Department shall pay indemnity if State funds are
    available and all of the following conditions are met:
    1) The infected flock is implicated through epidemiological evidence
        in a human disease outbreak;
    2) The flock owner voluntarily agrees to depopulate with appropriate
        State indemnity;
    3) The entire flock which is to be depopulated shall have originated
        from a flock that is classified "U.S. S. Enteritidis Monitored"
        for egg type birds and "U.S. S. Enteritidis Clean" for meat type
        birds under the National Poultry Improvement Plan and Auxiliary
        Provisions (9 CFR 145 and 147; 1997 1996);
    4) The flock owner must have been feeding the infected flock in
        accordance with the provisions of the National Poultry
        Improvement Plan and Auxiliary Provisions (9 CFR 145.23(d); 1997
        1996);
    5) The infected flock shall be slaughtered in accordance with 9 CFR
        82.33(b). Proof of kill will be reported to the Department by the
        meat and poultry inspector of the slaughtering establishment
        where the infected poultry is slaughtered;
    6) The premises has been disinfected in accordance with 9 CFR
        82.32(c); and
    7) Replacement poultry shall be from flocks that are classified
        "U.S. S. Enteritidis Monitored or "U.S. S. Enteritidis Clean"

DEPARTMENT OF AGRICULTURE

NOTICE OF ADOPTED AMENDMENT(S)

    under the National Poultry Improvement Plan and Auxiliary
    Provisions.

e) The amount of indemnity paid, based on the availability of State
    funds, shall be 75 percent of the fair market value and the health
    thereof at the time of slaughter, minus the salvage value. The
    following conditions shall be considered when determining the fair
    market value and health of the infected flock:
    1) Initial purchase price of each bird;
    2) Age of the bird and its egg production capabilities or value for
        producing progeny; and
    3) Feed and veterinary medical production costs as justified by
        documentation by the flock owner in the form of sales receipts
        and veterinary bills.

f) The Department and the infected flock owner must agree upon the value
    of the poultry destroyed, and in the case as agreement cannot be made,
    indemnity will not be paid for the flock.

(Source: Amended at   21   Ill.   Reg.   _____,   effective
_____ JAN 01 1998 ____)

Section 85.120 Cervidae

a) All cervidae (deer and elk) entering Illinois shall comply with the
    following:
    1) Be negative to a single cervical test using 0.1 PPD Bovis
        tuberculin in the midcervical region with reading by observation
        and palpation at 72 hours, plus or minus 6 hours within 60 days
        for all animals 6 months of age and over; and
    2) Be accompanied by a Certificate of Veterinary Inspection issued
        by an accredited veterinarian within 30 days of importation.

a)b) Elk In addition to the above requirements, elk entering Illinois shall
    be negative to a brucellosis card test or PCFIA test conducted within
    60 days on all animals 6 months of age and over.

b) Certified brucellosis-free cervid herds shall be established and
    maintained in accordance with the Brucellosis Uniform Methods and
    Rules as approved by the United States Animal Health Association (P.O.
    Box K227, Suite 114, 1610 Forest Avenue, Richmond, Virginia 23228;
    1997) and the United States Department of Agriculture.

c) All cervidae entering Illinois must also be in compliance with the
    Illinois Wildlife Code (520 ILCS 5).

(Source: Amended at   21   Ill.   Reg.   _____,   effective
_____ JAN 01 1998 ____)

Section 85.130 Vesicular Stomatitis

All veterinarians issuing Certificates of Veterinary Inspection for livestock

DEPARTMENT OF AGRICULTURE

NOTICE OF ADOPTED AMENDMENT(S)

including equine, bovine, porcine, caprine, ovine, and cervidae transported into Illinois from any state with a confirmed diagnosis of vesicular stomatitis within the past 30 days must include the following statement on the Certificate of Veterinary Inspection: "Vesicular stomatitis has not been diagnosed ~~on within ten miles~~ of the premises of origin within the past thirty days. I have examined the premises of origin and have found no signs of vesicular stomatitis."

[Source: Amended at 21 Ill. Reg. _____, effective JAN 0 1 1998)

Section 85.135 Requirements for Establishing and Maintaining a Herd or Flock Under the Voluntary Paratuberculosis (Johne's disease) Certification Program

<u>a) The following definitions shall be applicable to this Section:</u>

<u>1) "Accredited laboratory" means a laboratory operated by the Illinois Department of Agriculture, the University of Illinois College of Veterinary Medicine, or a laboratory approved by the Director (on the basis if its using USDA approved methods).</u>

<u>2) "Animal" means cattle, bison, buffalo, sheep, goats, llamas, or members of the cervid family.</u>

<u>3) "Herd" means all animals under common ownership or supervision that are grouped on one or more parts of any single premises (lot, farm, ranch), or all animals on two or more premises geographically separated, but on which animals have been interchanged or where there has been contact between the premises. Contact of animals between separated premises under common management shall be assumed to have occurred unless otherwise established by the herd owner or manager. Each separate species of animal shall be considered as a separate herd.</u>

<u>4) "Positive animal" means an animal infected with Mycobacterium paratuberculosis, only if M. paratuberculosis is demonstrated by an organism detection test on tissues or feces of the animal.</u>

<u>5) "M. paratuberculosis-Detection Test" or "organism detection test" means any test sufficiently sensitive and specific for detection of M. paratuberculosis in bovine or caprine fecal samples. Definitions of "sufficiently sensitive and specific" will be on the basis of results of performance of a check test and proficiency standards set by the National Paratuberculosis Certification Program. Any test approved by the U.S. Department of Agriculture for M. paratuberculosis organism detection (i.e., fecal culture test for M. paratuberculosis) is acceptable as long as it is performed at an accredited laboratory.</u>

<u>6) "Serum antibody test" means any test sufficiently sensitive and specific for detection of antibodies in bovine or caprine serum. Definition of "sufficiently sensitive and specific" will be on the basis of results of performance of a</u>

DEPARTMENT OF AGRICULTURE

NOTICE OF ADOPTED AMENDMENT(S)

<u>check test and proficiency standards set by the National Paratuberculosis Certification Program (1993), as recommended and approved by the U.S. Animal Health Association (P.O. Box #227, Suite 114, 1610 Forest Avenue, Richmond, Virginia 23228). Any test approved by the U.S. Department of Agriculture for serum antibody detection (i.e., ELISA for M. paratuberculosis) is acceptable as long as it is performed at an accredited laboratory.</u>

<u>7) "Test positive animal" means an animal that has been found positive on the serum antibody test or any other test for M. paratuberculosis.</u>

<u>b) Criteria for herds qualified to enter into the certification program:</u>

<u>1) Participation in this program is voluntary and the producer/owner is responsible for the cost of testing.</u>

<u>2) The herd has been in existence for at least one year or the herd was assembled with animals originating directly from paratuberculosis-certified herds only.</u>

<u>3) A herd assembled with animals originating directly from certified herds only shall start at the lowest certification level of the herds from which the assembled animals were acquired. A negative first-herd test will qualify the newly-assembled herd for the first certification level.</u>

<u>4) All animals must have permanent, unique, legible identification other than a plastic ear tag or neck chain. Acceptable means of permanent, unique, legible identification include registration or association numbers accompanied by identification document, ear tattoos, USDA uniform series ear tag (metal tags), freeze branding and electronic identification (microchips) as long as a reader is supplied by the owner or is readily available.</u>

<u>c) The following certification levels will be awarded compliance with certification requirements:</u>

<u>1) Level 1 - herd tested negative after one sampling.</u>

<u>2) Level 2 - herd tested negative after two samplings.</u>

<u>3) Level 3 - herd tested negative after three samplings.</u>

<u>4) Level 4 - herd tested negative after four samplings.</u>

<u>5) Level 5 - herd tested negative after five samplings.</u>

<u>6) Level 5 Monitored - herd tested negative after six or more samplings.</u>

<u>d) Certification requirements:</u>

<u>1) For annual certification, all animals 24 months of age and older must be tested.</u>

<u>2) Certified herds must be tested every 12 months (+/- 2 months).</u>

<u>3) All tests must be performed at an accredited laboratory.</u>

<u>4) The following annual testing protocol shall be followed for cattle and goats:</u>

<u>A) Levels 1, 3 and 5: blood for the detection of serum antibodies against M. paratuberculosis (i.e., ELISA).</u>

<u>B) Levels 2 and 4: feces for the detection of M.</u>

DEPARTMENT OF AGRICULTURE

NOTICE OF ADOPTED AMENDMENT(S)

paratuberculosis (i.e., fecal culture).

C) Level 5 Monitor: either type of test, at the option of the owner.

5) For all animals other than cattle and goats, an organism detection test for M. paratuberculosis (i.e., fecal culture) must be conducted.

6) All blood collection must be done by an accredited veterinarian. Fecal collection must be done either by, or under the direct supervision of, an accredited veterinarian who must verify that the samples were collected from the animals identified on the test documents.

7) The owner must certify:

A) At the initial test date, the herd has been in existence for at least one year or was assembled only from herds enrolled in a M. paratuberculosis program and are at the same or higher level than the herd. Animals purchased from herds participating in M. paratuberculosis programs outside of Illinois must have that state's program approved by the Director prior to certification.

B) At each test date, all animals in the herd 24 months of age or older were sampled and included in the herd test.

C) At each test date, a list identifying all animals previously tested but no longer in the herd must be provided to the Department.

D) At each test date, all animals added to the herd since the last herd test were natural additions to (born into) the herd, purchased from participating herds, or were tested at the time of arrival on the premises (see Section 85.135(h)).

E) At each test date, with a written statement sent to the Department certifying to the best of his/her knowledge no animal that left the herd tested positive for paratuberculosis or was exhibiting clinical signs of Johne's disease.

e) Upon completion of the required testing and review by the Director, the Department shall issue a certificate verifying the herd's status.

f) Handling of test positive animals:

1) All animals exhibiting clinical signs of M. paratuberculosis must be tested and isolated from the herd pending the test results. Either the serum antibody test or feces for organisms detection may be used for cattle and goats, and the feces for organisms detection test for other types of animals.

2) Cattle or goats found positive on a serum antibody test must be retested by a fecal M. paratuberculosis detection test as soon as possible but not more than 30 days after official notification from the Department.

3) The certified cattle or goat herd will maintain its present certification status pending the results of the M. paratuberculosis detection test.

DEPARTMENT OF AGRICULTURE

NOTICE OF ADOPTED AMENDMENT(S)

4) A negative result on the M. paratuberculosis detection test will allow the herd to move to the next certification level.

5) If cattle or goats are removed from the herd while waiting for serum antibody test results, a fecal sample shall be collected by an accredited veterinarian and submitted to an accredited laboratory. The sample will be tested for M. paratuberculosis if the antibody test is positive.

g) Suspension or revocation of herd certification:

1) Identification of a positive animal using the organism detection test during the certification herd test will result in the loss of certification status. The next negative test will qualify the herd for Level 1 certification.

2) Failure to collect a feces sample and submit it to an accredited laboratory within 30 days after notification of a test positive animal will result in loss of certification status. The next negative herd test will qualify the herd for Level 1 certification.

3) Herds not tested within 14 months after the last sampling will lose their certification status. The next negative herd test will qualify the herd for Level 1 certification.

h) Herd Additions. A negative serum antibody test is required for all cattle or goats being added to the herd prior to arrival on the premises, and an organism detection test must be submitted to an accredited laboratory no later than 15 days after arrival. For animals other than cattle or goats, animals purchased from another herd participating in a M. paratuberculosis certification program may enter the herd without further testing, and will be tested along with the herd at the next annual test. Animals originating from herds that are not participating in an M. paratuberculosis certification program must be isolated from the other members of the herd until a negative organism detection test has been received. Isolation means that the animal can have no opportunity to share feed or water receptacles with other members of the herd, and there can be no chance of fecal contamination from the animal.

i) Protocol if an animal sold from a certified herd is identified as positive:

1) If an animal sold from a certified negative herd is identified as positive by an organism detection test within 18 months after the date of sale, the selling certified herd may, within 120 days of being notified, be required to conduct a herd retest of all eligible animals by both the serum antibody and organisms detection tests. Determination of retesting of the herd will be made by the Director based upon, but not limited to, the level of certification of the herd, the last negative organism detection test of the herd and the status of the other animals in the purchasing herd, if known.

2) The selling certified herd will maintain its present certification status pending the results of the herd test or at

DEPARTMENT OF AGRICULTURE

NOTICE OF ADOPTED AMENDMENT(S)

the determination of the Director based on epidemiological
evidence provided by a state or federal veterinarian.

3) If the herd retest is negative, the herd will maintain its
"present" certification status. The herd owner/manager shall
then have the option of maintaining his/her present test schedule
or rescheduling his/her herd test date so that his/her next herd
test is not due until 12 months after the retest.

4) If a positive animal is identified on this retest, the selling
herd will lose its certification status. The next negative herd
test will qualify the herd for Level 1 certification.

(Source: Added at 21 Ill. Reg. _____, effective
JAN 0 1 1998)

DEPARTMENT OF AGRICULTURE

NOTICE OF ADOPTED AMENDMENT(S)

1) Heading of the Part: Feeder Swine Dealer Licensing

2) Code Citation: 68 Ill. Adm. Code 590

3) Section Numbers: Adopted Action:
   590.60   New Section

4) Statutory Authority: Illinois Feeder Swine Dealer Licensing Act [225
   ILCS 620]

5) Effective Date of amendments: January 1, 1998

6) Does this rulemaking contain an automatic repeal date? No

7) Does this proposed amendment contain incorporations by reference? No

8) Date Filed in Agency's Principal Office: January 1, 1998

9) Notices of Proposal Published in Illinois Register: September 5, 1997, 21
   Ill. Reg. 12027

10) Has JCAR issued a Statement of Objections to these rules? No

11) Differences between proposal and final version: Non-substantive editorial
    corrections have been made.

12) Have all the changes agreed upon by the agency and JCAR been made as
    indicated in the agreement letter issued by JCAR? N/A

13) Will this amendment replace an emergency amendment in effect? No

14) Are there any amendments pending on this Part? No

15) Summary and Purpose of amendments: Section 590.60 is being added to
    clarify the Department's role in the inspection of records.

16) Information and questions regarding this adopted amendment shall be
    directed to:

        Debbie Wakefield
        Illinois Department of Agriculture
        State Fairgrounds
        Springfield, IL 62794-9281
        217/785-5713
        Facsimile: 217/785-4505

The full text of Adopted Amendments begins on the next page:

DEPARTMENT OF AGRICULTURE

NOTICE OF ADOPTED AMENDMENT(S)

TITLE 68: PROFESSIONS AND OCCUPATIONS
CHAPTER II: DEPARTMENT OF AGRICULTURE

PART 590
FEEDER SWINE DEALER LICENSING

AUTHORITY: Implementing and authorized by the Illinois Feeder Swine Dealer
Licensing Act [225 ILCS 620].

SOURCE: Rules and Regulations Relating to Feeder Swine Dealer Licensing Act,
filed January 17, 1972, effective January 27, 1972; filed July 18, 1972,
effective July 28, 1972; Authority Note amended 2 Ill. Reg. 34, pg. 177,
effective August 24, 1978; codified at 5 Ill. Reg. 10571; amended at 10 Ill.
Reg. 70087, effective May 21, 1986; amended at 18 Ill. Reg. 1865, effective
January 24, 1994; amended at 20 Ill. Reg. 1532, effective January 12, 1996;
amended at 21 Ill. Reg. _____, effective _____JAN 01 1998_____.

Section 590.60 Maintenance of Records (Repealed)

Records and premises shall be open during regular business hours for inspection
by authorized Department inspectors.

    (Source: Old Section repealed at 10 Ill. Reg. 10087, effective May 21,
    1986; new Section added at 21 Ill. Reg. _____, effective
    _____JAN 01 1998_____)

DEPARTMENT OF AGRICULTURE

NOTICE OF ADOPTED AMENDMENTS

1) Heading of the Part: Illinois Bovine Tuberculosis Eradication Act

2) Code Citation: 8 Ill. Adm. Code 80

3) Section Numbers: Adopted Action:
    80.10   Amended
    80.20   Amended
    80.30   Amended
    80.40   Amended
    80.110   Amended
    80.120   Amended
    80.130   New Section
    80.140   New Section

4) Statutory Authority: Illinois Bovidae and Cervidae Tuberculosis
    Eradication Act [510 ILCS 35]

5) Effective Date of amendments: January 1, 1998

6) Does this rulemaking contain an automatic repeal date? No

7) Does this proposed amendment contain incorporations by reference? Yes

8) Date Filed in Agency's Principal Office: January 1, 1998

9) Notices of Proposal Published in Illinois Register: September 5, 1997, 21
    Ill. Reg. 12030

10) Has JCAR issued a Statement of Objections to these rules? No

11) Differences between proposal and final version: Non-substantive editorial
    corrections are made. In Sections 80.120(c), 80.130(a)(1), and 80.140(b),
    the following statement is added after the incorporation by reference:
    "This incorporation by reference does not include any future editions or
    amendments beyond the date specified." In 80.140(a)(1)(B), the second and
    third sentences become subsection (a)(1)(C).

12) Have all the changes agreed upon by the agency and JCAR been made as
    indicated in the agreement letter issued by JCAR? Yes

13) Will this amendment replace an emergency amendment in effect? No

14) Are there any amendments pending on this Part? No

15) Summary and Purpose of amendments: A legislative amendment to 510 ILCS 35
    (P.A. 90-192, effective July 24, 1997) includes bison, goats, sheep,
    antelope, and cervidae, and therefore this Part is being amended in
    accordance with the statutory change. The current edition of the Bovine

DEPARTMENT OF AGRICULTURE

NOTICE OF ADOPTED AMENDMENTS

Tuberculosis Eradication Uniform Methods and Rules is being adopted.

The fact that Illinois does not recognize brucellosis state classification for bison is added. This is necessary because Wyoming is Class Free for Bovine Brucellosis except for Yellowstone National Park where the bison are infected with brucellosis.

The regulations concerning accredited tuberculosis-free goat herds are moved from the Diseased Animals regulations to this Part.

The regulations concerning cervidae are moved from the Diseased Animals regulations to this Part, and regulations for the U.S. Department of Agriculture program for accrediting, qualifying, and monitoring tuberculosis-free cervidae herds are being adopted. The import testing requirements for cervidae have been changed to two negative tests prior to importation as recommended in the Uniform Methods and Rules for Tuberculosis Eradication of Cervidae.

16) Information and questions regarding this adopted amendment shall be directed to:

Debbie Wakefield
Illinois Department of Agriculture
State Fairgrounds
Springfield, IL 62794-9281
217/785-5713
Facsimile: 217/785-4505

The full text of Adopted Amendments begins on the next page:

DEPARTMENT OF AGRICULTURE

NOTICE OF ADOPTED AMENDMENTS

TITLE 8: AGRICULTURE AND ANIMALS
CHAPTER I: DEPARTMENT OF AGRICULTURE
SUBCHAPTER b: ANIMALS AND ANIMAL PRODUCTS
(EXCEPT MEAT AND POULTRY INSPECTION ACT REGULATIONS)

PART 80
ILLINOIS BOVIDAE AND CERVIDAE BOVINE TUBERCULOSIS ERADICATION ACT

Section
80.10   Requirements for Illinois Tuberculosis-Free Accredited Cattle and Bison Herds Herd
80.20   When Indemnity Will Be Paid on Tests
80.30   Herds Quarantined Because of Suspected Tuberculosis Infection
80.40   Identification Tags Not To Be Removed
80.50   Infected Herd Depopulation (Repealed)
80.60   Cattle for Immediate Slaughter (Repealed)
80.70   Feeding or Grazing Cattle (Repealed)
80.80   Female Cattle--Beef Breeds--18 Months and Over (Repealed)
80.90   Sale of Quarantined Feeding or Grazing Cattle (Repealed)
80.100   Release of Feeding or Grazing Cattle from Quarantine (Repealed)
80.110   Dairy or Beef Cattle, Bison or Steers
80.120   Tuberculin Tests
80.130   Establishing and Maintaining Accredited Tuberculosis-Free Goat Herds
80.140   Cervidae

AUTHORITY: Implementing and authorized by the Illinois Bovidae and Cervidae Tuberculosis Eradication Act [510 ILCS 35].

SOURCE: Regulations Relating to Bovine Tuberculosis, filed January 17, 1972, effective January 27, 1972; filed June 21, 1976, effective July 1, 1976; filed December 29, 1976, effective January 8, 1977; amended at 2 Ill. Reg. 24, p. 1, effective June 15, 1978; codified at 5 Ill. Reg. 10455; amended at 7 Ill. Reg. 1742, effective January 28, 1983; amended at 8 Ill. Reg. 17809, effective October 1, 1984; amended at 9 Ill. Reg. 4503, effective March 22, 1985; amended at 9 Ill. Reg. 18432, effective November 19, 1985; emergency amendment at 11 Ill. Reg. 5326, effective March 13, 1987, for a maximum of 150 days; amended at 11 Ill. Reg. 10183, effective May 15, 1987; amended at 12 Ill. Reg. 8295, effective May 2, 1988; amended at 13 Ill. Reg. 3676, effective March 13, 1989; amended at 14 Ill. Reg. 1931, effective January 19, 1990; amended at 21 Ill. Reg. _____, effective JAN 01 1998 .

Section 80.10 Requirements for Illinois Tuberculosis-Free Accredited Cattle and Bison Herds Herd

A cattle or bison herd qualifies as a tuberculosis-free accredited herd when it meets the requirements of the Bovine Tuberculosis Eradication Uniform Methods and Rules (June 1997 March 31, 1988, as amended February 3, 1989) for such herds as approved by the United States Animal Health Association (P.O. Box

DEPARTMENT OF AGRICULTURE

NOTICE OF ADOPTED AMENDMENTS

28176, Suite 205, 6924 Lakeside Avenue, Richmond, Virginia 23228-0176) and the United States Department of Agriculture, Animal and Plant Health Inspection Service, for the establishment and maintenance of a tuberculosis-free accredited herd of cattle or bison. This incorporation by reference does not include any future amendments or editions beyond the date specified.

(Source: Amended at 21 Ill. Reg. *17070*, effective JAN 0 1 1998)

Section 80.20 When Indemnity Will Be Paid on Tests

Indemnity will be paid to owners of dairy and breeding cattle, bison or cervidae which react to the tuberculin test administered by accredited veterinarians and are destroyed provided:

a) The entire herd is tuberculin tested. Tuberculosis reactors found when there is not a complete herd test are not eligible for indemnity.

b) Feeder cattle and steers are not eligible for indemnity except when an entire herd is depopulated due to tuberculosis infection.

c) The appraisal is made by a regularly employed State or Federal veterinarian and subject to the requirements of Sections 6, 7, and 8 of the Illinois Bovidae and Cervidae Bovine Tuberculosis Eradication Act (510 ILCS 35/6, 7 and 8) (111. Rev. Stat., 1987, ch. 8, pars. 92, 93, and 94). The appraisal value of the animal shall be based upon the breeding value of such animal at the moment of appraisal, taking into consideration the age, breed, health status, weight and market value at slaughter. *17070*

(Source: Amended at 21 Ill. Reg. , effective JAN 0 1 1998)

Section 80.30 Herds Quarantined Because of Suspected Tuberculosis Infection

a) Cattle, bison, goat, sheep, antelope or cervid herds or flocks suspected of being infected with bovine tuberculosis (Mycobacterium bovis) shall immediately be quarantined and the entire herd tuberculin tested. All tuberculin tests on such herds are to be conducted by veterinarians employed by the United States Department of Agriculture or the Illinois Department of Agriculture.

b) Procedures for release of quarantine on such herds are as follows:

1) If the initial herd test is negative, quarantine shall be released unless epidemiological evidence, such as infection in surrounding herds or continued exposure to tuberculosis, necessitates leaving the quarantine in place.

2) If a reactor is disclosed on the initial herd test, or on test of individual animals in the herd, but the slaughtered reactor does not exhibit gross lesions indicative of tuberculosis, the quarantine shall be released upon completion of one additional negative herd test conducted not less than 60 days following the

---

DEPARTMENT OF AGRICULTURE

NOTICE OF ADOPTED AMENDMENTS

initial herd test.

3) If a reactor is disclosed on initial herd test, or on test of individual animals in the herd, and the slaughtered reactor shows gross lesions indicative of tuberculosis, but Mycobacterium bovis is not confirmed by laboratory examination of tissues from the slaughtered animal, the quarantine shall be released following completion of two negative complete herd retests. The first herd retest shall be conducted not less than 60 days following the initial herd test on which the reactor was disclosed and the second herd retest shall be conducted not less than 6 months or more than one year following the first negative herd retest. After such herds have been released from quarantine, they must pass a negative herd test annually for two years following release of the quarantine.

4) If a reactor is disclosed on initial herd test, or on test of individual animals in the herd, and the slaughtered reactor shows gross lesions indicative of tuberculosis, with Mycobacterium bovis confirmed by laboratory examination of tissues from the slaughtered animal, the herd shall be depopulated if the owner is agreeable and if funds are available. If the herd is not depopulated, it shall remain under quarantine so long as it remains intact.

(Source: Amended at 21 Ill. Reg. *17070*, effective JAN 0 1 1998)

Section 80.40 Identification Tags Not To Be Removed

No person shall remove identification tags, numbers, or brands from cattle, bison, sheep, goats, antelope or cervidae.

(Source: Amended at 21 Ill. Reg. *17070*, effective JAN 0 1 1998)

Section 80.110 Dairy or Beef Cattle, Bison or Steers

All dairy or beef cattle or steers being exhibited in the State of Illinois from Accredited Tuberculosis Free States as defined under the Bovine Tuberculosis Eradication Uniform Methods and Rules (June 1997 March 31, 1988, as amended February 3, 1989) as approved by the United States Animal Health Association (P.O. Box 28176, Suite 205, 6924 Lakeside Avenue, Richmond, Virginia 23228-0176) and the United States Department of Agriculture shall be accompanied by an official certificate of health issued by an accredited veterinarian. This incorporation by reference does not include any future amendments or editions beyond the date specified. No tuberculin test is required for cattle originating from Accredited Tuberculosis Free States. Cattle being exhibited in Illinois from a state that is not Tuberculosis Accredited Free shall be accompanied by an official certificate of health

DEPARTMENT OF AGRICULTURE

NOTICE OF ADOPTED AMENDMENTS

issued by an accredited veterinarian showing:

a) Cattle originated from an accredited tuberculosis-free herd. Accredited herd number and date of last test shall be recorded on the certificate and the cattle shall be identified by ear tag number, tattoo number or registration name and number, OR

b) Cattle originating out-of-state were negative to a tuberculin test conducted within 60 days prior to exhibition, OR

c) If Illinois is not an Accredited Tuberculosis Free State, cattle originating in Illinois were negative to a tuberculin test conducted within 90 days prior to exhibition.

Accredited Tuberculosis Free State status is not recognized for bison but individual herd status for bison is recognized.

(Source: Amended at 21 Ill. Reg. _17070_, effective JAN 01 1998   )

Section 80.120 Tuberculin Tests

a) The caudal fold test shall be the official tuberculin test for testing of cattle, bison, sheep, goats, and antelope not known to be infected with, or exposed to, bovine tuberculosis. The caudal fold test shall be applied by accredited veterinarians OR by full-time State or Federal regulatory veterinarians.

b) The comparative cervical test shall be the official tuberculin test for retesting suspects. The comparative cervical test shall be applied only by full-time employed State or Federal regulatory veterinarians. The comparative cervical test must be applied within 10 OR not less than 60 days following the initial caudal fold injection.

c) The single cervical test shall be the official tuberculin test for retesting known infected herds and exposed cattle, bison, sheep, goats, antelope or cervidae which were once part of a known infected herd and is the official tuberculin test for any type of testing for cervidae. The single cervical test shall be applied only by full-time employed State or Federal regulatory veterinarians or by designated accredited veterinarians as defined by the Uniform Methods and Rules for Tuberculosis Eradication in Cervidae (effective May 15, 1994 and including 1996 amendments) as approved by the United States Animal Health Association (P.O. Box K227, Suite 114, 1610 Forest Avenue, Richmond, Virginia 23228) and/or the United States Department of Agriculture. This incorporation by reference does not include any future editions or amendments beyond the date specified.

(Source: Amended at 21 Ill. Reg. _17070_, effective JAN 01 1998   )

Section 80.130 Establishing and Maintaining Accredited Tuberculosis-Free Goat Herds

DEPARTMENT OF AGRICULTURE

NOTICE OF ADOPTED AMENDMENTS

a) General Requirements

1) Accredited tuberculosis-free herd certificates, which shall be valid for one year, unless revoked in accordance with the procedures outlined in the Bovine Tuberculosis Eradication Uniform Methods and Rules, effective June 1997, Part III B, Accredited Herd Plan for Dairy Goats (9 CFR 77.1, 1997), shall be issued by the Department. This incorporation by reference does not include any future editions or amendments beyond the date specified.

2) Certificates may be extended for a period of one year upon evidence of a negative herd retest and compliance with all requirements for maintenance of an accredited tuberculosis-free herd.

3) A "herd" shall be considered as including all animals 12 months of age and over and shall consist of at least 5 animals.

4) All animals in the herd shall be identified by registration number, individual tattoo, or ear tag.

5) All official tuberculin tests shall be conducted by an accredited veterinarian or a veterinarian in the employ of the Illinois Department of Agriculture or the United States Department of Agriculture.

b) To Qualify for Accreditation

1) Herds shall be accredited upon completion of 2 consecutive negative complete herd tests not less than 10 nor more than 14 months apart.

2) If a reaction to the tuberculin test is disclosed, the veterinarian reading the test shall, within 24 hours, notify the Department by collect telephone call and make arrangements for a veterinarian trained in conducting the comparative cervical test to retest the animal within 10 days after the original injection. If the animal is identified as a reactor as a result of the comparative cervical test, personnel from either the Illinois Department of Agriculture or the United States Department of Agriculture will issue a quarantine, supervise disposition of reactor animals, and conduct additional tests on members of the herd.

c) To Qualify for Reaccreditation

1) A negative herd test conducted within 60 days prior to the anniversary date is required for continuous accreditation. Upon receipt of a negative herd test, the Department shall extend accreditation for 12 months from the anniversary date.

2) If the annual test for reaccreditation is conducted within 60 days following the anniversary date, certification will be restored and the accreditation period will be 12 months from the anniversary date.

3) If the annual test for reaccreditation is not conducted within 60 days following the anniversary date, accreditation is cancelled and reaccreditation requirements are then the same as for initial

DEPARTMENT OF AGRICULTURE

NOTICE OF ADOPTED AMENDMENTS

accreditation.

4) If a reaction to the tuberculin test is disclosed at the time of the reaccreditation test, the procedure outlined in subsection (b)(2) of this Section shall be followed.

d) Additions to Accredited Tuberculosis-Free Herds

1) Animals originating from other accredited herds may be added without tests.

2) Animals originating from herds not accredited may be added, provided they are negative to an official test for tuberculosis within 60 days prior to addition and are retested and negative to an official tuberculin test not sooner than 60 days from the date the previous test was conducted.

3) Purchased additions shall not receive new herd status for sale or exhibition purposes until they have been members of the herd for at least 60 days and are included in a complete herd retest.

(Source: Added at 21 Ill. Reg. 17070; effective
    JAN 01 1998   )

Section 80.140 Cervidae

a) All cervidae entering Illinois shall comply with the following:

1) Be negative to two single cervical tests using 0.1 PPD Bovis tuberculin in the midcervical region with reading by observation and palpation at 72 hours, plus or minus 6 hours, no less than 90 days apart, with the second test conducted within 90 days prior to the movement, for all animals 12 months of age and over that were isolated from all other members of the herd during the testing period, unless they originate from an accredited, qualified or monitored herd.

A) Cervidae from an accredited herd may be moved into Illinois without further tuberculosis testing provided that they are accompanied by a certificate stating that such cervidae originated from an accredited herd.

B) Cervidae originating from qualified or monitored herds may enter Illinois with a negative test within 90 days prior to importation and a certificate stating that the animals originate from a monitored herd.

C) Institutions that have been accredited by the American Zoo and Aquarium Association (AZAA) are exempt from these requirements when movement is between accredited member facilities. All other movement from AZAA-accredited members must comply with these movement requirements.

2) Be accompanied by a Certificate of Veterinary Inspection issued by an accredited veterinarian within 30 days prior to importation.

3) Be individually identified by eartag or tattoo.

4) Be accompanied by a permit obtained from the Department as

DEPARTMENT OF AGRICULTURE

NOTICE OF ADOPTED AMENDMENTS

follows:

A) Applicant for permit shall furnish the following information to the Department:

i) Name and post office mailing address of Illinois destination;

ii) Name and post office mailing address of consignor;

iii) Number of cervidae in shipment.

B) Grounds for refusal to issue permit are:

i) Violation of the Act or any rule of this Part;

ii) Presence of a disease which might endanger the Illinois livestock industry;

iii) Refusal to provide required information for the permit.

C) Permits will be issued by telephoning or writing the Department.

b) Accredited, qualified and monitored tuberculosis-free cervidae herds shall be established and maintained in accordance with the Uniform Methods and Rules for Tuberculosis Eradication in Cervidae as approved by the United States Animal Health Association (P.O. Box K227, Suite 114, 1610 Forest Avenue, Richmond, Virginia 23228 (effective May 15, 1994 including 1996 amendments)) and/or the United States Department of Agriculture. This incorporation by reference does not include any future editions or amendments beyond the date specified.

c) Cervidae entering Illinois must also be in compliance with the Illinois Wildlife Code [520 ILCS 5].

(Source: Added at 21 Ill. Reg. 17070 , effective
    JAN 01 1998   )

DEPARTMENT OF AGRICULTURE

NOTICE OF ADOPTED AMENDMENT(S)

1) Heading of the Part: Illinois Pseudorabies Control Act

2) Code Citation: 8 Ill. Adm. Code 115

3)
Section Numbers:	Adopted Action:
115.10	Amended
115.70	Amended
115.80	Amended
115.90	Amended
115.100	Amended

4) Statutory Authority: Illinois Pseudorabies Control Act [510 ILCS 90]

5) Effective Date of amendments: January 1, 1998

6) Does this rulemaking contain an automatic repeal date? No

7) Does this proposed amendment contain incorporations by reference? Yes

8) Date Filed in Agency's Principal Office: January 1, 1998

9) Notices of Proposal Published in Illinois Register: September 5, 1997, 21
Ill. Reg. 12040

10) Has JCAR issued a Statement of Objections to these rules? No

11) Differences between proposal and final version: None

12) Have all the changes agreed upon by the agency and JCAR been made as
indicated in the agreement letter issued by JCAR? N/A

13) Will this amendment replace an emergency amendment in effect? No

14) Are there any amendments pending on this Part? No

15) Summary and Purpose of amendments: The Department is adopting the revised
Pseudorabies Eradication State-Federal-Industry Program Standards that
became effective January 1, 1997. The Department is updating citations to
the Code of Federal Regulations. The Department is clarifying the
exhibition testing requirements for Illinois swine and clarifying the
language concerning the movement of feeder swine from quarantined herds.

16) Information and questions regarding this adopted amendment shall be
directed to:

    Debbie Wakefield
    Illinois Department of Agriculture
    State Fairgrounds

DEPARTMENT OF AGRICULTURE

NOTICE OF ADOPTED AMENDMENT(S)

    Springfield, IL 62794-9281
    217/785-5713
    Facsimile: 217/785-4505

The full text of Adopted Amendments begins on the next page:

DEPARTMENT OF AGRICULTURE

NOTICE OF ADOPTED AMENDMENT(S)

TITLE 8: AGRICULTURE AND ANIMALS
CHAPTER I: DEPARTMENT OF AGRICULTURE
SUBCHAPTER b: ANIMALS AND ANIMAL PRODUCTS
(EXCEPT MEAT AND POULTRY INSPECTION ACT REGULATIONS)

PART 115
ILLINOIS PSEUDORABIES CONTROL ACT

Section
115.10   Definitions
115.15   Incorporation by Reference
115.20   Pseudorabies Quarantines
115.30   General Requirements for Qualified Pseudorabies Negative, Negative Gene-Altered Vaccinated and Feeder Swine Pseudorabies Monitored Herds
115.40   Requirements for Establishing and Maintaining Qualified Pseudorabies Negative Herds
115.50   Requirements for Establishing and Maintaining Pseudorabies Qualified-negative Gene-Altered Vaccinated (QNV) Swine Herds
115.60   Requirements for Establishing and Maintaining Feeder Swine Pseudorabies Monitored Herds (Repealed)
115.70   Pseudorabies Test Requirements for Intrastate Movement
115.80   Pseudorabies Testing of Feeder Swine
115.90   Feeder Swine
115.100   Breeding Animals Consigned to Slaughter

AUTHORITY: Implementing and authorized by the Illinois Pseudorabies Control Act [510 ILCS 90].

SOURCE: Adopted at 12 Ill. Reg. 3394, effective January 22, 1988; amended at 13 Ill. Reg. 3685, effective March 13, 1989; amended at 14 Ill. Reg. 1935, effective January 19, 1990; amended at 14 Ill. Reg. 5065, effective March 21, 1990; amended at 14 Ill. Reg. 15318, effective September 10, 1990; amended at 16 Ill. Reg. 11781, effective July 8, 1992; emergency amendment at 17 Ill. Reg. 5905, effective March 17, 1993, for a maximum of 150 days; amended at 17 Ill. Reg. 14006, effective August 16, 1993; amended at 20 Ill. Reg. 1542, effective January 12, 1996; amended at 21 Ill. Reg. 904, effective January 7, 1997; amended at 21 Ill. Reg. 17079, effective   JAN 01 1998   .

Section 115.10 Definitions

The definitions for this Part shall be as set forth in the general definitions Section (8 Ill. Adm. Code 20.1). Also, the following definitions shall apply to this Part:

"Act" means the Illinois Pseudorabies Control Act [510 ILCS 90].

"Official random-sample test (95/5)" means a sampling procedure utilizing official pseudorabies serologic tests that provide a 95

DEPARTMENT OF AGRICULTURE

NOTICE OF ADOPTED AMENDMENT(S)

percent probability of detecting infection in a herd in which at least 5 percent of the swine are seropositive for pseudorabies. Each separated group of swine on an individual premises must be considered a separate herd and sampled as follows:

Less than 100 head - test 45
100-200 head - test 51
201-999 head - test 57
1000 and over - test 59

"Official random-sample test (95/10)" means a sampling procedure utilizing official pseudorabies serologic tests that provide a 95 percent probability of detecting infection in a herd in which at least 10 percent of the swine are seropositive for pseudorabies. Each segregated group of swine on an individual premises must be considered a separate herd and sampled as follows:

Less than 100 head - test 25
100-200 head - test 27
201-999 head - test 28
1000 and over - test 29

"Official test" or "test" means any serologic test for the detection of pseudorabies (serum neutralization (SN), for example), as approved by the United States Department of Agriculture (9 CFR 85.1, 1997 1996) and conducted in an approved laboratory.

(Source: Amended at 21 Ill. Reg. 17079, effective   JAN 01 1998   )

Section 115.70 Pseudorabies Test Requirements for Intrastate Movement

No person shall lease, loan, trade, exhibit or sell any swine 4 months of age and over for breeding purposes, or offer or receive the services of any male swine for breeding purposes, unless such swine are accompanied by a health certificate, or an official pseudorabies test chart, or photocopy of such chart, showing that the swine have been tested and negative to an official test for pseudorabies within 60 days prior to the date of such transaction, with the test being recognized for one change of ownership or premises within the 60-day period, OR showing that the swine originated from a qualified pseudorabies negative herd OR showing that the swine are unvaccinated swine originating from an Illinois pseudorabies negative gene-altered vaccinated herd. Swine of any age being exhibited within the State must meet the above requirements except that the test is good for 90 days.

(Source: Amended at 21 Ill. Reg. 17079, effective   JAN 01 1998   )

DEPARTMENT OF AGRICULTURE

NOTICE OF ADOPTED AMENDMENT(S)

Section 115.80 Pseudorabies Testing of Feeder Swine

a) Swine for feeding purposes shall, in addition to complying with the
    other requirements of this Part and 8 Ill. Adm. Code 105.10, enter or
    move within Illinois without further testing requirements for
    pseudorabies if:
    1) The swine are from a qualified pseudorabies negative herd, a QNV
        herd, or a feeder swine pseudorabies monitored herd; or
    2) The swine are from a herd in which a representative sample of
        animals 6 months of age and over have been tested and are
        negative to an official serological test for pseudorabies within
        the preceding 12 months. In herds of 35 animals or less, a
        representative sample is all swine 6 months of age and over or at
        least 10 animals, whichever is less. In herds of 36 animals or
        more, a representative sample is a minimum of 30 percent or 30
        animals that are 6 months of age and over, whichever is less; or
    3) The swine originate from a state that has been classified as
        Stage III, IV or V under the Pseudorabies Eradication
        State-Federal-Industry Program Standards (Jan. 1997 #996) as
        approved by the United States Animal Health Association (P.O. Box
        28176, Suite 205, 6924 Lakeside Avenue, Richmond, Virginia
        23228-0176) or originate from a country that meets the
        requirements for Stage V. If there are multiple pseudorabies
        classifications within a state, the lowest classification shall
        be recognized by this Department as the classification for that
        entire state.
b) Swine tested for pseudorabies under a market swine testing program
    (Section 115.100) shall be included in the representative sample
    required in subsection (a)(2).

    (Source: Amended at 21 Ill. Reg. 17079 , effective
    JAN 01 1998   )

Section 115.90 Feeder Swine

No person shall offer for sale, sell, trade, lease or loan any feeder swine
unless the animals originate from a herd that is in compliance with Section
115.80, they are sold direct to slaughter, or they are sold and moved from a
quarantined herd to a quarantined herd under permit issued by the Department.
Feeder swine from a quarantined herd may be transferred, if accompanied by a
permit issued by the Department, to an unquarantined feeding swine herd,
provided there are no breeding swine on the premise or upon adjacent premises
within one mile, and such herd shall then be quarantined. Permits shall be
issued by the Department upon request and such request may be made either in
writing or by telephone (217-782-4944). Permits for such movement shall not be
issued, except for feeder swine moving from a herd which is under an approved
herd plan for eliminating pseudorabies infection.

DEPARTMENT OF AGRICULTURE

NOTICE OF ADOPTED AMENDMENT(S)

(Source: Amended at 21 Ill. Reg. 17079 , effective
JAN 01 1998   )

Section 115.100 Breeding Animals Consigned to Slaughter

Before being mixed with swine from any other source, all breeding animals
consigned to slaughter or offered for sale for slaughter shall be identified to
the herd of origin by an approved identification tag in accordance with the
Swine Identification Program (9 CFR 78.33, 1997 #996). The tag shall be
applied to the back of the neck of each animal. A report of such
identification shall be made on forms provided by the United States Department
of Agriculture and shall be submitted to the Department within 30 days of
application. If such swine are slaughtered in Illinois, the management of the
Illinois slaughter facility shall, upon written request from the Department or
from the U.S. Department of Agriculture, provide for or permit the collection
of blood samples for testing from the identified swine. 17079

    (Source: Amended at 21 Ill. Reg. 17079 , effective
    JAN 01 1998   )

DEPARTMENT OF AGRICULTURE

NOTICE OF ADOPTED AMENDMENT(S)

1) Heading of the Part: Livestock Auction Markets

2) Code Citation: 8 Ill. Adm. Code 40

3) Section Numbers: Adopted Action:
   40.60   Amended
   40.170   Amended

4) Statutory Authority: Livestock Auction Market Law [225 ILCS 640] and Section 40.23 of the Civil Administrative Code of Illinois [20 ILCS 205/40.23].

5) Effective Date of amendments: January 1, 1998

6) Does this rulemaking contain an automatic repeal date? No

7) Does this proposed amendment contain incorporations by reference? Yes

8) Date Filed in Agency's Principal Office: January 1, 1998

9) Notices of Proposal Published in Illinois Register: September 5, 1997, 21 Ill. Reg. 12046

10) Has JCAR issued a Statement of Objections to these rules? No

11) Differences between proposal and final version: Non-substantive editorial corrections have been made, and the Administrative Code reference was added in Section 40.170(e) and (f).

12) Have all the changes agreed upon by the agency and JCAR been made as indicated in the agreement letter issued by JCAR? N/A

13) Will this amendment replace an emergency amendment in effect? No

14) Are there any amendments pending on this Part? No

15) Summary and Purpose of amendments: In Section 40.60, the location of the brand for suspect animals is moved from the jaw to the hip as now required by the U.S. Department of Agriculture. Breeding swine are required to have a negative test for pseudorabies under the Illinois Pseudorabies Control Act and Swine Disease Control and Eradication Act, and references to the testing requirement are being added for clarification in Section 40.170.

16) Information and questions regarding this adopted amendment shall be directed to:

     Debbie Wakefield
     Illinois Department of Agriculture

DEPARTMENT OF AGRICULTURE

NOTICE OF ADOPTED AMENDMENT(S)

     State Fairgrounds
     Springfield, Illinois 62794-9281
     217/785-5713
     Fax: 217/785-4505

The full text of Adopted Amendments begins on the next page:

DEPARTMENT OF AGRICULTURE

NOTICE OF ADOPTED AMENDMENT(S)

TITLE 8: AGRICULTURE AND ANIMALS
CHAPTER I: DEPARTMENT OF AGRICULTURE
SUBCHAPTER b: ANIMALS AND ANIMAL PRODUCTS
(EXCEPT MEAT AND POULTRY INSPECTION ACT REGULATIONS)

PART 40
LIVESTOCK AUCTION MARKETS

AUTHORITY: Implementing and authorized by the Livestock Auction Market Law [225 ILCS 640] and Section 40.23 of the Civil Administrative Code of Illinois [20 ILCS 205/40.23].

SOURCE: Regulations Relating to Livestock Auction Markets, filed January 17, 1972, effective January 27, 1972; filed May 3, 1972, effective May 13, 1972; filed December 14, 1973, effective December 24, 1973; filed March 2, 1976, effective March 12, 1976; amended at 2 Ill. Reg. 24, p. 73, effective June 15, 1978; codified at 5 Ill. Reg. 10442; amended at 8 Ill. Reg. 5956, effective April 23, 1984; amended at 10 Ill. Reg. 9754, effective May 21, 1986; amended at 12 Ill. Reg. 3411, effective January 22, 1988; amended at 14 Ill. Reg. 1943, effective January 19, 1990; amended at 16 Ill. Reg. 11793, effective July 8, 1992; amended at 18 Ill. Reg. 1869, effective January 24, 1994; amended at 20

DEPARTMENT OF AGRICULTURE

NOTICE OF ADOPTED AMENDMENT(S)

Ill. Reg. 1546, effective January 12, 1996; amended at 20 Ill. Reg. 16192, effective January 1, 1997; amended at 21 Ill. Reg. 17085, effective JAN 01 1998 .

Section 40.60 Bovine Brucellosis

a) Cattle which, upon being tested for brucellosis at a livestock auction market, are classified as reactors to the official test shall be placed in the quarantine pen and sold for immediate slaughter.

b) The reactors when sold for slaughter shall be delivered to a public stockyard or recognized slaughtering establishment and be positively identified and branded as provided by Section 5 of the Illinois Bovine Brucellosis Eradication Act [510 ILCS 30/5]. The purchaser of the reactors shall sign a VS Form 1-27, "Permit For Movement of Animals." Illinois brucellosis reactors disclosed at other than a livestock auction market may be consigned to a livestock auction market designated as a marketing center if accompanied by official VS Form 1-27, "Permit For Movement of Animals". A new VS Form 1-27 shall be prepared by the livestock auction market veterinarian and shall accompany the reactor to slaughter and shall not be diverted en route and shall go only to the destination listed on the VS Form 1-27. No change of ownership of any reactor or suspect animal after the animal has been bought shall be allowed without the approval of the Department.

c) When one or more brucellosis reactors are disclosed in a group of cattle, the negative cattle which have been in contact with the reactors for more than 24 hours shall be either returned to the farm of origin under quarantine OR shipped directly to a recognized slaughtering establishment or a public stockyard, accompanied by VS Form 1-27 to be sold for slaughter only and shall not be diverted en route and shall go only to the destination listed on the VS Form 1-27. No change of ownership of any reactor or suspect animal after the animal has been returned to the farm of origin. Unless cattle are being returned to the farm of origin, they shall be identified by an ear tag provided by the Department and by branding with a hot iron the letter "S" on the left hip jaw in letters not less than 2 nor more than 3 inches in height, before the cattle leave the livestock auction market.

(Source: Amended at 21 Ill. Reg. 17085, effective JAN 01 1998)

Section 40.170 Swine

a) In no case shall swine remain on the livestock auction market premises for more than 10 days.

b) Out-of-state feeder swine shall enter Illinois accompanied by a health certificate and a permit (8 Ill. Adm. Code 105.10) and be ear tagged

DEPARTMENT OF AGRICULTURE

NOTICE OF ADOPTED AMENDMENT(S)

to show state of origin, except that feeder swine consigned from the
farm of origin directly to a federally approved market shall be tagged
immediately upon arrival at the market. Such swine shall move
directly into Illinois from the state of origin. A report of sale
shall be made within 48 hours of the time of sale (on Form I-5) to the
Department, stating name and address of purchaser and number of
animals purchased. Such swine shall be quarantined to the purchaser
for 21 days by the Department (8 Ill. Adm. Code 105.20).

c) Ear tag identification of swine, together with the name and address of
consignor and purchaser, date of sale, breed and number purchased,
shall be made a part of the records of the livestock auction market
before swine leave the livestock auction market.

d) In accordance with Section 2 of the Illinois Swine Brucellosis
Eradication Act (225 ILCS 95/2], all breeding swine 4 months of age
and over shall be negative to an official test for brucellosis within
60 days prior to sale or originate from a validated brucellosis-free
herd. Such test shall be recognized for one change of ownership or
premises only within the 60-day period.

e) In accordance with Section 115.70 of the regulations pertaining to the
Illinois Pseudorabies Control Act (8 Ill. Adm. Code 115.70), all
Illinois origin breeding swine must be accompanied by a health
certificate or an official pseudorabies test chart or photocopy of
such chart showing that the swine have tested negative to an official
test for pseudorabies within 60 days prior to the date of such
transaction with the test being recognized for one change of ownership
or premises within the 60-day period, or showing that the swine
originated from a qualified pseudorabies negative herd, or showing
that the swine are unvaccinated swine originating from an Illinois
pseudorabies negative gene-altered vaccinated herd.

f) In accordance with Section 105.30 of the regulations pertaining to the
Swine Disease Control and Eradication Act (8 Ill. Adm. Code 105.30),
the official health certificate shall show that any breeding swine
entering Illinois must be negative to an official test for
pseudorabies conducted by an approved laboratory within 30 days prior
to entry, or that the swine originated from a qualified pseudorabies
negative herd with the qualified herd number and qualification date
listed on the health certificate, or that the swine originated from a
country that meets the requirements for Stage V, or from a state that
has been classified as Stage IV or Stage V under the Pseudorabies
Eradication State-Federal-Industry Program Standards (January 1, 1997)
as approved by the United States Animal Health Association (P.O. Box
K227, Suite 114, 1610 Forest Avenue, Richmond, Virginia 23228). (This
incorporation by reference does not include any amendments or editions
beyond the date specified.) If there are multiple pseudorabies
classifications within a state, the lowest classification shall be
recognized by this Department as the classification for that entire
state.

(Source: Amended at 21 Ill. Reg.
JAN 01 1998)

DEPARTMENT OF AGRICULTURE

NOTICE OF ADOPTED AMENDMENT(S)

1) Heading of the Part: Livestock Dealer Licensing

2) Code Citation: 68 Ill. Adm. Code 610

3) Section Numbers: Adopted Action:
   610.30   Amended

4) Statutory Authority: Illinois Livestock Dealer Licensing Act [225 ILCS 645]

5) Effective Date of amendments: January 1, 1998

6) Does this rulemaking contain an automatic repeal date? No

7) Does this proposed amendment contain incorporations by reference? No

8) Date Filed in Agency's Principal Office: January 1, 1998

9) Notices of Proposal Published in Illinois Register: September 5, 1997, 21 Ill. Reg. 12052

10) Has JCAR issued a Statement of Objections to these rules? No

11) Differences between proposal and final version: None

12) Have all the changes agreed upon by the agency and JCAR been made as indicated in the agreement letter issued by JCAR? N/A

13) Will this amendment replace an emergency amendment in effect? No

14) Are there any amendments pending on this Part? No

15) Summary and Purpose of amendments: Breeding swine sold in Illinois must be in compliance with the Illinois Pseudorabies Control Act and therefore a reference to that Act is being added for clarification.

16) Information and questions regarding this adopted amendment shall be directed to:

    Debbie Wakefield
    Illinois Department of Agriculture
    State Fairgrounds
    Springfield, IL 62794-9281
    217/785-5713
    Facsimile: 217/785-4505

The full text of Adopted Amendments begins on the next page:

DEPARTMENT OF AGRICULTURE

NOTICE OF ADOPTED AMENDMENT(S)

TITLE 68: PROFESSIONS AND OCCUPATIONS
CHAPTER II: DEPARTMENT OF AGRICULTURE

PART 610
LIVESTOCK DEALER LICENSING

Section
610.5   Definitions
610.10   Entry Requirements
610.20   Breeding Cattle Health Requirements (Repealed)
610.30   Swine Health Requirements
610.40   Prevention of Spread of Livestock Diseases
610.50   Feeder Cattle
610.60   Slaughter Animals
610.70   Care of Livestock (Repealed)
610.80   Inspection
610.90   Identification Not to be Removed or Altered
610.100   Compliance with Market Cattle Identification Program
610.110   Surety Bonds and Other Pledged Security
610.120   Cancellation of Escrow Agreements (Personal Bonds) (Repealed)
610.130   Director as Trustee on Surety Bonds (Repealed)
610.140   Dealer's Agent (Repealed)
610.150   License Application

AUTHORITY: Implementing and authorized by the Illinois Livestock Dealer Licensing Act [225 ILCS 645].

SOURCE: Rules and Regulations Relating to the Livestock Dealer Licensing Act, filed January 17, 1972, effective January 27, 1972; amended May 3, 1972, effective May 13, 1972; June 20, 1973, effective July 1, 1973; April 5, 1976, effective April 15, 1976; amended at 2 Ill. Reg. 34, p. 166, effective August 24, 1978; codified at 5 Ill. Reg. 10573; amended at 8 Ill. Reg. 5973, effective April 23, 1984; amended at 13 Ill. Reg. 3690, effective March 13, 1989; amended at 18 Ill. Reg. 1875, effective January 24, 1994; amended at 20 Ill. Reg. 1552, effective January 12, 1996; amended at 20 Ill. Reg. 16197, effective January 1, 1997; amended at 21 Ill. Reg. _____, effective JAN 01 1998.

Section 610.30 Swine Health Requirements

a) All Illinois breeding swine 4 months of age and over purchased by a licensed livestock dealer shall comply with the Illinois Swine Brucellosis Eradication Act [510 ILCS 95] and the Illinois Pseudorabies Control Act [510 ILCS 90].

b) All breeding swine sold or purchased by a licensed livestock dealer through a livestock auction market shall comply with the requirements of the Livestock Auction Market Law and rules (8 Ill. Adm. Code 40.170[e]).

DEPARTMENT OF AGRICULTURE

NOTICE OF ADOPTED AMENDMENT(S)

(Source: Amended   at   21   Ill.   Reg. _____, effective
JAN 01 1998   )

DEPARTMENT OF AGRICULTURE

NOTICE OF ADOPTED AMENDMENTS

1) Heading of the Part: Swine Disease Control and Eradication Act

2) Code Citation: 8 Ill. Adm. Code 105

3) Section Numbers: Adopted Action:
   105.5   Amended
   105.10   Amended
   105.30   Amended

4) Statutory Authority: Illinois Swine Disease Control and Eradication Act
   [510 ILCS 100], the Illinois Pseudorabies Control Act [510 ILCS 90], and
   the Illinois Swine Brucellosis Eradication Act [510 ILCS 95]

5) Effective Date of amendments: January 1, 1998

6) Does this rulemaking contain an automatic repeal date? No

7) Does this proposed amendment contain incorporations by reference? Yes

8) Date Filed in Agency's Principal Office: January 1, 1998

9) Notices of Proposal Published in Illinois Register: September 5, 1997, 21
   Ill. Reg. 12056

10) Has JCAR issued a Statement of Objections to these rules? No

11) Differences between proposal and final version: In Section 105.10(b)(6),
    "This incorporation by reference does not include any future editions or
    amendments beyond the date specified." is added after the incorporation by
    reference to the January, 1997 edition of the Pseudorabies Eradication
    State-Federal-Industry Program Standards.   Non-substantive editorial
    corrections are also made.

12) Have all the changes agreed upon by the agency and JCAR been made as
    indicated in the agreement letter issued by JCAR? Yes

13) Will this amendment replace an emergency amendment in effect? No

14) Are there any amendments pending on this Part? No

15) Summary and Purpose of amendments: The Department is adopting the updated
    Pseudorabies Eradication State-Federal-Industry Program Standards that
    became effective January 1, 1997. The definition of tattoo is being
    amended to clarify the difference between a site tattoo, defined in the
    regulations as one assigned by a governmental agency and used exclusively
    with feeder pigs, and the breed registry tattoo that is used for breeding
    animals.

DEPARTMENT OF AGRICULTURE

NOTICE OF ADOPTED AMENDMENTS

TITLE 8: AGRICULTURE AND ANIMALS
CHAPTER I: DEPARTMENT OF AGRICULTURE
SUBCHAPTER b: ANIMALS AND ANIMAL PRODUCTS
(EXCEPT MEAT AND POULTRY INSPECTION ACT REGULATIONS)

PART 105
SWINE DISEASE CONTROL AND ERADICATION ACT

Section
105.5   Definitions
105.10   Swine Entering Illinois for Feeding Purposes Only
105.20   Quarantine of Imported Feeder Swine
105.30   Swine Entering Illinois for Breeding Purposes
105.40   Pseudorabies (Aujeszky's Disease) in Swine (Repealed)
105.41   General Requirements for Qualified Pseudorabies Negative, Controlled
         Vaccinated and Feeder Swine Pseudorabies Monitored Herds (Repealed)
105.42   Requirements for Establishing and Maintaining Qualified Pseudorabies
         Negative Herds (Repealed)
105.44   Requirements for Establishing and Maintaining Pseudorabies Controlled
         Vaccinated Swine Herds (Repealed)
105.46   Requirements   for   Establishing   and   Maintaining   Feeder   Swine
         Pseudorabies Monitored Herds (Repealed)
105.50   Official Pseudorabies Test (Repealed)
105.60   Pseudorabies Test Requirements for Intrastate Movement (Repealed)
105.70   Pseudorabies Testing of Feeder Swine (Repealed)
105.80   Feeder Swine (Repealed)
105.90   Feral Swine

AUTHORITY: Implementing and authorized by the Illinois Swine Disease Control
and Eradication Act [510 ILCS 100), the Illinois Pseudorabies Control Act [510
ILCS 90], and the Illinois Swine Brucellosis Eradication Act [510 ILCS 95].

SOURCE: Rules and Regulations Relating to the Illinois Swine Disease Control
and Eradication Act, filed February 24, 1975, effective March 6, 1975; 2 Ill.
Reg. 24, p. 31, effective June 15, 1978; 2 Ill. Reg. 46, p. 10, effective
November 11, 1978;   3 Ill. Reg. 33, p. 341, effective January 1, 1980; 5 Ill.
Reg. 3, p. 745, effective January 2, 1981; 5 Ill. Reg. 45, p. 12100, effective
October 27, 1981; codified at 5 Ill. Reg. 10461; amended at 5 Ill. Reg. 13619,
effective December 4, 1981; amended at 8 Ill. Reg. 5998, effective April 23,
1984;   amended at 9 Ill. Reg. 2236, effective February 15, 1985; amended at 9
Ill. Reg. 18435, effective November 19, 1985; amended at 10 Ill. Reg. 9758,
effective May 21, 1986; amended at 11 Ill. Reg. 10187, effective May 15, 1987;
amended at 11 Ill. Reg. 10538, effective May 21, 1987; amended at 12 Ill. Reg.
3440, effective January 22, 1988; amended at 13 Ill. Reg. 3715, effective March
13, 1989; amended at 14 Ill. Reg. 1981, effective January 19, 1990; amended at
14 Ill. Reg. 15322, effective September 10, 1990; amended at 16 Ill. Reg.
11799, effective July 8, 1992; emergency amendment at 17 Ill. Reg. 5910,
effective March 17, 1993, for a maximum of 150 days; amended at 17 Ill. Reg.

DEPARTMENT OF AGRICULTURE

NOTICE OF ADOPTED AMENDMENTS

14010, effective August 16, 1993; amended at 18 Ill. Reg. 1880, effective January 24, 1994; amended at 18 Ill. Reg. 17968, effective January 1, 1995; amended at 20 Ill. Reg. 1563, effective January 12, 1996; amended at 21 Ill. Reg. 917, effective January 7, 1997; amended at 21 Ill. Reg. _____, effective ___JAN 0 1 1998___ .

Section 105.5 Definitions

The definitions for this Part shall be as set forth in the general definitions Section (8 Ill. Adm. Code 20.1). Also, the following definitions shall apply to this Part:

    "Act" means the Illinois Swine Disease Control and Eradication Act [510 ILCS 100].

    "Feral swine" mean swine that have lived any part of their lives free roaming. Swine may lose their designation as feral if they are maintained in captivity for at least 30 days and are tested negative for pseudorabies and brucellosis.

    "Site tattoo<del>tattoo</del>" means a permanent mark in the right ear showing a unique number giving state and herd of origin. The unique number shall be assigned and approved by the Chief Animal Health Official of the state of origin or by the Federal Veterinarian in charge for that state.

(Source: Amended at 21 Ill. Reg. 17094 , effective ___JAN 0 1 1998___)

Section 105.10 Swine Entering Illinois for Feeding Purposes Only

a) Feeder swine, except feral swine, may enter Illinois provided they are identified by an ear tag or site tattoo in the right ear showing state of origin and accompanied by a permit from the Department and an official health certificate.
b) Official health certificate shall:
    1) Be issued by an accredited veterinarian of the state of origin or a veterinarian in the employ of the United States Department of Agriculture;
    2) Be approved by the Animal Health Official of state of origin;
    3) Show that the feeder swine are free from visible evidence of any contagious, infectious, or communicable disease or exposure thereto;
    4) Show that the feeder swine are not from a quarantined herd and/or area;
    5) List number and description of the feeder swine, site tattoos, ear tag series or location of ear tag records when pigs originate from cooperative feeder pig sales; and

DEPARTMENT OF AGRICULTURE

NOTICE OF ADOPTED AMENDMENTS

    6) Show that the swine originated from a herd in which a representative sample of the breeding herd has been tested and found negative for pseudorabies (8 Ill. Adm. Code 115.80), originate from a qualified pseudorabies negative or pseudorabies negative gene-altered vaccinated herd or originate from a state that has been classified as Stage III, IV or V under the Pseudorabies Eradication State-Federal-Industry Program Standards (January Jan., 1997 1996) as approved by the United States Animal Health Association (P.O. Box 28176, Suite 205, 6924 Lakeside Avenue, Richmond, Virginia 23228-0176) or originate from a country that meets the requirements for Stage V. This incorporation by reference does not include any future editions or amendments beyond the date specified. If there are multiple pseudorabies classifications within a state, the lowest classification shall be recognized by this Department as the classification for that entire state.
c) Permits:
    1) Permits to import feeder swine shall only be issued to:
        A) An Illinois licensed feeder swine dealer; and
        B) A person importing pigs to feed on his own premises and not for resale other than to slaughter.
    2) Applicant for permit shall furnish the following information to the Department:
        A) Name and complete mailing address of Illinois destination.
        B) Name and address of consignor.
        C) Number of swine in shipment.
    3) Grounds for refusal to issue a permit are:
        A) Violation of the Act or any rule of this Part.
        B) If a person should be licensed under the Illinois Feeder Swine Dealer Licensing Act [225 ILCS 620] and his or her license is not in good standing with the Department.
        C) Presence of a disease which might endanger the Illinois swine industry.

(Source: Amended at 21 Ill. Reg. _____ , effective ___JAN 0 1 1998___)

Section 105.30 Swine Entering Illinois for Breeding Purposes

a) Swine for breeding purposes, except feral swine, may enter Illinois provided they are accompanied by a permit from the Department and an official health certificate.
b) Official health certificate shall:
    1) Be issued by an accredited veterinarian of the state of origin or by a veterinarian in the employ of the United States Department of Agriculture;
    2) Be approved by the Animal Health Official of the state of origin;
    3) Identify each animal by registration number, ear tag, breed

DEPARTMENT OF AGRICULTURE

NOTICE OF ADOPTED AMENDMENTS

registry tattoo, or ear notch approved by the respective breed
registry;

4) Show the swine are free from visible evidence of contagious,
infectious, or communicable diseases;

5) Show that the swine are not from a quarantined herd and/or area;

6) Show any swine more than 4 months of age to be negative to an
official test for brucellosis, conducted by an approved
laboratory within 30 days prior to entry, OR that the swine
originate from a validated brucellosis-free herd, with validated
herd number and validation date listed on the health certificate,
OR that the swine originate from a validated brucellosis-free
state (Swine Brucellosis Eradication Uniform Methods and Rules
(February 1995; as approved by the United States Animal Health
Association, P.O. Box K227, Suite 114, 1610 Forest Avenue,
Richmond, Virginia 23228)). Incorporation by reference does not
include any amendments or editions beyond the date specified; and

7) Show any swine to be negative to an official test for
pseudorabies conducted by an approved laboratory within 30 days
prior to entry OR that the swine originated from a qualified
pseudorabies negative herd, with the qualified herd number and
qualification date listed on the health certificate, OR that the
swine originated from a country that meets the requirements for
Stage V or from a state that has been classified as Stage IV or
Stage V under the Pseudorabies Eradication State-Federal-Industry
Program Standards (January ~~1~~ 1997 1996) as approved by the
United States Animal Health Association (P.O. Box K227, Suite
114, 1610 Forest Avenue, Richmond, Virginia 23228). If there are
multiple pseudorabies classifications within a state, the lowest
classification shall be recognized by this Department as the
classification for that entire state. Incorporation by reference
does not include any amendments or editions beyond the date
specified.

c) Permits:

1) Permits to import breeding swine shall be issued by telephoning
or writing the Department.

2) Applicant for permit shall furnish the following information to
the Department:
Name and complete mailing address of Illinois destination;
Name and address of consignor; and
Number of swine in shipment.

3) Grounds for refusal to issue a permit are:
A) Violation of the Act or any rule of this Part; and
B) Presence of a disease which might endanger the Illinois
swine industry.

d) Imported breeding animals shall be kept isolated until a percentage of
the imported breeding swine are retested and negative to an official
test for pseudorabies conducted not less than 21 days nor more than 90
days after entering Illinois. If the number of imported breeding

DEPARTMENT OF AGRICULTURE

NOTICE OF ADOPTED AMENDMENTS

animals is 35 or less, all or at least 10 animals, whichever is less,
are to be tested. If more than 36 imported breeding animals are
involved, a minimum of 30 percent or 30 animals, whichever is less, is
to be tested. Swine originating from a country that meets the
requirements for Stage V or a state that has been classified as Stage
IV or Stage V under the Pseudorabies Eradication
State-Federal-Industry Program Standards are exempt from the isolation
and retest provisions. If there are multiple pseudorabies
classifications within a state, the lowest classification shall be
recognized by this Department as the classification for that entire
state.

(Source: Amended   at   21   Ill.   Reg. _____,   effective
~~JAN 01 1990~~   )

ILLINOIS COMMERCE COMMISSION

NOTICE OF ADOPTED RULES

1) Heading of the Part: Universal Service

2) Code Citation: 83 Ill. Adm. Code 765

3) Section Numbers: Adopted Action:
   765.10   New Section

4) Statutory Authority: Implementing Section 254 of the Communications Act
   of 1934 (47 U.S.C. 254) and authorized by Section 10-101 of the Public
   Utilities Act [220 ILCS 5/10-101].

5) Effective Date of Rule: December 10, 1997

6) Does this rulemaking contain an automatic repeal date? No

7) Does this rule contain incorporations by reference? No

8) Date filed in Agency's Principal Office: December 3, 1997

9) Notice of Proposal Published in Illinois Register: August 15, 1997, 21
   Ill. Reg. 11378

10) Has JCAR issued a Statement of Objections to this rule? No

11) Differences between proposal and final version: None

12) Have all the changes agreed upon by the agency and JCAR been made as
    indicated in the agreement letter issued by JCAR? No changes required.

13) Will this rule replace an emergency rule currently in effect? No

14) Are there any amendments pending on this part? No

15) Summary and Purpose of Rule: The rule incorporates by reference the FCC
    rule that sets discounts for eligible entities ranging from 20 percent to
    90 percent for all telecommunication services, internet access, and
    internal connections. These State-set discounts would be available for
    intrastate services.

16) Information and questions regarding this adopted rule shall be directed
    to:
            Conrad Rubinkowski
            Office of General Counsel
            Illinois Commerce Commission
            527 East Capitol Avenue
            P.O. Box 19280
            Springfield, IL 62794-9280
            Phone: (217)785-3922

ILLINOIS COMMERCE COMMISSION

NOTICE OF ADOPTED RULES

The full text of the Adopted Rule begins on the next page:

ILLINOIS COMMERCE COMMISSION

NOTICE OF ADOPTED RULES

TITLE 83: PUBLIC UTILITIES
CHAPTER I: ILLINOIS COMMERCE COMMISSION
SUBCHAPTER f: TELEPHONE UTILITIES

PART 765
UNIVERSAL SERVICE

Section
765.10 · Discounts for Entities Eligible for Universal Service Support

AUTHORITY: Implementing Section 254 of the Communications Act of 1934 (47
U.S.C. 254) and authorized by Section 10-101 of the Public Utilities Act (220
ILCS 5/10-101).

SOURCE: Emergency rules adopted at 21 Ill. Reg. 11611, effective July 31, 1997,
for a maximum of 150 days; adopted at 21 Ill. Reg. 17103, effective
DEC 1 0 1997 .

Section 765.10 Discounts for Entities Eligible for Universal Service Support

  a) The Illinois Commerce Commission adopts the amounts specified in 47
     CFR 54.505 as of July 17, 1997 for the discounts on intrastate
     telecommunications services available to those entities that qualify
     for such universal service discounts on intrastate telecommunications
     services pursuant to 47 CFR 54.501. ·
  b) No later amendments or editions are incorporated by this Part.

OFFICE OF THE COMPTROLLER

NOTICE OF ADOPTED AMENDMENTS

1) Heading of the Part: Illinois Funeral or Burial Funds Act

2) Code Citation: 38 Ill. Adm. Code 610

3) Section Numbers: Adopted Action:
   610. Exhibit A   New

4) Statutory Authority: 225 ILCS 45 ·

5) Effective Date of Rule: December 5, 1997

6) Does this rulemaking contain an automatic repeal date? No

7) Does this proposed rule contain incorporations by reference? No

8) Date filed in Agency's Principal Office: December 4, 1997

9) Notice(s) of Proposal Published in Illinois Register: October 24, 1997,
   21 Ill. Reg. 11829

10) Has JCAR issued a Statement of Objections to these rule(s)? No

11) Difference(s) between proposed and final version:

    1) Under the "What Services and Merchandise Are Covered By The Funeral Or
       Burial Funds Act" heading, the text was revised to more precisely
       clarify and distinguish among the coverages of the Illinois Funeral or
       Burial Funds Act, the Illinois Pre-Need Cemetery Sales Act, and the
       Cemetery Care Act.

    2) The heading "Pre-need funeral and burial planning" was changed to
       "Pre-need funeral burial purchases" to better reflect the purpose and
       scope of the statute. Under this heading, "planning" was changed to
       "purchasing" to better reflect the purpose and scope of the statute.

    3) Under the "Be Sure To Read Your Contract" heading, "selection" was
       changed to "purchase" and "services to be provided" was changed to
       "and/or services purchased".

    4) Under the "What Is A Guaranteed Price" heading, the text was revised
       to provide a clearer explanation of the definition of a non-guaranteed
       contract.

    5) Under the "Consumer Payments On Pre-need Services And Merchandise Must
       be Placed In A Trust Account" heading, the text was revised to provide
       a clearer explanation of the law on the basis of suggestions by the
       IFDA and ICFRA.

OFFICE OF THE COMPTROLLER

NOTICE OF ADOPTED AMENDMENTS

12) Have all the changes agreed upon by the agency and JCAR been made as indicated in the agreement letter issued by JCAR? Yes

13) Will these rules replace an emergency rule currently in effect? No

14) Are there any rules pending on this Part? No

15) Summary and Purpose of Rules: The Comptroller has jurisdiction over the administration and enforcement of the Illinois Funeral or Burial Funds Act. The pre-need booklet sets forth rights protecting consumers who purchase funeral and burial services and/or merchandise in advance of need (pre-need).

16) Information and questions regarding these adopted rules shall be directed to:

   Mr. John E. Stevens
   Legal Counsel
   Illinois Office of the Comptroller
   201 State Capitol
   Springfield, IL 62706-0001
   (217) 782-5328

The full text of the adopted rules begins on the next page.

OFFICE OF THE COMPTROLLER

NOTICE OF ADOPTED AMENDMENTS

TITLE 38: FINANCIAL INSTITUTIONS
CHAPTER V: COMPTROLLER

PART 610
ILLINOIS FUNERAL OR BURIAL FUNDS ACT

Section
610.10   Statutory Authority
610.20   Application
610.30   Definitions
610.40   Classification of Pre-Need Contract by Funding Methods
610.50   Requirements for all Pre-Need Contracts
610.60   Trust Investment in Life Insurance or Annuities
610.70   Requirements for Pre-Need Booklet
610.80   Licensing of Sellers of Pre-Need Contracts Funded by Life Insurance or Tax-Deferred Annuity
610.90   Schedule of Charges for Examinations for Licensee of Pre-Need Contracts Funded by Life Insurance or Tax-Deferred Annuity
EXHIBIT A   Illinois Consumers Guide to Pre-Need Funeral and Burial Planning

AUTHORITY: Implementing Sections 1a-1, 2(d), 2a, 3, 3f, and 4a and authorized by Sections 1a-1, 2 and 3 of the Illinois Funeral or Burial Funds Act [225 ILCS 45/1a-1, 2, 2(d), 2a, 3, 3f, and 4a].

SOURCE: Adopted at 20 Ill. Reg. 9530, effective July 3, 1996; amended at 21 Ill. Reg. 1̲ ̲ ̲ ̲, effective **DEC 0 5 1997**.

OFFICE OF THE COMPTROLLER

NOTICE OF ADOPTED AMENDMENTS

Section 610.EXHIBIT A Illinois Consumers Guide to Pre-Need Funeral and Burial Purchases

ILLINOIS CONSUMERS GUIDE TO PRE-NEED
FUNERAL AND BURIAL PURCHASES

The Illinois Funeral or Burial Funds Act, 225 ILCS 45 (the law) sets forth rights protecting consumers who purchase funeral services and/or merchandise in advance of need (pre-need). The State Comptroller has jurisdiction over the administration and enforcement of this law.

This guide is intended to assist you in making decisions in connection with the purchase of funeral services and merchandise -- pre-need -- and to advise you of your rights and protections under Illinois law.

What is "Pre-Need" Funeral or Burial Purchasing?

A pre-need funeral or burial purchase is purchasing, in advance, funeral services and merchandise that you select for yourself or loved ones. In connection with the purchase of pre-need services and merchandise, you enter into a pre-need contract with the seller, funeral home or cemetery.

What are Some of the Protections Provided to you by Illinois Law?

Sellers of pre-need services and/or merchandise must be licensed by the State of Illinois through the Office of the Comptroller. You should verify that the person with whom you are doing business is licensed to sell pre-need services and merchandise before you make your purchase. You may contact the Comptroller's Office to verify whether a seller is licensed.

What Services and Merchandise are Covered by the Funeral or Burial Funds Act?

The law covers the purchase of funeral services, clothing, caskets, burial containers commonly referred to as burial vaults and urns. Sales of cemetery services and merchandise are not covered by the law. The purchase of cemetery services and merchandise may be covered by the Illinois Pre-Need Cemetery Sales Act and Cemetery Care Act. Those laws are also administered by the Comptroller. If you have any questions concerning those laws, you should contact the Comptroller's Office.

Be Sure to Read Your Contract

All pre-need contracts sold in Illinois must contain disclosures to assist consumers in their purchase of pre-need services and merchandise. Required disclosures include: a clear identification of the seller's name and address, the purchaser and the beneficiary; a complete description of the goods and/or services purchased; clear notice as to whether the contract is for a guaranteed or non-guaranteed price; how you will pay for the services and/or merchandise

OFFICE OF THE COMPTROLLER

NOTICE OF ADOPTED AMENDMENTS

(i.e., trust account, life insurance policy or annuity); and the cancellation and penalty policy of the seller.

What are Guaranteed and Non-Guaranteed Contracts?

A "Guaranteed" Contract means that the cemetery or funeral home guarantees to provide you with the services and/or merchandise you selected for the amount of money stated in the contract. This means that you or your estate will not be required to pay any additional costs for the items guaranteed, except for unexpected charges incurred (which may include, for example, the need for shipment of remains from a distance).

If the contract does not guarantee the prices charged it must be clearly identified as a "Non-Guaranteed Contract." The amount you pay will be determined at the time the services and/or the merchandise are needed. Any amount you pay pre-need will be consider a deposit to be used toward the purchase price, which will earn interest.

Consumer Payments on Pre-need Services and Merchandise Must Be Placed in a Trust Account.

When you purchase pre-need services and merchandise, the seller must place a certain percentage of the costs of the purchase price in a trust account to ensure delivery at the time of need; 95% of the purchase price of all services and merchandise and 85% of the purchase price of outer burial containers (burial vaults) must be placed into trust.

May I Fund a Pre-need Arrangement with a Life Insurance Policy or Annuity?

Yes, under Illinois law a pre-need contract may be funded through an insurance policy or tax deferred annuity. The insurance policy or annuity may or may not be sold in connection with a commitment from a licensed funeral establishment or cemetery to provide you with specific services and/or merchandise. If there is no provider of funeral services and/or merchandise, this fact must be disclosed in your contract. Without a provider you may only be purchasing insurance coverage providing a payout of a certain amount, and not entering into an actual pre-need contract that guarantees the actual provision and price for the services and/or merchandise. Be sure to read your contract or insurance policy carefully.

Can I Get My Money Back If I Change My Mind?

Yes, depending on the circumstances, The penalties for cancelling a pre-need contract may be different depending upon when the contract is cancelled. If a pre-need contract is subject to the Federal Trade Commission (FTC) three-day cancellation rule (which applies to door-to-door sales or other sales made at a place other than the seller's place of business) you may cancel the contract within three business days after it is signed without any penalty.

OFFICE OF THE COMPTROLLER

NOTICE OF ADOPTED AMENDMENTS

If a pre-need contract is funded by an insurance policy, Illinois law allows you to cancel the insurance policy within 30 days without penalty. Cancellation of an insurance policy does not necessarily serve to cancel the pre-need contract. After 30 days you are entitled to the accrued "cash surrender value" of the policy upon cancellation.

Unless made irrevocable, you may cancel a pre-need contract at any time. If cancellation occurs as a result of your default on payments, the seller is permitted to retain the lesser of 25% of the sales proceeds or $300.

The seller cannot otherwise cancel the contract. If you cancel the contract after it is paid in full, the seller may retain the lesser of 10% of the sales proceeds or $300.

What Can I Do If I Believe I Am Treated Unfairly?

If you think that you have been a victim of unfair or illegal practices in the handling of pre-need funds, you may file a written complaint with the Office of the Comptroller, Department of Cemetery and Burial Trust, James R. Thompson Center, Suite 15-500, 100 West Randolph Street, Chicago, Illinois 60601. In addition, the State Attorney General can seek a court order for restitution and issuance of fines. If you believe that improprieties exist in connection with the sale of insurance used to fund a pre-need contract, you can file a complaint with the Illinois Department of Insurance, 320 West Washington, Floor 4, Springfield, Illinois 62767.

For more information on preplanning or prepaying, see your local cemetery or funeral director or the:

Illinois Funeral Director's Association
215 South Grand Avenue West
Springfield, Illinois 62704

or

Funeral Directors Services Association
499 Northgate Parkway
Wheeling, Illinois 60090-2646

or

Illinois Cemetery and Funeral Home Association
P.O. Box 267
Belvidere, Illinois 61008-0267

(Source: Added at 21 Ill. Reg. _____, effective DEC 05 1997)

DEPARTMENT OF STATE POLICE

NOTICE OF ADOPTED AMENDMENT(S)

1) **Heading of the Part:** Sample Collection for Genetic Marker Indexing

2) **Code Citation:** 20 Ill. Adm. Code 1285

3) **Section Numbers:** **Adopted Action:**
   1285.10 Amendment
   1285.80 Amendment

4) **Statutory Authority:** Implementing and authorized by Section 5-4-3 of the Unified Code of Corrections [730 ILCS 5/5-4-3] and authorized by Section 55a of the Civil Administrative Code of Illinois [20 ILCS 2605/55a].

5) **Effective Date of Amendments:** December 11, 1997

6) **Does this rulemaking contain an automatic repeal date?** No

7) **Does this amendment contain incorporation by reference?** Yes

8) **Date filed in Agency Principal Office:** December 10, 1997

9) **Notice of Proposal published in Illinois Register:** 21 Ill. Reg. 5469, May 2, 1997

10) **Has JCAR issued a Statement of Objection to these rule(s)?** No

11) **Difference(s) between proposal and final version:** Editing and formatting changes recommended by JCAR were made.

    Section 1285.80(b) changed to "Access to the State genetic marker database shall be denied to those forensic laboratories that do not comply with the FBI's requirements for DNA indexing entitled "CODIS Standards for Acceptance of DNA Data at NDIS"; FBI Laboratory Division, Forensic Science System Unit, 935 Pennsylvania Avenue N.W., Room GRB-3R, Washington D.C. 20535 (November 1996). This incorporation by reference contains no further editions or amendments."

12) **Have all the changes agreed upon by the agency and JCAR been made as indicated in the agreement letter issued by JCAR?** Yes

13) **Will this amendment replace an emergency rules currently in effect?** No

14) **Are there any amendments pending on this Part?** No

15) **Summary and purpose of amendment:** This amendment ensures Illinois State Police procedures are consistent with the national guidelines relating to genetic marker data management in the context of the CODIS program.

16) **Information and questions regarding this adopted amendment shall be**

DEPARTMENT OF STATE POLICE

NOTICE OF ADOPTED AMENDMENT(S)

directed to:

Mr. James W. Redlich
Chief Legal Counsel
Illinois State Police
124 East Adams Street, Room 102
P.O. Box 19461
Springfield, IL 62794-9461
(217)782-7658

The full text of the Adopted Amendments begins on the next page:

DEPARTMENT OF STATE POLICE

NOTICE OF ADOPTED AMENDMENT(S)

TITLE 20: CORRECTIONS, CRIMINAL JUSTICE AND LAW ENFORCEMENT
CHAPTER II: DEPARTMENT OF STATE POLICE

PART 1285
SAMPLE COLLECTION FOR GENETIC MARKER INDEXING

SUBPART A: PROMULGATION

Section
1285.10   Purpose
1285.20   Definitions

SUBPART B: OPERATIONS

Section
1285.30   Responsibilities
1285.40   Voluntary Samples
1285.50   Procedures for Collection
1285.60   Privacy Protection
1285.70   Expungement of Records
1285.80   Non-participation

AUTHORITY: Implementing and authorized by Section 5-4-3 of the Unified Code of
Corrections [730 ILCS 5/5-4-3] and authorized by Section 55a of the Civil
Administrative Code of Illinois [20 ILCS 2605/55a].

SOURCE: Adopted at 16 Ill. Reg. 12595, effective July 23, 1992; amended at 17
Ill. Reg. 22571, effective December 15, 1993; amended at 21 Ill. Reg.
_ _ _ _ , effective ____DEC 1 1 1997____

SUBPART A: PROMULGATION

Section 1285.20 Definitions

Unless specified otherwise, all terms shall have the meaning set forth in
Section 5-4-3 of of the Unified Code of Corrections [Ill. Rev. Stat. 1991, ch.
38, par. 1005-4-3 [730 ILCS 5/5-4-3]. For purpose of the Part, the following
additional definitions apply:

"Act" means the Unified Code of Corrections [Ill. Rev. Stat. 1991, ch.
38, par. 1001-1 et seq.] [730 ILCS 5].

"CODIS" means the Combined DNA Index System.

"Department" means the Illinois Department of State Police.

"Designated Agency" means the entity designated by these rules to be
responsible for the collection of blood specimens.

DEPARTMENT OF STATE POLICE

NOTICE OF ADOPTED AMENDMENT(S)

"FBI" means the Federal Bureau of Investigation.

"Kit" means the Genetic Marker Indexing Kit provided by the
Department.

Qualifying offender" means any person described at Section 5-4-3(a) of
the Act.

"Sample" means specimens of blood collected from a qualifying
offender.

(Source: Amended at 21 Ill. Reg. *17110*, effective
DEC 11 1997   )

SUBPART B: OPERATIONS

Section 1285.80 Non-participation

a) Results of genetic marker grouping analysis and access to the State
genetic marker database information may be denied to any agency which
fails to comply with these Rules.

b) Access to the State genetic marker database shall be denied to those
forensic laboratories that do not comply with the FBI's requirements
for DNA indexing entitled "CODIS Standards for Acceptance of DNA Data
at NDIS"; FBI Laboratory Division, Forensic Science System Unit, 935
Pennsylvania Avenue N.W., Room GRB-3R, Washington D.C. 20535 (November
1996). This incorporation by reference contains no further editions
or amendments.

(Source: Amended at 21 Ill. Reg. *17110*   , effective
DEC 11 1997   )

BOARD OF TRUSTEES OF THE UNIVERSITY OF ILLINOIS

NOTICE OF ADOPTED AMENDMENTS

1) Heading of the Part: Program Content and Guidelines for Division of
Specialized Care for Children

2) Code Citation: 89 Ill. Adm. Code 1200

3)
Section Numbers:	Adopted Action:
1200.10	Amendments
1200.20	Amendments
1200.30	Amendments
1200.40	Amendments
1200.50	Amendments
1200.60	Amendments
1200.70	Amendments
1200.80	Amendments
1200.90	Amendments
1200.110	Amendments
1200.Appendix A	Amendments
1200.Appendix B	Amendments

4) Statutory Authority: Implementing Section 1 of the Specialized Care for
Children Act [110 ILCS 345] and authorized by Section 1 of the University
of Illinois Act [110 ILCS 305].

5) Effective Date of Rulemaking: December 11, 997

6) Does this rulemaking contain an automatic repeal date? No

7) Does this rulemaking contain incorporations by reference? No

8) Date Filed in Agency's Principal Office: December 11, 1997

9) Notice of Proposal Published in Illinois Register: May 30, 1997 (21 Ill.
Reg. 6404)

10) Has JCAR issued a Statement of Objections to these rules? No

11) Difference(s) between proposal and final version:
 - Section 1200.30, line 404, delete ", as determined by the Director"
 - Section 1200.80, line 1312, add "see Section 1200.50)" before the period.
 - Section 1200.90, line 1572, add "National Drug Code" before "NDC" and add
   parentheses around "NDC"
 - Lines 1604 and 1648, strike "state" and add "State"
 - Lines 1690-1691, strike "and Illinois Clinical Laboratories Code" and
   delete the comma after Code.
 - Line 1717, strike "57 Fed. Reg. 6614" and add "62 Fed Reg. 12651 (1997)"

12) Have all the changes agreed upon by the agency and JCAR been made as
indicated in the agreement letter issued by JCAR? Yes

BOARD OF TRUSTEES OF THE UNIVERSITY OF ILLINOIS

NOTICE OF ADOPTED AMENDMENTS

13) Will this rulemaking replace an emergency rule currently in effect? No

14) Are there any amendments pending on this Part? No

15) Summary, and Purpose of Rulemaking: To encourage the development of
comprehensive systems of care for children with special health care needs;
to change "disabled children" to "children with disabilities"; to make
medically necessary diagnostic services accessible to families by
supporting needed transportation costs; to change the limit of continuation
of a treatment plan from six months after the child's 18th birthday to the
child's 21st birthday; to clarify conditions under which treatment services
and financial support can be provided when LRAs are not residents of
Illinois; to make an adjustment in the Income Scale to reflect 65% of gross
median income instead of the current 58%. Deletion of reference to the
Illinois Comprehensive Health Insurance Program. Addition to the reasons
LRAs may lose financial assistance. Deletion of statement regarding
reimbursement for minor occasional costs of a Recipient Child's treatment.
Clarification of payment for drugs. Addition of statement regarding
negotiation of payment amounts for services in out-of-state facilities.
Clarification of treatment facilities providing in-hospital, inpatient
care. Changes in the Income and Payment scales.

16) Information and questions regarding these adopted amendments shall be
directed to:

    Name: Thomas M. Wilkin, Associate Director
    Address: Division of Specialized Care for Children
              2815 West Washington, Suite 300
              P.O. Box 19481
              Springfield, Illinois 62794-9481
    Telephone: (217)793-2350   Fax: (217)793-0773

The full text of the Adopted Amendment begins on the next page:

BOARD OF TRUSTEES OF THE UNIVERSITY OF ILLINOIS

NOTICE OF ADOPTED AMENDMENTS

TITLE 89: SOCIAL SERVICES
CHAPTER X: THE BOARD OF TRUSTEES OF THE UNIVERSITY OF ILLINOIS

PART 1200
PROGRAM CONTENT AND GUIDELINES FOR DIVISION
OF SPECIALIZED CARE FOR CHILDREN

Section	
1200.10	Purpose and Description
1200.20	Definitions
1200.30	Eligibility: General
1200.40	Medical Eligibility
1200.50	Financial Eligibility
1200.60	Appeal Process
1200.70	Payment for Services
1200.80	Availability of Services
1200.90	Rates of Payment
1200.100	Standards for Health Care Professionals
1200.110	Standards for Health Care Facilities
1200.120	Records
1200.130	Reports
APPENDIX A	Income Scale
APPENDIX B	Payment Scale

AUTHORITY: Implementing Section 1 of the Specialized Care for Children Act
[110 ILCS 345] and authorized by Section 1 of the University of Illinois Act
[110 ILCS 305].

SOURCE: Adopted at 11 Ill. Reg. 3508, effective February 10, 1987; amended at
13 Ill. Reg. 9283, effective June 6, 1989; amended at 14 Ill. Reg. 5135,
effective March 22, 1990; amended at 17 Ill. Reg. 1137, effective March 8,
1993; emergency amendment at 17 Ill. Reg. 9735, effective July 1, 1993, for a
maximum of 150 days; amended at 18 Ill. Reg. 2104, effective January 24, 1994;
amended at 21 Ill. Reg. _____, effective ____ DEC 11 1997 ____.

Section 1200.10 Purpose and Description

    a) General Program
        1) The Division of Specialized Care for Children (hereinafter
            referred to as "DSCC" or "the Division") is the department of the
            University of Illinois designated to receive and administer funds
            and aid under Federal and State programs, including the Maternal
            and Child Health Services Block Grant (42 U.S.C. 701 et seq.) as
            implemented by 42 C.F.R. Part 51a et seq., for the purpose of
            providing habilitative, rehabilitative, and medical treatment to
            children with disabilities disabled children, as provided in
            Section 1 of the Specialized Care for Children Act [110 ILCS 345]
            {Ill. Rev. Stat. 1991, ch. 144, par. 67.1} ("the Act"). The

BOARD OF TRUSTEES OF THE UNIVERSITY OF ILLINOIS

NOTICE OF ADOPTED AMENDMENTS

objectives of DSCC are as follows:
A) to provide for early evaluation of ~~disabled~~ children with conditions eligible for the services of the Division;
B) to develop and implement a mechanism for evaluation and diagnosis required to carry out the purposes of this Part;
C) to offer or arrange for the necessary specialized medical care and related habilitative services for eligible ~~disabled~~ children with disabilities;
D) to develop, promote or improve the standards of care required by ~~disabled~~ children with disabilities;
E) to make efforts, within the resources of DSCC, to coordinate benefits for children who are eligible for other State ~~state~~ programs providing benefits to children with health problems; and,
F) to encourage the development of comprehensive systems of care for children with special health care needs that are coordinated, community-based, culturally competent and family centered.

2) All services are provided subject to budgetary limitations and annual appropriations to the State ~~state~~ and federal programs through which DSCC is funded.

b) Supplemental Security Income - Disabled Children's Program (SSI-DCP)
1) DSCC administers this program for the State of Illinois in accordance with Section 1615(a)(2) of "Subchapter XVI - Supplemental Security Income for Aged, Blind, and Disabled" (42 U.S.C. 1382d(a)(2)) to the extent provided in this Part.
2) Children are evaluated as eligible for this program by the Social Security Administration of the U.S. Government and its regional offices as well as the Department of Rehabilitation Services of the State of Illinois through its Disability Adjudication Unit. Children so deemed eligible by those agencies are referred to DSCC for disposition.
3) An SSI-DCP-eligible child with a Medically Eligible Condition shall be deemed to be entitled to DSCC benefits in accordance with and subject to this Part. (See Section 1200.40 of this Part.) All other SSI-DCP-eligible children will be referred by DSCC to programs, services, or institutions providing assistance to said children whenever such programs, services, or institutions are available.

c) Service Population
Children suspected of having Medically Eligible Conditions represent the potential service population. Such children, if not already specifically diagnosed, may be referred to DSCC for a diagnostic evaluation.

d) Availability of Information
1) All information distributed by DSCC about its programs, as well as all official DSCC forms and/or applications are available in both English and Spanish.

BOARD OF TRUSTEES OF THE UNIVERSITY OF ILLINOIS

NOTICE OF ADOPTED AMENDMENTS

2) For further descriptions of available DSCC information and DSCC information dissemination techniques, see DSCC Internal Operating Rules (2 Ill. Adm. Code 5155).

(Source: Amended at 21 Ill. Reg. 1....., effective DEC 11 1997)

Section 1200.20 Definitions

Adjusted Family Income: The amount equal to the family's annual Total Income as defined in Section 1200.50(d)(2) less allowable expenses as determined pursuant to Section 1200.50(d)(3).

Advisory Board: As established in Section 2 of the Act, physicians or surgeons appointed by the University of Illinois Board of Trustees who advise the University of Illinois and the Division on qualifying for Federal funds, make recommendations to the University and the Division regarding the provision of services to ~~disabled~~ children with disabilities, and consult with the Division and the University regarding general policy considerations.

Allowable Expenses: Deductions from the annual Total Income as specified in Section 1200.50(d)(3).

Amenable to Treatment: Reasonable medical certainty of long term ~~developmental~~ improvement in health status or function as determined by the treating physician.

Annual Total Income: The amount of a family's income determined pursuant to Section 1200.50(d)(2).

Applicant: One applying for DSCC eligibility. The term as used in this Part refers to the child.

Assistive Appliance: Equipment intended to support, replace or augment a dysfunctioning or non-functioning part of the body. Such appliances -- which may be mechanical, structural or electrical -- are intended to support specific habilitative objectives determined by the child's health care providers.

Authorized Services: Direct medical care and related care for a Recipient Child, as more completely set forth in Section 1200.80(e) of this Part, which DSCC staff has approved ~~provided~~ for payment.

Child with Disability: An individual below the age of 21 who has a physical impairment or an organic disease, function, defect, or condition which may hinder the achievement of normal growth and/or development.

BOARD OF TRUSTEES OF THE UNIVERSITY OF ILLINOIS

NOTICE OF ADOPTED AMENDMENTS

Chronic Condition: Condition which is expected to be long lasting or to be lifelong.

Completed Application: A signed and dated request for program benefits made by the LRA on a form specified by the agency which contains current, accurate and relevant information in every space required by the form.

Consent: An agreement by a Legally Responsible Adult to a certain course of action involving him/herself or his/her Recipient Child. Such consent will only be valid when the consenting person:

> has been informed by the physician(s) treating a Recipient Child of such foreseeable risks, results, and alternatives to a proposed medical procedure as a reasonable medical practitioner of the same school, in the same or similar circumstances, would make known to his/her patients;

> agrees in writing to the performance of the procedure for which consent was sought;

> has been informed that the granting of consent is voluntary and may be revoked at any time.

Disabled--Child--An-individual-below-the-age-of-21-who-has-a-physical impairment-or-an-organic-disease,-function,-defect,-or-condition-which may-hinder-the-achievement-of-normal-growth-and/or-development.

Diagnostic Services: Those medical services which provide information necessary to determine a child's medical eligibility for participation in the DSCC treatment program, i.e., whether an Applicant has a Medically Eligible Condition. See Section 1200.40 of this Part. Diagnostic Services shall also include any initial interviews provided as a part of the application process.

Emergency: A medical situation requiring immediate medical care and services to avoid loss of life, permanent loss of good health, or permanent degradation of state of health.

Field Clinic: A community-based clinic which meets on a periodic basis for the purpose of diagnosis and treatment. Such clinics are organized and operated by DSCC and utilize DSCC approved providers.

Financial Participation Agreement (FPA): The agreement between DSCC and the Legally Responsible Adult(s) which specifies the family's monetary obligation to pay for a specified portion of approved direct medical care and/or related care for their Recipient Child, which agreement must be signed prior to receiving DSCC benefits. This

BOARD OF TRUSTEES OF THE UNIVERSITY OF ILLINOIS

NOTICE OF ADOPTED AMENDMENTS

amount is determined according to the Payment Scale, Appendix B, of this Part and through the rules established in this Part.

Full Financial Assistance: When DSCC pays, to the extent provided for in this Part, for all of a Recipient Child's DSCC authorized services not covered by the family's insurance. To determine eligibility see Section 1200.50 of this Part.

Health Care Facility: Any Diagnostic and Treatment Facility within the contemplation of Section 1200.110(a) and any Outpatient Therapy Center within the contemplation of Section 1200.110(b) of this Part.

Health Care Professional: Any individual or corporation licensed or certified to provide health care services to a patient and practicing in a commonly recognized field of knowledge. The term shall include but shall not be limited to Physicians and Other Health Care Professionals as defined in Section 1200.100(a)(3).

Health--Care--Facility:--Any--Diagnostic-and-Treatment--Facility-within the-contemplation-of-Section-1200.110(a)-and--any--Outpatient--Therapy Center-within-the-contemplation-of-Section-1200.110(b)-of-this-Part.

Health Care Provider: Any Health Care Professional, Health Care Facility, or any Medical Equipment Supplier within the meaning of Section 1200.110(c) of this Part.

Income: Money received by an Applicant, Recipient Child, or his family which can be applied directly to meet basic needs for food, shelter, and medical expenses. Total income is defined at Section 1200.50(d)(2) of this Part. Adjusted family income, i.e., net income, is figured by reference to Section Sections 1200.50(d)(3) of this Part.

Income Scale: The schedule, adjusted for family size, used to determine financial eligibility.

Individual Service Plan: A document describing a child's health and developmental status which serves as a basis for a plan of specific services and monitoring. The Plan is developed by the DSCC professional staff based upon the demonstrated health care needs of the child and the availability of services to meet those needs.

Legally Responsible Adult (LRA): A person who is legally required to provide for and entitled to make decisions about the DSCC service Applicant or Recipient Child. This person may be a parent (biological or adoptive) or legally appointed guardian. The LRA may also be the DSCC service Applicant or Recipient Child under the following circumstances:

BOARD OF TRUSTEES OF THE UNIVERSITY OF ILLINOIS

NOTICE OF ADOPTED AMENDMENTS

If he/she has been emancipated in accordance with the provisions of the Emancipation of Mature Minors Act [750 ILCS 30] (Ill. Rev. Stat. 1991 ch. 40, par. 2201 et seq.) provided that the order of emancipation contemplates that the Applicant or Recipient Child is empowered to act in the manner required.

If he/she is authorized to consent to health care services in accordance with the Consent by Minors to Medical Procedures Act [410 ILCS 210] (Ill. Rev. Stat. 1991 ch. 111, par. 4501 et seq.).

If he/she is over the age of 18 years and has the legal capacity to act in the manner required, provided that, if any Applicant or Recipient Child is partially or wholly financially dependent on his/her parents or guardian, the parents or guardian shall be considered the LRA for purposes of making financial determinations hereunder. Medical consent is required from only one Legally Responsible Adult in the event that the Recipient Child or Applicant is not legally entitled to consent.

Medically Eligible Condition: That medical condition which renders the child eligible for DSCC services. Specific conditions are enumerated at Section 1200.40 of this Part.

Parent: The biological or adoptive parent of the Applicant or Recipient Child receiving or seeking DSCC services.

Partial Financial Assistance: The amount that DSCC pays over and above the amount for which the family is obligated and over and above the amount which is covered by insurance.

Payment Scale: The schedule indicating an amount the family is expected to contribute toward the medically related costs of care for their Recipient Child during a twelve - (12) month period. This contribution is required from all families who have not been categorized as fully financially eligible.

Principal Medical Condition: The medical condition which exerts the most pervasive impact on the child's function, state of health or well-being or anatomic structure. Usually the condition which requires the most immediate and extensive medical attention at the time.

Programmatic Assistance: A process undertaken by professional staff of the Division on behalf of children with Medically Eligible Conditions, which may include procedures for evaluation of the child's condition, development of an Individual Service Plan, recommendations of health care providers and facilities, assistance in arrangement of

BOARD OF TRUSTEES OF THE UNIVERSITY OF ILLINOIS

NOTICE OF ADOPTED AMENDMENTS

such care, and subsequent monitoring of the status of the child and family. The level of programmatic assistance required will be based on the medical needs of the child as determined by usual and customary medical standards.

Recipient Child: A child who is currently receiving DSCC services or whose Health Care Providers are being paid, in whole or part, by DSCC.

Referral: A procedure by which any person can introduce a child to the DSCC program. See Section 1200.80(c)(5)(A) and (B) of this Part.

Reimbursement Agreement: Written agreement signed by the LRA(#) and/or attorney(s) for the LRA or eligible child specifying that any money recovered as judgment or settlement of a lawsuit or from an insurance or personal settlement arising from a claim relating to the child's medical condition for which DSCC is providing care or reimbursing Health Care Providers will be used to reimburse DSCC for its payment of the child's medical and related care costs, which funds will then be replaced into the DSCC program and used to further benefit eligible children.

Resident(s) of Illinois:

Any person living in the State of Illinois with the intent to remain in the State indefinitely. The term "living in the State of Illinois" shall be limited to all persons whose primary domicile is located within the State. Intent to remain indefinitely is established through a showing that a person has significant contacts with the State of Illinois as evidenced by indicia thereof, such as maintaining a bank account in the State, registering to vote in the State, paying Illinois income taxes, obtaining permanent employment within the State, owning real estate within the State, and possessing an Illinois driver's license or similar permits; or

Any person who is present in the State of Illinois for the purpose of performing migrant agricultural labor and who evidenced a pattern of regularly returning to the State to perform such work or who expresses an intention to establish a pattern of regularly returning to the State to perform such work. Migrant agricultural labor is defined as agricultural work of a seasonal or temporary nature which requires that the worker be away from his/her permanent place of residence to perform said work more than overnight. A pattern of regularly returning to the State to perform such work shall be considered to have been established if a person is present in the State of Illinois to perform migrant agricultural work for two successive growing seasons; or

BOARD OF TRUSTEES OF THE UNIVERSITY OF ILLINOIS

NOTICE OF ADOPTED AMENDMENTS

Any person who is an active duty member of the U.S. military and on official military assignment within the State of Illinois, whether or not they maintain residence in another state, or any person who is an active duty member of the U.S. military on official military assignment in another state or country who pays Illinois income taxes.

Retroactive Authorization: Authorizations which occur, under specified circumstances, after medical service has been provided to a Recipient Child. See Section 1200.80(c)(5) for enumeration of the circumstances in which this will be considered.

Retroactive Financial Eligibility: Financial eligibility which reaches· back no more than 30 days prior to the date of completed application. See Section 1200.50(c)(7)(A) and (B).

(Source: Amended at 21 Ill. Reg. _____, effective
DEC 1 1 1997   )

Section 1200.30 Eligibility: General

a) Program Purpose
   The purpose of the Illinois Division of Specialized Care for Children is to provide diagnostic and treatment services for children who are disabled as a result of congenital and/or acquired states or have a condition which may lead to disability. The objective is to provide a program of comprehensive evaluation, medical care and related habilitative services appropriate to their various needs and to financially support such care to the extent that ·their Legally Responsible Adults (LRAs) require such financial assistance as determined by the Financial Eligibility Criteria (Section 1200.50 of this Part). Children who are eligible for Programmatic Assistance only will be served without regard to a financial means test. Due to financial limitations, DSCC will only provide assistance to children with certain categories of disabling conditions as defined in Section 1200.40 of this Part.

b) Eligibility Criteria for Diagnostic Services
   1) Initial diagnostic services are provided without regard to ability to pay to the extent medically necessary applying usual and customary medical standards to determine whether the child has one of the conditions enumerated in Section 1200.40, Medically Eligible Conditions. Whenever eligibility or ineligibility is established based upon an interview with the child or the LRA, which occurs when a diagnosis has already been established, DSCC shall not be required to provide further initial medical diagnostic services.
   2) Children may be but need not be referred for said services by an individual or agency.

BOARD OF TRUSTEES OF THE UNIVERSITY OF ILLINOIS

NOTICE OF ADOPTED AMENDMENTS

   3) To make medically necessary diagnostic services accessible to families, DSCC will support needed transportation costs.
c) Eligibility Criteria for Other DSCC Services
   1) Programmatic Assistance
      To be eligible for Programmatic Assistance a child must meet the following requirements:
      A) Be under 21 years of age;
      B) Be a Resident of Illinois;
      C) Have a Medically Eligible Condition.
   2) Treatment Services and Financial Support
      It is recognized that it·is the duty and responsibility of the LRAs to pay for necessary health care services for their children. DSCC will assist the LRA with this responsibility by providing treatment services and financial assistance, provided the LRAs are Residents of Illinois, and provided the child:
      A) Be under 18 years· of age (except that DSCC shall provide services beyond the child's 18th birthday when necessary to complete a treatment plan developed before that time if cessation of treatment would cause an immediate threat to or damage to the child's life or good health or would negate gains resulting from previous rehabilitative efforts. In no event may said extension continue beyond six-months-after the child's 21st 18th birthday);
      B) Be a Resident of Illinois;
      C) Have a Medically Eligible Condition· and in addition:
         i) The LRAs are lawfully admitted to the United States on a visa or ·permit which contemplates that the LRA will be entitled to permanently remain in the United States or has been admitted under color of law; or
         ii) The child aforedescribed is a United States citizen.
   3) In addition, whenever payment for treatment services or financial support is desired, the LRA must:
      A) Meet the financial eligibility criteria set forth at Section 1200.50 of this Part;
      B) Make maximum use of insurance benefits, if any, as well as any other form of payment (such as trust funds, gifts, or fund raising drives) available for the child and/or make the payments toward the support of the child's treatment as are determined by his or her FPA;
      C) Sign a Reimbursement Agreement, if the injuries for· which treatment is sought were caused by any alleged negligent act (including products liability) whenever litigation is pending or contemplated.
   4) Further, any attorney retained to represent the child on any claim relating to the child's medical condition for which DSCC will provide care must separately sign the Reimbursement Agreement. Failure to comply with this requirement will not, however, delay or hinder the application process.

BOARD OF TRUSTEES OF THE UNIVERSITY OF ILLINOIS

NOTICE OF ADOPTED AMENDMENTS

5) When the LRAs are not residents of Illinois, treatment services and financial support can be provided for a limited period of time when all the following conditions are met:
   A) The child remains a resident of Illinois;
   B) The child's LRAs were residents of Illinois at the time the child was registered with DSCC;
   C) An active DSCC supported treatment plan for the child's eligible condition was in progress at the time the LRAs left Illinois;
   D) Discontinuation of treatment would result in probable harm to the child or an adverse outcome of treatment; and
   E) Legal action is in progress that will establish legal guardianship of the child with a person or agency located in Illinois.

d) Application Process: Initial and Continuing Eligibility

   1) No person participating in or wishing to participate in the Division's programs shall be denied benefits of the program or shall be discriminated against on the basis of sex, religion, race, color, national origin or handicap not related to program eligibility.

   2) General responsibilities of Applicants, Recipient Children, and LRAs:
      A) Applicants/Recipients and LRAs requesting assistance shall furnish requested factual information regarding eligibility and shall keep DSCC informed of any changes in financial status (defined as any change in financial circumstances which would affect financial eligibility for DSCC benefits as set forth in Section 1200.50 including, but not limited to changes in family size, income, or expenses).
      B) The application process requires consent by the LRA(s) to release or to verify medical data and financial information provided as a part of the application process.

   3) An LRA shall complete and sign a written application on behalf of the Applicant on forms specified by DSCC. DSCC shall inform the Applicant of all relevant time deadlines with respect to filing of an application and appealing any adverse decision. An LRA may choose a person to assist in completing the application. A representative of a public agency may complete and sign the application for a child in that agency's custody. A representative of a private agency may complete and sign the application for a child if he/she is the authorized guardian for the child.

   4) A completed application must be submitted to DSCC within the following time periods:
      A) In all cases, a completed application for initial financial eligibility must be received by DSCC within thirty (t 30) days from the date of services for which assistance is desired. Applications not received within the said 30 day

BOARD OF TRUSTEES OF THE UNIVERSITY OF ILLINOIS

NOTICE OF ADOPTED AMENDMENTS

period shall be processed for reimbursement of treatment services provided no more than 30 days prior to the actual date of receipt. This time period shall be adjusted by DSCC for good cause if DSCC is notified of the circumstances within the 30 day time period (for purposes of this clause, "good cause" shall include, but shall not be limited to, a family emergency, demonstrated delays caused by the U.S. Postal Service, and demonstrated delays caused by the Internal Revenue Service in providing a copy of an income tax return).

      B) Applications for continuing financial eligibility must be received by DSCC within the current period of eligibility. If an application is received after said eligibility time period, continuing eligibility shall recommence no more than thirty (t 30) days prior to the date the application is actually received by DSCC.

   5) If financial support is desired, the LRA shall complete and sign a financial application on behalf of the Applicant on forms specified by DSCC, which shall be submitted within the time periods specified in Section 1200.30(d)(4).
      A) Such statement shall include a copy of the LRA's most recent filed federal income tax return. If an LRA is not required to file with the Internal Revenue Service, verification of income must be submitted.
      B) DSCC shall accept other supporting documents from the LRA to verify level of income if DSCC determines that the documents provided prove the information sought and if the LRA has demonstrated diligence in attempting to obtain federal tax returns or pay stubs but has been unsuccessful in doing so.
      C) DSCC shall accept supporting documentation from the LRA that reflects financial eligibility for services being provided by or reimbursed by the Illinois Department of Public Aid (IDPA) or any other State state agency using criteria the same as or more stringent than DSCC.

   6) If financial support is not desired, no financial application is required. Applicants with a Medically Eligible Condition who either do not desire or do not qualify for DSCC financial support shall be eligible for Programmatic Assistance.

   7) Determination of eligibility is performed at the regional offices. (See 2 Ill. Adm. Code 5155.Appendix A.)
      A) The DSCC staff shall verify the information provided on behalf of the Applicant. This may include discussion, including an interview with the LRA, if the application is not complete. The interview shall be conducted at a place and time convenient to all parties.
      B) If supplemental information required by DSCC to determine eligibility is not provided within thirty (t 30) days after the LRA receives notice of a requirement that the said

BOARD OF TRUSTEES OF THE UNIVERSITY OF ILLINOIS

NOTICE OF ADOPTED AMENDMENTS

information is needed to complete this application, DSCC shall then advise the LRA that the application will be invalidated and not given further consideration unless the LRA was precluded, due to causes beyond his/her control, from providing the information required.

C) A written decision regarding eligibility shall be sent to the LRA and any referring medical care provider or referring agency within ~~thirty~~ 30† days ~~after~~ of receipt of the completed application unless the emergent nature of the child's condition requires a decision in a more timely fashion.

(Source: Amended at 21 Ill. Reg. _1711_ , effective ~~DEC 11 1997~~)

Section 1200.40 Medical Eligibility

a) Eligible Medical Conditions

1) Within the resources available, the Division of Specialized Care for Children has determined that it can best serve children who: have disabling impairments that are expected to be chronic; involve multiple physical defects/ disabilities/handicaps; are amenable to treatment as determined by the treating physician; have a need for long-term highly specialized medical care including, as necessary, related habilitative services; and in the judgement of the treating physician have life expectancy sufficient to realize benefit from the treatment.

2) Currently, DSCC serves children whose disabling impairments are enumerated in the list which follows. These conditions were determined as covered by the Director, in consultation with and upon advice of the Advisory Board.

b) Medically Eligible Conditions

1) ORTHOPEDIC IMPAIRMENTS are defined as those affecting bone, joint or muscle are eligible. Such impairments may be of congenital origin, or may be manifestations of an active chronic disease, or may represent a persisting result of previous infection, trauma, toxicity, disease or malignancy, which are determined to be chronic orthopedic impairments amenable to treatment requiring long-term management involving specialist care and required related habilitative or rehabilitative services.

2) NERVOUS SYSTEM IMPAIRMENTS which are defined as those affecting the brain, spinal cord or peripheral nerves, and present as persistent or recurring loss of consciousness, coordination, strength or sensation, but not cognitive or emotional disability, are eligible. Such impairments may be of congenital origin, or may be manifestations of an active chronic disease, or may represent a persisting result of previous infection, trauma,

BOARD OF TRUSTEES OF THE UNIVERSITY OF ILLINOIS

NOTICE OF ADOPTED AMENDMENTS

toxicity, disease or malignancy, which are determined to be chronic neurologic impairments responsive to medical treatment requiring long-term management involving specialist care and required related habilitative services. Children in a chronic vegetative state would be eligible upon medically determined emergence of recovery and sufficient health stability for a program of active habilitation to be instituted (for purposes of this clause, a chronic vegetative state is defined as a condition in which a child displays no evidence of progressive positive developmental or neurological improvement, as determined by usual and customary medical standards).

3) CARDIOVASCULAR IMPAIRMENTS which are defined as primarily affecting the heart and/or the larger blood vessels are eligible. Such impairments may be of congenital or acquired origin, the latter representing a persisting result of previous infection, trauma, toxicity or disease or malignancy, and which are determined to be a chronic cardiovascular impairment responsive to treatment requiring multispecialist intervention and a program of extended supervision and/or long-term active management, specialized medical care and such related habilitation services as may be necessary. Children with a disease or past infection known to primarily affect the heart and/or larger blood vessels which predispose to chronic heart and/or larger blood vessels impairment and which requires specialist management to minimize or preclude such impairment would be eligible.

4) EXTERNAL BODY IMPAIRMENTS, including the oral and nasal structures with their extension into the mouth, pharynx, larynx, major bronchi and esophageal structures, defined as significant defects affecting the skin and/or its underlying structures and defects of the mucosa and/or its underlying structures of the above internal parts which may affect breathing, speech and eating. Such impairments must be determined to be beyond the normal range of acceptable external appearances or adequate function, as determined by a medical specialist, responsive to specialist(s) intervention and a program of long-term management with related habilitation services or subject to correction which would preclude chronic physical or functional impairment, and may be of congenital origin, or may be manifestations of an active chronic disease, or may represent a persisting result of previous infection, disease, trauma, toxicity or malignancy. External body defects to be considered as beyond the normal range of accepted appearance are those defects considered to be major in the customary characterization of congenital defects or, if acquired, to be defects which fall outside of acceptable appearance as defined by the Division in consultation with its advisers. Defects of dentition and occlusion associated with severe oro-craniofacial structural deformities or if causative to impairment of intelligible speech are included.

BOARD OF TRUSTEES OF THE UNIVERSITY OF ILLINOIS

NOTICE OF ADOPTED AMENDMENTS

5) HEARING IMPAIRMENTS which are defined as a loss of hearing or
    deafness of at least 30 decibels in two frequencies or a 35
    decibel loss in one speech frequency involving one or both ears,
    as determined by audiometric testing are eligible. Such hearing
    loss may be of congenital origin, or may be a manifestation of an
    active chronic disease, or may represent a persisting result of
    previous infection, trauma, toxicity, disease or malignancy and
    which are determined to be chronic hearing impairments responsive
    to treatment requiring otological intervention and a program of
    extended supervision and/or long-term active management.
    Children with middle ear infection and/or middle ear effusion
    persisting for longer than three months and who have received
    medical treatment are eligible for special medical and hearing
    assessment and evaluation of communicative skills. If a hearing
    impairment is defined, otologic treatment, monitoring of
    communicative skills and provision of hearing aids shall be
    provided if determined medically necessary in accordance with
    usual and customary standards. Children considered to be
    profoundly deaf and not amenable to otologic intervention and/or
    hearing aids, as determined through the application of usual and
    customary medical standards, shall be eligible for assistance to
    enhance the communication skills of the child (and family) if
    such assistance is not available from other agencies or sources.
6) SPEECH IMPAIRMENTS which are defined as an impairment of
    intelligibility arising from any structural defect of the organs
    responsible for vocalization or neurological defects specific to
    orderly speech development are eligible. Such speech impairments
    may be of congenital origin, or may be manifestations of an
    active chronic disease, or represent a persisting result of
    previous infection, trauma, disease or malignancy determined to
    be responsible for the chronic speech impairment which is
    responsive to medical treatment requiring long-term management
    involving specialist care and related habilitative services and
    equipment. Developmental language deficits are not eligible (for
    purposes of this clause, a developmental language deficit is
    defined as a condition, as determined by the application of usual
    and customary medical standards, that can be expected to correct
    itself with maturation or with such therapy as is generally
    available through the public school system).
7) CYSTIC FIBROSIS. Children with cystic fibrosis are eligible if
    they manifest symptoms amenable to specialized medical care and
    long-term management by a team of specialists organized for this
    purpose.
8) HEMOPHILIA and similar chronic defects of coagulation or chronic
    hemorrhagic conditions are eligible. Eligibility for services
    shall be established in accordance with Rules ~~of--the--Illinois
    Department--of--Public--Health~~ under the Hemophilia Care Act [410
    ILCS 420] ~~{Ill.-Rev.-Stat.-1991,-ch.-111-1/2,-pars.-2900-et-seq.}~~

BOARD OF TRUSTEES OF THE UNIVERSITY OF ILLINOIS

NOTICE OF ADOPTED AMENDMENTS

    ~~and--Rules--promulgated--thereunder;~~ [77 Ill. Adm. Code 705].
    Eligible persons shall receive such services as may be provided
    with those rules ~~by-the--Illinois-Department-of-Public--Health--in
    accordance--with--the--rules--aforedescribed~~. DSCC shall provide
    children case management and financial support of
    hospitalization, outpatient care and such additional services as
    may be required for specialized medical and related habilitative
    services, including home management, except that a Recipient
    Child not eligible for services under the Hemophilia Care Act
    ~~from--the--Illinois-Department-of-Public-Health~~ as provided above
    shall receive required services through the Division.
9) INBORN ERRORS OF METABOLISM which are defined as those newborn
    conditions leading to severe neurological, mental and physical
    deterioration for which there are acceptable treatments which,
    when promptly instituted, would preclude or significantly
    minimize the adverse effects of the metabolic defect are
    eligible.
10) EYE IMPAIRMENTS which are defined as those affecting the eye
    and/or eye muscles, but excluding isolated refractive errors, are
    eligible. Such impairments must lead to or cause a significant
    risk of loss of vision and be chronic impairments which are
    determined to be responsive to treatment requiring medical or
    surgical ophthalmology ~~medical-or-surgical~~ intervention and a
    program of extended supervision and/or long-term active
    management. In determining whether an eye impairment may be
    responsive to a program of extended supervision and/or long-term
    active management, the following factors must be present: that
    without treatment, the condition would be expected to last at
    least six months; and that extended and long-term active
    management shall require medical supervision of at least six
    months. Such impairments may be of congenital origin, or may be
    a manifestation of an active chronic disease, or may represent a
    persisting result of previous infection, trauma, toxicity or
    disease. When required as part of an approved management program
    not involving services or equipment prohibited by Section
    1200.80(a) and approved pursuant to Sections 1200.80(b) and (c),
    and prescribed by the managing ophthalmologist, treatment of
    associated refractive errors is eligible. Children considered to
    be blind and not amenable to ophthalmologic intervention, as
    determined through the application of usual and customary medical
    standards, are not eligible under this category.
11) URINARY SYSTEM IMPAIRMENTS which are defined as those chronic
    organic impairments affecting the kidney, ureter, bladder, and/or
    urethra, but excluding urinary tract infections, and isolated
    ureteral urinary reflux unless associated with a persistent
    structural defect, are eligible. Such impairments may be of
    congenital origin, or may be manifestations of an active chronic
    disease, or may represent a persisting result of previous

BOARD OF TRUSTEES OF THE UNIVERSITY OF ILLINOIS

NOTICE OF ADOPTED AMENDMENTS

infection, trauma, toxicity, disease or malignancy, which are determined to be chronic, amenable to treatment requiring long-term medical or surgical management involving specialist care and required related habilitative or rehabilitative services. Children requiring chronic renal dialysis and/or renal transplantation are not eligible under this category.

c) Health care services defined as "well child care," routine medical and dental treatment, medical care of acute childhood illnesses (defined as diseases which are not normally chronically disabling and which are not unusual in the course of a child's maturation) or trauma or short-term complications related thereto, are not provided by DSCC.

d) Health care services for children whose impairment is considered to be "acute" as an immediate associated consequence of infection, trauma, disease, toxicity or malignancy, would be considered eligible after completion of medical treatment of such acute condition and determination of a resulting persisting disability.

e) Care Beyond Medical Eligible Conditions
Children with the chronic disabilities which are defined in this Section as Medically Eligible Conditions may have associated health impairments which, as isolated health impairments, would not be considered as medically eligible for DSCC services. However, in order to achieve successful treatment of the eligible condition, if medically recommended, the services required to treat such associated health impairments will be provided to Recipient Children, except those related to a malignancy or to a chronic vegetative state. Treatment of such associated health impairments must be necessary for successful treatment of the Medically Eligible Condition and will continue to be provided only so long as the Recipient Child has a Medically Eligible Condition which is under continuing and active medical treatment. Further, if at any time, one of these other than Medically Eligible Conditions becomes the Recipient Child's principal medical condition, these additional services will be discontinued.

(Source: Amended at 21 Ill. Reg. _____, effective ___DEC 11 1997___)

Section 1200.50 Financial Eligibility

a) The LRA has an obligation to meet the cost of medical care for his/her Recipient Child to the extent they are able. Full or partial financial assistance, in the form described in Section 1200.90 of this Part, is provided to LRAs who are unable to meet such expenses from their own resources as established through a financial need determination Financial Need Determination performed pursuant to criteria established in subsections Section 1200.50(c) and (d) of this Section.

b) Exceptions to Financial Need Determination
1) DSCC provides diagnostic services necessary to determine medical

BOARD OF TRUSTEES OF THE UNIVERSITY OF ILLINOIS

NOTICE OF ADOPTED AMENDMENTS

eligibility without regard to the economic status of an Applicant's LRAs.

2) Financial information is not required from LRAs when:
A) medical eligibility is uncertain;
B) no expenditure of DSCC funds is anticipated;
C) the child is a ward of the State state agency which is financially responsible for the child's medical care;
D) the child has been determined eligible for services being provided by or reimbursed by a State state agency using criteria the same as, or more stringent than, DSCC. However, if such LRAs elect to provide financial information and complete the financial need process, they may do so and the period of eligibility established will be determined in accordance with subsection (c)(7) below.

c) Criteria for Financial Assistance
1) Financial eligibility is based upon the financial status of the LRA requesting financial assistance.

2) The Income Scale (Appendix A) and the Payment Scale (Appendix B) are used to determine financial eligibility. The Income Scale represents 65% 58% of the gross median family income adjusted for family size as developed for the State of Illinois by the U.S. Department of Health and Human Services, Family Support Administration under the provisions of Section 2603(7) of Title XXVI of the Omnibus Budget Reconciliation Act of 1981 (P.L. 97-35). Although this scale is derived from gross income figures, for purposes of financial eligibility, a family is placed on the scale according to its Adjusted Family Income and family size.

3) Full financial assistance is provided when the Adjusted Family Income considering family size is equal to or less than that which is allowable in accordance with the Income Scale. The LRA and attorney must submit a Reimbursement Agreement, if applicable, as provided in Section 1200.30(c)(3)(C).

4) Partial financial assistance is provided when the Adjusted Family Income considering family size exceeds the amount allowable on the Income Scale, subject to the following conditions:
A) A determination that the annual family payment as established in the Payment Scale is less than the anticipated cost of services for the proposed period of eligibility;
B) Completion of a Financial Participation Agreement (FPA) by the LRA. An FPA will be required whenever the LRA of a Recipient Child is eligible for partial financial assistance. The FPA shall be signed and returned to DSCC within thirty (30) days after of its receipt by the LRA.
i) The FPA obligates an LRA to pay for DSCC approved care for the Recipient Child. The amount will be equal to the annual family payment described by the Payment

BOARD OF TRUSTEES OF THE UNIVERSITY OF ILLINOIS

NOTICE OF ADOPTED AMENDMENTS

      Scale. DSCC will use this money to pay for the child's direct and related care.

    ii) The FPA shall cover all Recipient Children in one family.

  C) Submission of a Reimbursement Agreement by the LRAs and attorney(s), as provided in Section 1200.30(c)(3)(C), if applicable.

  D) Adjustments to the annual family payment shall be made by DSCC if there is evidence in the application or through additional information that indicates the LRA has the ability to assume cost-sharing beyond the amount previously indicated based upon application of the financial eligibility criteria in this Section 1200.50.

5) The LRA shall be determined ineligible for financial assistance from DSCC when:

  A) It is determined that the Adjusted Family Income is in excess of $10,499 of that which is allowable in accordance with Appendix A, the Income Scale.

  B) An LRA has failed within the time periods established in Section 1200.30(d) to provide sufficient information to determine eligibility. In such instances, eligibility shall commence up to 30 days prior to the postmark date or, if unavailable, the date of receipt of a new application with such information sufficient necessary to establish eligibility.

  C) An LRA has failed within the time period established in Section 1200.30(d) to complete and sign the application (including the financial application), the Reimbursement Agreement (Section 1200.30(c)(3)(C)), if applicable, and an FPA, if applicable (Section 1200.50(c)). In such instances, eligibility shall commence up to 30 days prior to the postmark date or, if unavailable, the date of receipt of a new the signed application, and/or Reimbursement Agreement, and/or FPA.

  D) The family is fully enrolled in the Illinois Comprehensive Health Insurance Program or a Health Maintenance Organization (HMO) which has responsibility for provision of medical care for the Applicant or Recipient Child. However, families with HMO coverage are eligible for financial assistance to the extent that the HMO has no responsibility for such care.

  D)E) In addition, the LRAs shall lose their financial assistance if:

    i) Medical insurance payments or other forms of payment available or paid directly to the LRA to meet the cost of care for the Recipient Child have not been applied to the cost of care arranged, authorized, and paid by DSCC for that child. In such instances, the LRA may

BOARD OF TRUSTEES OF THE UNIVERSITY OF ILLINOIS

NOTICE OF ADOPTED AMENDMENTS

    reapply for assistance upon repayment to DSCC of an amount equal to the medical insurance payments made available but not applied toward the child's cost of care.

  ii) An LRA has not complied with the payment schedule established in the FPA with DSCC. In such instances, the LRA may reapply for assistance once the required payment has been made to DSCC.

  iii) An LRA fails to notify DSCC within thirty (30) days of any change in the child's medical insurance which results in medical coverage for costs which are currently paid for by DSCC.

  iv) An LRA fails to submit a Reimbursement Agreement in accordance with Section 1200.30(c)(3)(C), if applicable.

  v)iv) It is determined that the LRA has in any way falsified documents used to determine eligibility.

6) LRAs determined to be wholly or partially ineligible shall be advised of the right to appeal the determination in accordance with the procedures as set forth in Section 1200.60.

7) Period of Financial Eligibility

  A) Financial eligibility shall be established for a period of up to twenty-four (24) months commencing no sooner than thirty (30) days prior to the date a completed application is received by DSCC if applicants are able to provide current federal tax information. For purposes of this Section, current federal tax information shall be defined as the tax information for the calendar year prior to the year of application; or

  B) Financial eligibility shall be established for a period of up to twelve (12) months commencing no sooner than thirty (30) days prior to the date a completed application is received by DSCC under the following circumstances:

    i) Applicants able to provide federal tax information not older than one (1) year prior to the current federal tax information.

    ii) Applicants not required to file federal income tax forms as defined by the federal Internal Revenue Service. Income must be verified using two (2) consecutive pay stubs that are within two (2) months of application.

    iii) Applicants determined to have a Financial Participation Agreement.

    iv) Applicants determined financially eligible on the basis of eligibility for services being provided by or reimbursed under the Hemophilia Care Act (410 ILCS 420). by the Illinois Department of Public Aid (IDPA) or any other state agency using criteria the same as

BOARD OF TRUSTEES OF THE UNIVERSITY OF ILLINOIS

NOTICE OF ADOPTED AMENDMENTS

~~or more stringent than DSCC.~~

C) When more than one child in a family is eligible for financial assistance, the period of eligibility for all eligible children will be for the same period.

D) Financial eligibility shall be redetermined subject to the date established at subsection (c)(7)(A) and (B) above.

E) The period of financial eligibility may be <u>decreased</u> ~~less than 12 months~~ under the following circumstances:
   ~~i) DSCC eligibility was based upon eligibility with the Illinois Department of Public Aid (IDPA) or any other state agency and such eligibility has been cancelled. Eligibility for DSCC benefits shall be cancelled at the same time that IDPA or the other state agency eligibility is cancelled.~~
   ~~ii~~i) The Recipient Child, at the time of financial evaluation, was a ward of an agency or court because adoption had not been finalized, and the adoption is finalized. DSCC eligibility shall terminate on the effective date of the finalization of the adoption.
   ~~iii~~ii) Supplemental information submitted pursuant to Section 1200.30(d)(2)(A) of this Part causes a change in financial eligibility.
   iii) <u>The Recipient Child loses DSCC General or Medical Eligibility. Eligibility for DSCC benefits shall terminate at the time that DSCC General or Medical Eligibility is determined to have been lost.</u>

F) In the event that an LRA submits information, at any time, which, upon verification by DSCC, establishes that the LRA is eligible or ineligible for financial assistance at a level in excess of that previously approved by DSCC, a new period of eligibility shall begin on the date <u>the</u> ~~said~~ information is received by DSCC, provided that the LRA has <u>met all prior financial obligations to DSCC and</u> signed a <u>new</u> ~~revised~~ FPA, if one is required pursuant to subsection (c)(4)(B).

d) Financial Determination Calculations
   1) Family Size
      A) Family size shall be determined by the sum of the number of persons in each of the following categories when they share the same household. However, if a person falls into more than one category, that person shall be counted only once:
         i) The Applicant or Recipient Child;
         ii) The Applicant or Recipient Child's spouse;
         iii) An LRA and his/her spouse;
         iv) Other persons who, for Federal Income Tax purposes, are deemed dependents of the applying LRA.
   2) The family's annual Total Income shall be the sum of all income of persons comprising the family unit, as determined above but excluding income of dependent children except income of the

BOARD OF TRUSTEES OF THE UNIVERSITY OF ILLINOIS

NOTICE OF ADOPTED AMENDMENTS

dependent Applicant or Recipient Child and his/her spouse. Total Income shall include all income as <u>defined</u> by the Internal Revenue Service for federal income tax reporting purposes.
   3) The following are allowable expenses which the family may deduct from their annual Total Income in determining financial eligibility:
      A) The larger of:
         i) The federal income tax Standard Deduction Rate based on the LRA's federal income tax filing status used to determine financial eligibility; <u>or</u> ~~or~~
         ii) The total itemized deductions as reported on Schedule A of the LRA's federal filed income tax return used to determine financial eligibility.
      B) Child and dependent care costs in accordance with the guidelines established by the Internal Revenue Service for federal income tax reporting purposes.

(Source: Amended at 21 Ill. Reg. _____, effective
_____DEC 11 1997_____)

Section 1200.60 Appeal Process

a) Notice of Determination
   1) Except as otherwise provided in <u>this Part</u> ~~these Rules~~, the Division shall notify the Applicant's LRA in writing within ~~thirty (~~ 30<u>)</u> days <u>after</u> ~~of~~ the receipt of the completed application that the Division has determined that the Applicant is eligible or ineligible, and the amount, if any, of the LRA's required financial contribution to the cost of the Applicant's medical care. If the Applicant or LRA is determined to be ineligible, the Notice of Determination shall state the reasons for <u>the</u> ~~said~~ determination.
   2) In the event that DSCC has requested additional information in order to determine eligibility, or has requested the LRA to sign a Reimbursement Agreement or an FPA and the request has not been complied with within the time period set forth in Section 1200.50, DSCC shall notify the LRAs that the application shall be considered inactive and provide the reasons therefor.
   3) The Division shall notify a Recipient Child's LRA in writing of any action which the Division intends to take which adversely affects ~~the LRA's financial~~ eligibility. This written notification shall provide specific reasons for the action being taken. This written notification shall be sent to the Recipient Child's LRA at least ~~thirty (~~ 30<u>)</u> days prior to ~~the~~ effective date of the proposed action.
   4) An explanation of the LRA's right to appeal shall be sent with each Notice of Determination provided pursuant to <u>subsections</u> ~~subsection~~ (<u>a</u>)(1)-(3) ~~immediately~~ above.

BOARD OF TRUSTEES OF THE UNIVERSITY OF ILLINOIS

NOTICE OF ADOPTED AMENDMENTS

    5) The Notice of Determination described at subsection (a)(3) immediately above and all further written notices which bear on it shall be sent by certified or registered mail to the LRA at his/her last known address. If the Applicant or Recipient Child has a designated representative, a copy of all written notices will also be sent to that designated representative.

b) Right to Reapply

    1) If the Applicant or Recipient Child's LRA has been determined to be ineligible, they may reapply at any time they believe they have become eligible.

    2) If the Recipient Child's financial eligibility has been reduced or has been set at a level less than full financial assistance, the LRA may submit additional financial information at any time their financial situation changes.

c) Right to Meeting and Appeal Conference

    1) The Applicant or Recipient Child's LRA, or designated representative, has a right to a meeting with the DSCC staff person responsible for a decision reflected in any Notice of Determination issued pursuant to subsections subsection (a)(1)-(3).

      A) The request for such a meeting must be made in writing and must identify the decision which is being questioned.

      B) The request must be made within 14 days after of receipt of the said Notice of Determination.

      C) DSCC shall contact the requester within five (5) days after of receipt of the request in order to schedule a meeting date, time and place.

      D) Within seven (7) days after the meeting, DSCC shall notify the Applicant or Recipient Child's LRA of the result of the meeting. Such notification shall be in the manner set forth at subsection Subsection (a)(5) immediately above and shall state the reasons for the decision made.

    2) The Applicant or Recipient Child's LRA, or designated representative, has a right to appeal the results of a meeting decision to the Director in a conference with the Director or his/her designee held for that purpose. The Director shall not take part in any original decision or any initial meeting held under subsection (c)(1).

      A) The request for such an appeal conference must be made in writing and must identify the meeting decision which is being appealed.

      B) The request must be made within 14 days after of receipt of notification of result of the subsection (c)(1) meeting.

      C) DSCC shall contact the requester within five (5) days after of receipt of the request in order to schedule a meeting date, time and place.

      D) The Director or his/her designee shall consider the decision issued pursuant to subsection (c)(1)(D), any written

BOARD OF TRUSTEES OF THE UNIVERSITY OF ILLINOIS

NOTICE OF ADOPTED AMENDMENTS

    material presented at the meeting provided for in subsection (c), any evidence presented at the conference, and all other information which the Director or his/her designee obtains through an independent investigation of the issues raised by the appeal.

      E) Within seven (7) days after the appeal conference, DSCC shall notify the Applicant or Recipient Child's LRA of the result of the appeal conference. Such notification shall be in the manner set forth at subsection (a)(5) above and shall state the reasons for the decision made.

      F) The decision rendered by the Director or his designee is final.

d) Procedural Rights at Meeting and Conference

    The Applicant or Recipient Child's LRA, or designated representative, has the following rights:

    1) The right at any time to inspect and copy the contents of the Applicant or Recipient Child's case file and any other documents used by DSCC in making its determination or proposing its action; and

    2) The right to appear on their own behalf and/or to be represented, advised and/or accompanied by a relative, friend, lawyer or advocate; and

    3) The right to present relevant information, witnesses and evidence in any form; and

    4) The right to ask questions of the Division staff present.

e) DSCC may deny or dismiss a meeting or appeal conference if:

    1) The Applicant or Recipient Child's LRA, or designated representative, withdraws the request for the meeting or appeal conference in writing; or

    2) The Applicant or Recipient Child's LRA, or designated representative, fails without good cause (defined as any reason which a prudent person would deem to be an adequate and complete excuse for failure to act, such as emergencies and family deaths) to appear at the scheduled meeting or appeal conference.

f) Benefits While Awaiting Decision

    1) LRAs of Applicants who are denied financial assistance benefits may appeal the denial but shall not receive any financial benefits in behalf of the Applicant while awaiting the meeting or appeal conference.

    2) LRAs of Applicants who are granted less than full financial assistance may appeal the decision but the LRA in behalf of the Applicant will only receive such partial financial assistance as originally determined while awaiting the outcome of the said meeting or appeal conference.

    3) An LRA who is notified of a termination or reduction of financial assistance benefits shall continue at his/her prior level of financial assistance while awaiting the meeting or appeal conference, provided that the LRA requests the said meeting and

BOARD OF TRUSTEES OF THE UNIVERSITY OF ILLINOIS

NOTICE OF ADOPTED AMENDMENTS

appeal conference within the time limits designated in subsections subsection (c)(1)[B][b] and [c][C](2)(B).

g) Effective Dates of DSCC Decisions

1) If the decision of a meeting or appeal conference is in favor of an applicant's LRA, the financial assistance benefits determined appropriate as a result of the appeal shall be effective from the date of the completed application.

2) If a Recipient Child's LRA does not appeal, a Notice of Determination of termination or reduction of DSCC benefits, the effective date thereof shall be as provided for in subsection (a)(3).

3) If a Recipient Child's LRA appeals a Notice of Determination of termination or reduction of DSCC benefits, no such termination or reduction shall be effective until ten [10] days after all appeal rights have been waived or exhausted.

(Source: Amended at 21 Ill. Reg. _____ , effective
DEC 11 1997   )

Section 1200.70 Payment for Services

a) With respect to Medicaid, Medicare, any other medical insurance plan or policy or other third-party payers, unless prohibited by law, DSCC shall be deemed the payer of last resort. Nothing contained in these regulations shall authorize or require DSCC to provide payment for medical services, hospital services, supplies or appliances which would otherwise be paid by Medicaid, Medicare, any other medical insurance plan or policy or other third-party payers, including donated funds and such other funds available for medical care derived from settlement of injury claims.

b) Payments for services are subject to the availability of funds as determined by the University of Illinois in its sole discretion.

1) If DSCC determines, based upon its own internal auditing and record keeping systems, at any time, that it does not have or will not have sufficient funds to provide payments for authorized services for additional Applicants, DSCC shall:

A) Cease accepting applications.

B) Post notices in conspicuous places in DSCC offices and clinics and in other places where such notices are likely to be seen by Applicants. The notices shall state that DSCC is no longer accepting applications because of insufficient funds, and shall state the probable date on which DSCC shall again accept applications. Notices will also be posted in a like manner when funding again becomes available.

C) DSCC employees shall inform clinic patients and other persons that DSCC is no longer accepting applications because of insufficient funds, and shall inform such persons of the probable date on which the Division shall again

BOARD OF TRUSTEES OF THE UNIVERSITY OF ILLINOIS

NOTICE OF ADOPTED AMENDMENTS

accept applications.

D) Cease authorizing additional health care services for Recipient Children whose LRAs are eligible for DSCC financial assistance.

2) If DSCC determines, based upon its own internal auditing and record keeping systems, at any time that it does not have or will not have sufficient funds to provide payments for authorized services for Applicants who have applied, but with respect to whom no determination of eligibility has been made, DSCC shall nevertheless finish processing those applications and determine the eligibility or ineligibility of each such Applicant and his/her LRA for use in the event that additional funds become available. In such event, the LRAs of eligible applicants, shall be provided funding in the order received unless a child's life or good health is threatened in which event the said child's application will be given priority.

3) DSCC shall make payments for authorized services in the order in which DSCC receives bills for such services.

4) If DSCC determines due to nonavailability of funds that it is unable to pay for an authorized service. it shall cancel the authorization and any related purchase order any time up to the point at which services have been provided. For this purpose, the authorization and related Purchase Order shall contain the following statement: "This authorization is subject to all of the various rules and procedures set forth at 89 Ill. Adm. Code 1200." In the event any authorization is cancelled pursuant to this limitation, any charges incurred for services rendered after the date of cancellation shall not be the obligation of DSCC.

5) Except as otherwise specifically provided herein in the event that DSCC determines that it does not or will not have sufficient funds to provide payments for all Applicants, present and future, as well as to make payments in behalf of all Recipient Children, it shall first cease accepting applications in accordance with subsection (b)(1) above. If after taking such action, it is still determined that sufficient funds are not available, it shall take the actions set forth in subsection (b)(2) above. If after taking such action, it is still determined that sufficient funds are not available, it shall take the actions set forth in subsections (b)(3) and (4) above. In the event that the life or good health of a child is threatened if a procedure is not performed, DSCC shall give funding such procedure priority over other procedures not posing such threat.

c) The Director shall establish maximum dollar amounts for payment of authorized services per fiscal year which shall be applied to each child. DSCC shall provide notice of the limit to all Recipients and Health Care Facilities who may be affected.

d) By accepting a DSCC authorization, the Health Care Provider agrees not to seek further payment from the patient or the patient's family for

BOARD OF TRUSTEES OF THE UNIVERSITY OF ILLINOIS

NOTICE OF ADOPTED AMENDMENTS

such authorized services beyond the amounts available from insurance, DSCC, Medicare, or Medicaid. In those cases where DSCC has notified the Provider that money is no longer available from DSCC, the Provider shall not be so restricted.

e) Insurance

1) Maximum insurance benefits must be used. The LRA is responsible for complying with insurance contract provisions required to maximize the level of insurance benefits.

2) Payment for authorized services for children with insurance benefits shall not be made until insurance has paid or rejected the claim. Subject to all the limits on benefits as contained in this Part these Rules, DSCC will pay the cost of all required services above that reimbursed by insurance up to an established rate of payment. The Director shall approve payment for authorized services prior to settlement of the insurance claims if such is necessary to avoid undue suffering or to preserve life and good health, and if immediate payment will cause DSCC funds to be utilized in the most efficient and effective fashion, all as determined based on usual and customary medical standards.

3) The family shall notify DSCC within thirty (30) days of any change in the child's medical insurance coverage which results in coverage of costs which are currently paid for by DSCC.

f) DSCC will not provide reimbursement for minor occasional costs of a Recipient. Child's treatment. For purposes of this clause "minor costs" shall be defined as charges for supplies, equipment replacement parts, repair and replacement of equipment, and drugs less than $25 each. "Occasional costs" shall be defined as costs occurring less frequently than once per month. In the event that minor costs are not occasional, they may be aggregated by the LRA and will be authorized by DSCC.

f) g) Submittal of Claims

1) In order to be eligible for payment consideration, a provider's/vendor's payment claim or bill, either initial or resubmittal following prior rejection, must be received by DSCC no later than nine (9) months from the date on which medical services, appliances or supplies are provided. This includes third party payment or denial information.

2) Claims which are not submitted and received by DSCC in compliance with the requirements of subsection (f)(1) (g)(1) will not be eligible for payment under DSCC's medical program. DSCC and the patient or patient's family or guardian shall have no liability for any payment thereof.

(Source: Amended at 21 Ill. Reg. 17142, effective DEC 11 1997)

Section 1200.80 Availability of Services

BOARD OF TRUSTEES OF THE UNIVERSITY OF ILLINOIS

NOTICE OF ADOPTED AMENDMENTS

a) Limitations

DSCC will not provide the following:

1) Organ transplants and related anti-rejection drugs.

2) Surgery or other treatment which is primarily for cosmetic purposes.

3) Research or experimental medical or professional services, hospital services, drugs, devices or equipment.

A) Research or experimental medical or professional services, hospital services, drugs, devices or equipment is defined to include services, drugs, devices or equipment which have not been recognized as having a proven rehabilitative value as determined by the professional standards of the applicable medical or health care specialty groups, including but not limited to:

i) equipment or appliances that do not have the approval of the Department of Health and Human Services, Food and Drug Administration or other appropriate federal agency (Investigational New Drugs and Devices and investigational services and treatments shall not be deemed to have received such approval);

ii) medical and/or other health related services, including drugs, food supplements, equipment or appliances not reported on, described, or discussed in published and recognized professional journals which have an advisory board passing on its publications;

iii) services, drugs, devices, equipment or appliances that have not been recognized by appropriate national professional organizations.

B) If a Health Care Provider wishes to utilize medical services, equipment or appliances which are identified as possibly research or experimental, the Provider must provide a written justification for doing so. Other pertinent information from knowledgeable professional sources may be obtained by the Health Care Provider. The DSCC Director shall determine whether services, equipment or appliances are, in fact, experimental or research based on the information supplied and the criteria at subsections (a)(3)(A)(i) (iii), immediately above.

C) If DSCC authorizes a Health Care Provider to perform medical services or hospital service, or to purchase equipment or supplies later determined by DSCC as research or experimental, and if said Provider has failed to notify DSCC in advance of the possible experimental or research nature thereof, the Provider shall be obligated to refund any monies paid to it by DSCC or the LRA to perform such procedure or purchase such item.

b) Authorization: General

1) Except as otherwise specifically provided in subsection Section

BOARD OF TRUSTEES OF THE UNIVERSITY OF ILLINOIS

NOTICE OF ADOPTED AMENDMENTS

1200.98(c)(5) of this Section, all health care services, equipment or drugs to be purchased for individuals by DSCC, including diagnostic evaluation services (see subsection (d) See;--Section---1200.98(d)), must be preauthorized, i.e., authorized by DSCC before their delivery. Such authorizations shall be to specific Health Care Providers and shall specify the services to be provided.

2) Prior to any services, equipment or drugs being authorized by DSCC, a completed application must have been submitted to DSCC and eligibility established for the DSCC program (see Section 1200.50).

3) All authorizations are recorded as part of the individual patient's case record.

c) Authorization Procedure

1) An authorization for health care services, equipment or drugs must be requested from DSCC.

A) Any person may request that DSCC issue an authorization, but authorizations will not be effective until DSCC receives notice from a Health Care Provider which documents the need for and extent of the services, equipment or drugs to be provided to the Recipient Child. This notice may be either written or oral.

B) Services, drugs or equipment which are duplicative of those authorized or exceed authorized limits or are arranged without prior notification to and concurrence by DSCC shall not be authorized.

2) Authorizations will be issued for health care services, drugs or equipment only to a specific Health Care Provider and then only if Provider meets the criteria established in this Part, has evidenced a willingness to participate in the DSCC program, agrees to accept DSCC rates of payment, and agrees to abide by DSCC administrative procedures, as set forth in this Part.

A) DSCC maintains lists of qualifying, currently participating, Health Care Providers.

B) If the LRA or Recipient Child wishes to use a particular Health Care Provider, not currently participating in the DSCC program, that Provider will be added to the DSCC program upon confirmation that said Provider meets all the standards enumerated above.

3) All hospitalizations and all equipment purchases are subject to separate authorizations for each occasion of such service.

4) Children receiving DSCC services shall be preauthorized for a certain set number of professional outpatient service visits if such is determined medically necessary and the said services will be furnished by a specific Health Care Professional or Facility. Upon medical recommendation for additional services, separate issuance of authorization(s) will be required.

5) Exceptions to the pre-authorization requirement:

BOARD OF TRUSTEES OF THE UNIVERSITY OF ILLINOIS

NOTICE OF ADOPTED AMENDMENTS

A) The initial medical referral of a child to DSCC may be concurrent with the first visit to an approved Health Care Professional or Health Care Facility. Upon submission of a completed application by an LRA (within thirty--(30) days of the time services were rendered), an authorization for the aforedescribed initial medical service will be issued if the applicant and LRA are determined eligible for the DSCC program and if the services provided are determined by DSCC to be medically necessary through the application of usual and customary medical criteria. (Note: payment for such services is subject to the time limits on retroactive benefits.)

B) Retroactive authorizations for services provided may be made unless:

i) the service was not provided during a period of eligibility except as provided in (c)(5)(A), immediately-above;

ii) DSCC was not notified within thirty--(30) days after the service was provided;

iii) funds are not available to make the reimbursement, as determined by DSCC in accordance with Section 1200.70(b));

iv) the service was provided by a Health Care Facility or by a Health Care Professional not pre-approved by DSCC as meeting the Standards for Medical Personnel (Section 1200.100) or Standards for Facilities (Section 1200.110); unless the service provided was an emergency, as determined by usual and customary medical standards, in which case the service will be retroactively authorized if the Facility or Professional providing the service is deemed by DSCC to meet the standards of this Part after the request for reimbursement is received;

v) the LRA has privately arranged for services with a Health Care Provider expecting private sources of reimbursement at the level of their usual and customary charges; unless the said Provider subsequently agrees to accept the DSCC level of reimbursement.

d) The Diagnostic Evaluation Program (Diagnostic Services)

1) DSCC provides for early identification and diagnostic evaluation of children eligible for the DSCC treatment program through the qualified professional and support staff within DSCC, through a clinic system which is organized and operated in cooperation with Health Care Providers from various regions and through relationships with Health Care Providers in the private-voluntary sector throughout the State state.

2) Services necessary to determine medical eligibility are provided

BOARD OF TRUSTEES OF THE UNIVERSITY OF ILLINOIS

NOTICE OF ADOPTED AMENDMENTS

without charge above available insurance or other forms of reimbursement regardless of family financial circumstances.

3) In specified areas outside of Chicago, DSCC arranges for field clinics with special or general scope to meet on a periodic basis. These clinics are staffed by Health Care Professionals participating in the DSCC program and are available for Diagnostic Services as well as certain treatment services.

4) In the City of Chicago, DSCC utilizes established outpatient clinics associated with DSCC approved Health Care Facilities to perform Diagnostic Services. This list is available to the general public and these facilities may be utilized at any time, since there are not specific "DSCC clinic times" at these Facilities.

5) All Applicants requiring Diagnostic Services must receive an Authorization from DSCC and must make a specific appointment for the evaluation, in accordance with the rules and procedures of that Health Care Facility.

6) If DSCC is able to determine, from an interview or from other existing information, that an Applicant is ineligible, Diagnostic Services shall not be performed.

7) All Diagnostic Services must be provided on an outpatient basis unless inpatient services for this purpose are specifically approved by the Director who shall approve such services when they are medically required to complete the diagnostic evaluation.

e) The Treatment Program

1) DSCC provides for treatment and follow-up services through qualified professional and support staff within DSCC, through the field clinic system outside the City of Chicago, through DSCC approved Health Care Professionals and Facilities in Chicago, and through Health Care Providers throughout the **State** state. The DSCC program is oriented in large part around a clinic or 'specialized centers" model to encourage coordinated multi-specialist involvement with DSCC Recipient Children recipient children.

2) The services provided through the DSCC Treatment Program include, when determined medically necessary by a Recipient Child's treating physician(s), the following:

A) Consultative services through a Health Care Professional or Facility.

B) Continuing outpatient supervision furnished by Health Care Professionals including office visits or by a Health Care Facility in a clinic, if such would more adequately meet the health care needs of the Recipient Child based on all applicable medical criteria than would a DSCC field clinic.

C) Hospitalization and inpatient medical and/or surgical treatment including special rehabilitation services. Provided, however, that procedures, tests, or services shall

BOARD OF TRUSTEES OF THE UNIVERSITY OF ILLINOIS

NOTICE OF ADOPTED AMENDMENTS

not be performed on an inpatient basis if, under medical professional standards such procedures, tests, or services are usually and customarily performed in outpatient facilities. except that such procedures, tests, or services shall be performed on an inpatient basis if determined to be medically indicated by the Director based on the recommendation of the Recipient Child's treating physician(s).

D) Convalescent care to the extent available and required as an intermediate service to continued hospitalization.

E) Home based care intended to prevent continued hospitalization or similar-type medical placement, as determined desirable and feasible applying all medical standards. Such care is limited to training of parents and/or community health care providers; provision of recommended equipment and supplies; and, as necessary, periodic visiting nurse and/or related health personnel supervision. DSCC does not provide continuing care nursing, life support systems, or high technology equipment and related supplies but will help the LRA locate funding sources for these services, if they are determined to be medically necessary.

F) Assistive appliances, approved by DSCC, such as braces, prosthetic limbs, hearing aids, wheelchairs and related adaptive devices and special supplies determined medically necessary to accomplish rehabilitation goals. Excluded are fixed architectural modifications of the LRA's dwelling in which the child resides, and property related thereto. External ramps and/or mechanical lifts needed to provide the child access to the dwelling are not excluded.

G) Speech and hearing therapy, physical and occupational therapy.

H) Nutrition evaluation, guidance and provision of special dietary substances upon medical recommendation, excepting those dietary substances available through programs of public or private agencies established for such purposes.

I) Specialized dental care, such as orthodontia, prosthodontia, or oral surgery as required to further the treatment plan of children with severe oro-craniofacial deformities (e.g., cleft lip-cleft palate). Routine preventive or restorative dentistry is not provided except for children for whom this service is a specific recommendation to be integrated into an authorized orthodontic or prosthodontic plan.

J) Arrangements for home follow-up services by public health and/or related habilitative services personnel.

K) Specialized prescriptive drugs integral to the treatment program of a chronic disability, subject to the limitations of Section 1200.70(f).

BOARD OF TRUSTEES OF THE UNIVERSITY OF ILLINOIS

NOTICE OF ADOPTED AMENDMENTS

L) Genetic evaluation and family counseling.
M) Psychological/psychiatric evaluation as medically recommended for diagnosis and treatment planning.
N) Referral to other public or private agencies as required to further support the special needs of the family and/or child.

f) Transportation Assistance

1)~3~ In order to make recommended services accessible to families, DSCC will support necessary transportation, lodging, meals, and parking costs ~if the annual Total Income is at or below 133% of Poverty Income Guidelines (57 Fed. Reg. 5455)~. DSCC shall be obligated to provide the ~said~ support only if no other sources are available for this purpose.

A) DSCC shall support necessary transportation by the most economically appropriate method and at a cost not exceeding limitations as set forth in the Reimbursement Schedule of the Travel Regulation Council at 80 Ill. Adm. Code 3000.Appendix A. DSCC will prescribe the form and procedure which families must follow in order to receive and verify expenses.

B) Support will be available for the following individuals: LRAs; the child Recipient ~Child~; any additional caretaker whose presence is medically required to provide care for the child Recipient ~Child~ during transportation.

C) When circumstances so dictate to meet the health care needs of the child, the Director shall authorize payments in excess of the amount stated above.

(Source: Amended at 21 Ill. Reg. _____ , effective DEC 1 1 1997)

Section 1200.90 Rates of Payment

a) All services subject to payment by DSCC shall be authorized by DSCC in accordance with Section 1200.80(c). All payments shall be approved and made in accordance with all applicable State ~state~ laws relating to making disbursements of public funds.

b) Methods of Payment

1) The rate of payment for the services of Health Care Professionals shall be established by the Director at a level not in excess of the usual and customary fee for the service to be performed as determined by all data, information and value scales bearing on the appropriateness of the fee. Dental services shall have the same reimbursement arrangement. DSCC will negotiate other reimbursement formulae or fee schedules if it determines that such will be required to meet the needs of children with complex impairments.

BOARD OF TRUSTEES OF THE UNIVERSITY OF ILLINOIS

NOTICE OF ADOPTED AMENDMENTS

2) Payments for other medically necessary treatment or services appropriate for the condition being treated whether at the patient's home, a private office, hospital, extended care facility or outpatient therapy center, shall be determined by the Director utilizing the criteria described in subsection (b) Subsection(1) ~immediately above~.

3) Payments for hospital services, including hospital outpatient clinics, shall be the lower of the hospital's reimbursable costs as determined by cost reports filed by the hospital with the Illinois Department of Public Aid or similar agency or its charges. Hospitals shall be entitled to interim payments in amounts not to exceed their billed charges. In the event that these interim payments to the hospital exceed the hospital's verified allowable costs, the hospital shall reimburse any overpayment to DSCC. All payments made to hospitals shall be deemed subject to this provision.

4) Payments for outpatient services such as x-rays and laboratory procedures shall be made in accordance with fee schedules established by DSCC utilizing criteria described in subsection (b) Subsection(1) ~immediately above~.

5) Payments for drugs shall be made in accordance with a fee schedule based upon a net dispensing fee and a percentage of the average wholesale price as determined from the National Drug Code (NDC) Product and Pricing Database, upon billing ~at rates which are the lower of those established in accordance with 42 C.F.R. 447.331 (Maximum Allowable Costs); 42 C.F.R. 447.332 (Estimated Acquisition Costs); 42 C.F.R. 447.333 (Dispensing Fee); and with P.A. 83-333 adding Section 5-5.12 to Chapter 23 of the Illinois Public Aid Code, effective January 1, 1984; or a usual and customary charge as established in accordance with the law and the regulations aforementioned~.

6) Payments for braces, prostheses, hearing aids, and related assistive appliances and medical supplies shall be made in accordance with the laws of the State of Illinois relating to purchasing and finance.

7) Payment amounts for services in out-of-state facilities not otherwise included in subsection (b)(3) Subsection (3) of this Section shall be the ~said~ facility's charge unless DSCC determines that the charge exceeds the usual and customary level of reimbursement. When possible, the amount will be determined in advance of the authorization for services through direct negotiation with the provider.

(Source: Amended at 21 Ill. Reg. _____ , effective DEC 1 1 1997)

Section 1200.110 Standards for Health Care Facilities

BOARD OF TRUSTEES OF THE UNIVERSITY OF ILLINOIS

NOTICE OF ADOPTED AMENDMENTS

a) Diagnostic and Treatment Facilities - General
   1) All such facilities utilized by DSCC must carry adequate malpractice insurance in such amounts as are determined by the Director from time to time and must give DSCC assurance of this coverage.
   2) All hospital and extended care facilities utilized by DSCC for the provision of patient care services shall conform to the following standards:
      A) Licensure by the appropriate State state licensing body;
      B) Accreditation by the Joint Commission on Accreditation of Healthcare Organizations; or; the American Osteopathic Association when providing in-hospital care;
      C) Recipient Children shall be provided inpatient care in hospital facilities with a physically definable pediatric unit to which only children are admitted. In making the selection and designation of such approved patient care facilities, DSCC shall give priority to those facilities which demonstrate emphasis on quality children's medical services pursuant to standards enumerated in subsection (a)(2)(D) immediately below. In a particular service area in which only a single hospital is utilized to admit all Recipient Children, these standards shall be waived when determined by the DSCC Director to be medically indicated to meet the needs of the Recipient Child;
      D) All patient care facilities, programs and specialized patient care centers shall meet national standards whenever possible, including those promulgated by the American Medical Association, the American Hospital Association, American College of Surgeons, the American Academy of Pediatrics, the Joint Commission on the Accreditation of Healthcare Organizations Hospitals, the Commission for the Accreditation of Rehabilitation Facilities, the Inter-Society Committee on Congenital Heart Disease and the American Heart Association.
   3) Priority shall be given to those facilities Facilities affiliated with a medical school. DSCC shall refer children to designated regional or statewide referral centers when medically indicated utilizing usual and customary medical standards.
   4) The above standards shall be waived by the DSCC Director when necessary to meet the medical needs of the child utilizing usual and customary medical standards.
b) Outpatient therapy centers Therapy Centers, defined as facilities, not directly associated with approved hospital facilities, which are organized to provide habilitative services such as physical, occupational, speech and hearing therapy (including applicable diagnoses), at the community level, will be available to patients under DSCC authorization provided that:
   1) Such facilities carry adequate malpractice insurance in such

BOARD OF TRUSTEES OF THE UNIVERSITY OF ILLINOIS

NOTICE OF ADOPTED AMENDMENTS

   amounts as are determined by the Director from time to time and DSCC is given assurances of this coverage;
   2) Such facilities and staff meet appropriate State state certification whenever such standards exist;
   3) Such facilities and staff meet accreditation standards of the Commission for Accreditation of Rehabilitation Facilities,; where they exist;
   4) Utilization of outpatient therapy centers Outpatient Therapy Centers or individual therapist Health Care Professionals must be prescribed by the Recipient Child's DSCC-authorized physician responsible for the overall management of the physical impairment requiring the habilitative service.
c) Medical Equipment Suppliers
   1) All medical equipment suppliers must carry adequate insurance in such amounts as are determined by the Director from time to time and must give DSCC assurance of this coverage.
   2) A facility providing braces, appliances and/or prostheses must be currently approved under the Facility Certification Program administered by the American Board of Certification in Orthotics and Prosthetics, Incorporated, and have in their employ an orthotist and/or prosthetist who has successfully completed a training program recognized by the American Board of Orthotists and Prosthetists, Incorporated, and who is certified by the said Board. Providers of specialized medical equipment shall be authorized or approved dealers for such equipment as defined by the manufacturer and shall meet the manufacturer's standards for servicing and repairing such equipment.
   3) The above services must be requested by the Recipient Child's DSCC-authorized physician.
   4) A provider of hearing instruments aids must be licensed certified by the Department of Public Health as a hearing instrument aid dispenser as provided in the Hearing Instrument Aid Consumer Protection Act [225 ILCS 50] (Ill. Rev. Stat. 1991, ch. 111 1/2, par. 7401 et seq.).
d) Clinical Laboratories
   1) All clinical laboratories must carry adequate insurance in such amounts as are determined by the Director from time to time and must give DSCC assurance of this coverage.
   2) All such laboratories utilized by DSCC must meet the standards and be appropriately licensed by the state in which they operate. Laboratories in Illinois must have a current license maintained in accordance with the Clinical Laboratory and Blood Bank Act [310 ILCS 25] (Ill. Rev. Stat. 1991, ch. 111 1/2, par. 621-101 et seq.) and Illinois Clinical Laboratories Code or; be fully certified to perform tests of moderate or high complexity under the Clinical Laboratory Improvement Amendments of 1988 (CLIA).
e) Hospitals and other treatment facilities are responsible for informing DSCC of changes in professional staff providing services to any

BOARD OF TRUSTEES OF THE UNIVERSITY OF ILLINOIS

NOTICE OF ADOPTED AMENDMENTS

Recipient Child.

(Source: Amended at 21 Ill. Reg. 17151 , effective
    DEC 11 1997   )

BOARD OF TRUSTEES OF THE UNIVERSITY OF ILLINOIS

NOTICE OF ADOPTED AMENDMENTS

Section 1200.APPENDIX A Income Scale

Family Size of Household	~~Income Scale~~	Income Allowance* ~~(FY-93)~~
1		$18,200 ~~13,300~~
2		23,800 ~~17,400~~
3		29,400 ~~21,500~~
4		35,000 ~~25,600~~
5		40,600 ~~29,800~~
6		46,200 ~~33,900~~
7		47,300 ~~34,600~~
8		48,300 ~~35,400~~
9		49,400 ~~36,200~~
10		50,400 ~~36,900~~
11		51,500 ~~37,700~~
12		52,500 ~~38,500~~

This table is based upon 65% 50% of the gross median family income adjusted for
family size as developed for the State of Illinois by the U.S. Department of
Health and Human Services, using the Federal Register's updated table for gross
median family income (62 Fed. Reg. 12851 (1997) 57 Fed. Reg. 6114). In order to
find 65% 50% of State state median income for households with greater than 12
members, perform the following calculation:

    1) Begin with 1.50 150%;
    2) Add 0.03 point 3 percentage points for each additional family
        member (above 12 members);
    3) Multiply figure obtained at step (2) by $35,000 25,600 (i.e., the
        4 person household amount);
    4) Round the figure obtained at step (3) to the nearest $100.

*Maximum allowable Allowable Adjusted Family Income which results in full
financial assistance.

    (Source: Amended at 21 Ill. Reg. _____, effective
        DEC 11 1997   )

BOARD OF TRUSTEES OF THE UNIVERSITY OF ILLINOIS

NOTICE OF ADOPTED AMENDMENTS

Section 1200.APPENDIX B   Payment Scale*

$ Amount in Excess of Adjusted
~~Family Income in Excess~~
of Income Scale

		Annual Payment
1	999 ~~499~~	None ~~20%-of-amount-in~~ ~~excess-of-Income-Scale~~
500	999	~~$105~~
1,000	1,499	$ 20 ~~220~~
1,500	1,999	45 ~~345~~
2,000	2,499	80 ~~480~~
2,500	2,999	125 ~~625~~
3,000	3,499	180 ~~780~~
3,500	3,999	245 ~~945~~
4,000	4,499	320 ~~1,120~~
4,500	4,999	405 ~~1,305~~
5,000	5,499	500 ~~1,500~~
5,500	5,999	605 ~~1,700~~
6,000	6,499	720 ~~2,040~~
6,500	6,999	845 ~~2,340~~
7,000	7,499	980 ~~2,660~~
7,500	7,999	1,125 ~~3,000~~
8,000	8,499	1,280 ~~3,360~~
8,500	8,999	1,445 ~~3,740~~
9,000	9,499	1,620 ~~4,140~~
9,500	9,999	1,805 ~~4,560~~
10,000 - 10,499		2,000 ~~5,000~~
10,500 and above		no DSCC financial payment

*Derived from U.S. Department of Health and Human Services publication;
"Setting Fees Based on a Family's Ability to Pay: A Guide for Agency Decision
Making" (An Administrative Publication for State MCH Agencies, "Measure of
Ability to Pay," December 1982).
†456/U;

(Source: Amended   at   21   Ill.   Reg. _____,   effective
DEC 11 1997   )

DEPARTMENT OF INSURANCE

NOTICE OF EMERGENCY RULES

1)   Heading of the Part: Investment Fee Disclosure Requirements For Pension
Funds

2)   Code Citation: 50 Ill. Adm. Code 4430

3)   Section Numbers: Emergency Action:
4430.10   New Section
4430.20   New Section
4430.30   New Section
4430.40   New Section

4)   Statutory Authority: Implementing Sections 1-113.5(b)(3), (d) and (e) and
also 1-113.6, and authorized by Section 1-113.11 of the Illinois Pension
Code (40 ILCS 5/113.5(b)(3), (d) and (e), 1-113.6 and 1-113.11, as added
by P.A. 90-507, effective August 22, 1997].

5)   Effective Date of Emergency Rule: December 16, 1997

6)   If this emergency rule is to expire before the end of the 150-day period,
please specify the date on which it is to expire: This emergency rule
will not expire before the end of the 150 day period.

7)   Date Filed in Agency's Principal Office: December 16, 1997

8)   Reason for Emergency: This emergency rule is being initiated to implement
P.A. 90-507, which became effective on August 22, 1997. Within this bill,
many new Sections were added to the Pension Code which allow pension funds
to make permitted investments beginning January 1, 1998. At a minimum,
the Department is promulgating this fee disclosure rule to ensure that
pension funds obtain adequate information about the actual fees and costs
that will be incurred in conjunction with investment transactions.
Pension funds must obtain a disclosure statement to be in compliance with
this Part.

9)   A Complete Description of the Subjects and Issues Involved: Beginning
January 1, 1998, police and firefighter pension funds established under
either Article 3 or 4 of the Pension Code may now draw pension funds out
for investment purposes. Pursuant to the requirements of this Part,
pension funds must obtain a fee disclosure statement from any investment
advisor, registered broker-dealer, bank, insurer or any other person used
for investment-related services. This rule sets forth the minimum
information that must be contained in a disclosure statement and further
identifies what recordkeeping requirements pension funds must meet to be
in compliance with this Part.

10)   Are there any proposed amendments to this Part pending?   No

11)   Statement of Statewide Policy Objectives: This emergency rule will not

97

DEPARTMENT OF INSURANCE

NOTICE OF EMERGENCY RULES

ernment to establish, expand or modify its activities
s to necessitate additional expenditures from local

stions re ardin this amendment:

on

o:

DEPARTMENT OF INSURANCE

NOTICE OF EMERGENCY RULES

TITLE 50: INSURANCE
CHAPTER I: DEPARTMENT OF INSURANCE
SUBCHAPTER aaa: PENSIONS

PART 4430
INVESTMENT FEE DISCLOSURE
REQUIREMENTS FOR PENSION FUNDS

Section
4430.10   Scope
EMERGENCY
4430.20   Required Disclosures
EMERGENCY
4430.30   Recordkeeping
EMERGENCY
4430.40   Penalties
EMERGENCY

AUTHORITY: Implementing Sections 1-113.5(b)(3), (d) and (e) and also 1-113.6,
and authorized by Section 1-113.11 of the Illinois Pension Code [40 ILCS 5/1-
113.5(b)(3), (d) and (e), 1-113.6 and 1-113.11, as added by P.A. 90-507,
effective August 22, 1997].

SOURCE: Emergency rules adopted at 22 Ill. Reg. _____, effective
____DEC 16 1997____, for a maximum of 150 days.

Section 4430.10 Scope
EMERGENCY

This Part is applicable to all police and firefighter pension funds and pension
fund boards which are subject to the provisions of Sections 1-113.1 through
113.10 of the Illinois Pension Code [40 ILCS 5/1-113.1 through 1-113.10].

Section 4430.20 Required Disclosures
EMERGENCY

No pension fund shall engage an investment advisor, registered broker-dealer,
bank, insurer or any other person for the purposes of providing investment
services unless the following written disclosure requirements are met:
   a) A description, expressed as a set amount or range in dollars or as a
       percentage of the dollar value of a particular transaction or
       transactions, of any and all commissions, fees, penalties, or any
       other items of compensation related to a particular transaction that
       may be received by any such person from the pension fund. The written
       description must be furnished by any such person effectuating any
       transaction with a pension fund, and the written description need not
       be furnished with respect to each subsequent transaction to which the

DEPARTMENT OF INSURANCE

NOTICE OF EMERGENCY RULES

description applies.

b) If the investment service contemplated is one which might result in the pension fund acquiring an asset from any inventory held by an investment advisor, registered broker-dealer, bank, insurer, or other person; the written engagement or contract must also include a statement disclosing:

1) The possibility that the investment advisor, registered broker-dealer, bank or insurer may obtain a financial benefit from such sale beyond the items listed under subsection (a) above; and

2) That the realization and extent of any such benefit is dependent upon market valuations as of the date the inventoried asset was acquired as compared to the price at which the pension fund acquires the asset; and

3) That the pension fund should take steps to familiarize itself with the market in which any such acquisitions or investments are to be made.

Section 4430.30 Recordkeeping
EMERGENCY

When authorizing any investment transaction, every pension fund subject to the provisions of Sections 1-113.1 through 1-113.10 of the Illinois Pension Code shall:

a) Establish, maintain and file with the Pension Division of the Department of Insurance by no later than April 1, 1998, its current investment policy as required by Section 1-113.6 of the Illinois Pension Code. In addition, every pension fund shall file revisions to their investment policy with the Pension Division of the Department of Insurance 30 days after such revision is adopted by the pension fund board; and

b) Establish and maintain such books, receipts, confirmations, statements, or other records in sufficient detail to verify and support all annual statements and investment and financial reports required to be filed with the Pension Division. Such records shall include, but are not limited to, any of the following records received by the pension fund;

1) The minutes of any meeting of the board wherein investment matters are discussed;

2) All correspondence, orders or directions to, or from any person providing investment or custodial services;

3) Any documentation concerning the letting and acceptance of bids for investment services;

4) Any bank, brokerage, policy, contract or other account statement reporting the status of a pension fund investment;

5) Any receipt, confirmation, transmittal advice, binder or other record which confirms, verifies or reports any investment transaction; any investment cost, expense, fee or penalty; or any

DEPARTMENT OF INSURANCE

NOTICE OF EMERGENCY RULES

investment transaction profit or loss.

Section 4430.40 Penalties
EMERGENCY

If any party fails to comply with the requirements of this Part, including either the substance or filing requirements contained herein, such party shall be subject to the penalty provisions of the Illinois Pension Code [40 ILCS 5/1A-101 through 1A-113].

TEACHERS' RETIREMENT SYSTEM OF THE STATE OF ILLINOIS

NOTICE OF EMERGENCY AMENDMENTS

1) Heading of the Part: The Administration and Operation of the Teachers' Retirement System

2) Code Citation: 80 Ill. Adm. Code 1650

3) Section Numbers: Emergency Action:
   1650.346   New Section
   1650.575   New Section
   1650.595   New Section

4) Specific statutory citation upon which the rule is based and authorized:
   1650.346   40 ILCS 5/16-127(b)(5)(iv)
   1650.575   40 ILCS 5/16-140(4)
   1650.595   30 ILCS 210/5; 40 ILCS 5/16-172

5) Effective date of the rule: December 9, 1997

6) If this emergency rule is to expire before the end of the 150-day period (other than by means of adopting the rule through the general rulemaking process), please specify the date: This rule will expire at the end of the 150-day period.

7) Date filed in agency's principal office: December 5, 1997

8) The reason for the emergency: The new Sections 1650.346 and 1650.575 are in response to recently enacted legislation (P.A. 90-32 and 90-448, respectively). The new Section 1650.595 is in response to recently adopted rules by the Debt Collection Board (74 Ill. Adm. Code 910).

9) A Complete Description of the Subjects and Issues Involved: Section 1650.346 defines terms used in 40 ILCS 5/16-127(b)(5)(iv), which was added by P.A. 90-32 and which gives teachers who left teaching prior to 1983 to adopt an infant under age three the right to purchase optional service credit.

   Section 1650.575 defines the term "full-time student" used in 40 ILCS 5/16-140(4), which was added by P.A. 90-448 and which provides increased survivor benefits to dependent children ages 18 to 22 who are full-time students.

   Section 1650.595 establishes the collection parameters for receivables of the System from members, annuitants, or beneficiaries who received benefits in excess of the amount due them. The collection parameters are in harmony with the recently adopted rules of the Debt Collection Board and the authorizing language of 30 ILCS 210/5 and recognize the somewhat unique nature of those receivables.

10) Whether there are any proposed amendments pending on this Part other than

TEACHERS' RETIREMENT SYSTEM OF THE STATE OF ILLINOIS

NOTICE OF EMERGENCY AMENDMENTS

those appearing in the same issue of the Register as the emergency rules. If so, please specify Section numbers, the proposed action and the Register citation to the Notice of Proposed Rules: None

11) Statement of Statewide Policy Objectives, if applicable: Not Applicable

12) Name, address and telephone number of the person to whom information and questions regarding this adopted rule shall be directed:

   Carl Mowery, General Counsel
   Erin Smith, Legal Assistant
   Teachers' Retirement System
   2815 West Washington, P. O. Box 19253
   Springfield, IL 62794-9253
   (217) 753-0961

The full text of the Emergency Amendments begins on the next page:

TEACHERS' RETIREMENT SYSTEM OF THE STATE OF ILLINOIS

NOTICE OF EMERGENCY AMENDMENTS

TITLE 80: PUBLIC OFFICIALS AND EMPLOYERS
SUBTITLE D: RETIREMENT SYSTEMS
CHAPTER III: TEACHERS' RETIREMENT SYSTEM OF
THE STATE OF ILLINOIS

PART 1650
THE ADMINISTRATION AND OPERATION OF THE
TEACHERS' RETIREMENT SYSTEM

SUBPART A: REPORTS BY BOARD OF TRUSTEES

TEACHERS' RETIREMENT SYSTEM OF THE STATE OF ILLINOIS

NOTICE OF EMERGENCY AMENDMENTS

TEACHERS' RETIREMENT SYSTEM OF THE STATE OF ILLINOIS

NOTICE OF EMERGENCY AMENDMENTS

Section
1650.605   Policy of the Board Concerning Attorney Generals' Opinion (Repealed)

SUBPART H: ADMINISTRATIVE REVIEW

Section
1650.610   Staff Responsibility
1650.620   Right of Appeal
1650.630   Form of Written Request
1650.640   Prehearing Procedure
1650.650   Hearing Procedure
1650.660   Rules of Evidence

SUBPART I: AMENDMENTS TO BYLAWS AND RULES

Section
1650.710   Amendments

SUBPART J: RULES OF ORDER

Section
1650.810   Parliamentary Procedure

SUBPART K: FREEDOM OF INFORMATION ACT REQUESTS

Section
1650.910   Summary and Purpose
1650.920   Definitions
1650.930   Submission of Requests
1650.940   Form and Content of FOIA Requests
1650.950   Appeal of a Denial
1650.960   Executive Director's Response to Appeal
1650.970   Response to FOIA Requests
1650.980   Inspection of Records at System Office
1650.990   Copies of Public Records
1650.995   Materials Available Under Section 4 of FOIA

SUBPART L: BOARD ELECTION PROCEDURES

Section
1650.1000   Nomination of Candidates
1650.1010   Petitions
1650.1020   Eligible Voters
1650.1030   Election Materials
1650.1040   Marking of Ballots
1650.1050   Return of Ballots
1650.1060   Observation of Ballot Counting
1650.1070   Certification of Ballot Counting

TEACHERS' RETIREMENT SYSTEM OF THE STATE OF ILLINOIS

NOTICE OF EMERGENCY AMENDMENTS

1650.1080   Challenges to Ballot Counting

SUBPART M: RETIREMENT BENEFITS

Section
1650.2900   Excess Benefit Arrangement

AUTHORITY: Implementing and authorized by Article 16 of the Illinois Pension
Code [40 ILCS 5/Art. 16]; Freedom of Information Act [5 ILCS 140]; Internal
Revenue Code [26 U.S.C. 1, et seq.]; Section 5-15 of the Illinois
Administrative Procedure Act [5 ILCS 100/5-15].

SOURCE: Filed June 20, 1958; emergency rules adopted at 2 Ill. Reg. 49, p.
249, effective November 29, 1978, for a maximum of 150 days; adopted at 3 Ill.
Reg. 9, p. 1, effective March 3, 1979; codified at 8 Ill. Reg. 16350; amended
at 9 Ill. Reg. 20885, effective December 17, 1985; amended at 12 Ill. Reg.
16896, effective October 3, 1988; amended at 14 Ill. Reg. 18305, effective
October 29, 1990; amended at 15 Ill. Reg. 16731, effective November 9, 1991;
amended at 17 Ill. Reg. 1631, effective January 22, 1993; amended at 18 Ill.
Reg. 6349, effective April 15, 1994; emergency amendment at 18 Ill. Reg. 8949,
effective May 24, 1994, for a maximum of 150 days; emergency modified at 18
Ill. Reg. 12880; amended at 18 Ill. Reg. 15154, effective September 27, 1994;
amended at 20 Ill. Reg. 3118, effective February 5, 1996; emergency amendment
at 21 Ill. Reg. 483, effective January 1, 1997, for a maximum of 150 days;
amended at 21 Ill. Reg. 2422, effective January 31, 1997; amended at 21 Ill.
Reg. 4844, effective March 27, 1997; emergency amendment at 21 Ill. Reg.
17180, effective December 9, 1997, for a maximum of 150 days.

SUBPART D: MEMBERSHIP AND SERVICE CREDITS

Section 1650.346 Service Credit for Periods Away From Teaching Due to Adoption

    a) Service credit of up to three years shall be granted for periods
        beginning prior to July 1, 1983, during which a teacher ceased covered
        employment for the purpose of adopting an infant under three years of
        age or caring for a newly adopted infant under three years of age.
    b) For purposes of determining eligibility to receive optional service
        credit under the provisions of 40 ILCS 5/16-127(b)(5)(iv), the
        following definitions shall apply:
        1) "Ceased covered employment" shall mean the submission of a
            resignation that terminated employment in a position requiring
            membership contributions to the System as a condition of
            employment.
        2) "For the purpose of adopting an infant under three years of age"
            shall mean the termination of covered employment:
            A) to meet the requirements of an adoption agency or similar
                entity resulting in the adoption of an infant who is under
                the age of three at the time the member terminates covered

TEACHERS' RETIREMENT SYSTEM OF THE STATE OF ILLINOIS

NOTICE OF EMERGENCY AMENDMENTS

employment; or

B) to formally commence judicial or administrative proceedings to adopt an infant who is under the age of three at the time the adoption proceedings were initiated; or

C) to care for an infant under the age of three while an adoption proceeding is ongoing which results in the adoption of the infant.

3) "Caring for a newly adopted infant under three years of age" shall mean providing care to an adopted infant of less than three years of age when the interruption of service begins within 180 days of the court order declaring the member the adoptive parent of such an infant.

4) "Teaching service creditable under this System or the State Universities Retirement System" means employment in a position requiring membership contributions to the System or the State Universities Retirement System as a condition of employment.

c) The documents necessary to establish service credit under this Section shall include:

1) Employment records;

2) Birth certificates;

Court records;

Adoption agency records;

Governmental records; and/or

6) Other documentation, such as corroborating affidavits, that are based upon actual knowledge and are sufficiently specific as to times, dates, places and surrounding circumstances so that the proof of service submitted to the System reliably documents the service credit to be established while eliminating the possibility of mistake or fraud.

d) For purposes of granting service credit for periods away from teaching due to adoption, the statutory return-to-teaching requirement is met when the member returns to teaching service creditable under this System or the State Universities Retirement System for the period the member was away from teaching due to adoption or one year, whichever is less.

(Source: Emergency amendment at 21 Ill. Reg. 17159, effective December 9, 1997, for a maximum of 150 days)

SUBPART F: RULES GOVERNING ANNUITANTS AND BENEFICIARIES

Section 1650.575 Full-time Student - Receipt of Survivors Benefits Until Age 22

a) For purposes of 40 ILCS 5/16-140(4), a full-time student shall be one who is enrolled in a course of study in an accredited educational institution (other than a program of study by correspondence), and who is carrying a full-time workload as determined by the educational

TEACHERS' RETIREMENT SYSTEM OF THE STATE OF ILLINOIS

NOTICE OF EMERGENCY AMENDMENTS

institution during the regular school year for the course of study the student is pursuing.

b) Accredited educational institutions include schools, colleges, universities, and post-secondary vocational institutions whose courses of study are approved by appropriate state or federal educational accreditation authorities.

c) A regular school year is the eight to nine months which includes two semester terms or three quarter terms (or their equivalent), excluding the summer term. Terms that begin after April 15 and end before September 16 are considered summer terms.

d) Survivors benefits shall be payable during the period between regular school years if the benefit recipient was a full-time student during the preceding semester term or quarter term (or their equivalent).

e) To verify that an eligible child is a full-time student, the System must receive a certification signed by an official of the educational institution confirming that the student is a full-time student as provided in subsection (a) above.

(Source: Emergency amendment at 21 Ill. Reg. _____, effective December 9, 1997, for a maximum of 150 days)

Section 1650.595 Overpayments

a) When the System determines benefits, except for an impermissible refund as defined in Section 1650.240, have been paid erroneously in an amount greater than $50 to a member, annuitant or beneficiary (recipient), the System shall record such overpayment as an accounts receivable and make demand upon the recipient for the amount due.

b) Interest shall accrue on overpayments at the rate of 0.83% per month beginning on the first day of the month following 30 days from the date of notification to the recipient of the overpayment.

c) The System shall use its best efforts to ensure repayment of overpayments within 36 months of such overpayment.

d) If the recipient of an overpayment fails to repay the amount due plus any applicable interest within 36 months, the System will collect any amount plus applicable interest outstanding at the time the recipient next receives a benefit from the System by withholding 10% of the recipient's gross payment if a periodic payment including any reciprocal system payment or 100% if a lump sum payment.

e) The System shall retain the option to refer any debt due the System to the Attorney General, the Debt Collection Board, the Comptroller's Offset System, or private collection agencies at any time it deems appropriate.

(Source: Emergency amendment at 21 Ill. Reg. _____, effective December 9, 1997, for a maximum of 150 days)

DEPARTMENT OF CENTRAL MANAGEMENT SERVICES

NOTICE OF PEREMPTORY AMENDMENTS

1) Heading of the Part: Pay Plan

2) Code Citation: 80 Ill. Adm. Code 310

3) Section Numbers: Peremptory Action:
310.Appendix A, Table O   Amended
310.Appendix A, Table P   Amended

4) Reference to the specific State or Federal Court Order, Federal Rule or Statute which requires this Peremptory Rulemaking: Section 1-5(d) of the Illinois Administrative Procedure Act [5 ILCS 100/1-5(d)]

5) Statutory Authority: Authorized by Sections 8 and 8a of the Personnel Code [20 ILCS 415/8 and 8a.]

6) Effective Date: December 9, 1997

7) A Complete Description of the Subjects and Issues Involved:

In Section 310. Table O RC-028 (Paraprofessional Human Services Employees, AFSCME), the Crime Studies Associate title is being replaced by the State Police Crime Information Evaluator with the monthly salary range of $1,800 - 2,504, effective December 1, 1997.

In Section 310. Table P RC-029 (Paraprofessional Investigatory and Law Enforcement Employees, IFPE), the Illinois Federation of Public Employees Association negotiated a new three year contract which reflects that those employees whose retirement formula rates were changed shall receive a one-time lump sum payment of $565 for Fiscal Year 1998. Employees receiving the alternative pension formula shall receive a 3% wage increase on July 1, 1997.

Effective July 1, 1997, the Plant and Pesticide Specialist I and II titles shall receive a salary adjustment of one pay grade. The Product and Standards Inspector title shall be increased two pay grades. Also, the Vehicle Compliance Inspector's monthly salary range is being corrected from $2,354 - 3,060 to $2,463 - 3,121.

Effective July, 1998 and July, 1999, the salary schedules shall receive a 3% across-the-board increase.

Effective July 1, 1998, the Environmental Protection Legal Investigator I and II titles shall receive a salary adjustment of two pay grades. The Warehouse Examiner I title will be reclassified to Warehouse Examiner with the monthly salary range of $2,537 - 3,215. The Warehouse Examiner II and III titles will be reclassified to Warehouse Examiner Specialist with the monthly salary range of $2,799 - 3,571.

DEPARTMENT OF CENTRAL MANAGEMENT SERVICES

NOTICE OF PEREMPTORY AMENDMENTS

Employees employed as Arson Investigators I, II, Commerce Commission Police Officers I, II and Police Officers I, II and III shall receive an increase of $50 per month longevity pay as outlined in the Alternative pension formula schedule upon reaching 10 years, 13 years and 15 years service in the same classification series.

Those employees (non-sworn) on Step 7 who have attained 15 years of service and have 3 or more years of creditable service on Step 7 in the same pay grade shall receive a longevity increase of $50 per month.

8) Does this rulemaking contain an automatic repeal date? No

9) Date Filed in Agency's Principle Office: December 9, 1997

10) Is this Rule in compliance with Section 5-50 of the Illinois Administrative Procedure Act? Yes

11) Are there any proposed amendments pending to this Part? Yes

Section Numbers	Proposed Action	Ill. Reg. Citation
310. Appendix D	Amended	21 Ill. Reg. 12859 (September 8, 1997)
310. Appendix G	Amended	21 Ill. Reg. 12859 (September 8, 1997)
310.230	Amended	21 Ill. Reg. 14648 (November 14, 1997)
310.270	Amended	21 Ill. Reg. 14648 (November 14, 1997)
310.280	Amended	21 Ill. Reg. 14648 (November 14, 1997)

12) Statement of Statewide Objectives: These amendments to the Pay Plan pertain only to State employees subject to the Personnel Code and do not set out any guidelines that are to be followed by local or other jurisdictional bodies within the State.

13) The name, address and telephone number of the person to whom information and questions concerning this peremptory rule shall be directed to: Within 45 days, comments should be written and addressed to:

Mr. Michael Murphy
Department of Central Management Services
Division of Technical Services
504 William G. Stratton Building
Springfield, IL 62706
Telephone: (217) 782-5601

DEPARTMENT OF CENTRAL MANAGEMENT SERVICES

NOTICE OF PEREMPTORY AMENDMENTS

The full text of the Peremptory Amendments begins on the next page:

DEPARTMENT OF CENTRAL MANAGEMENT SERVICES

NOTICE OF PEREMPTORY AMENDMENTS

TITLE 80: PUBLIC OFFICIALS AND EMPLOYEES
SUBTITLE B: PERSONNEL RULES, PAY PLANS, AND
POSITION CLASSIFICATIONS
CHAPTER I: DEPARTMENT OF CENTRAL MANAGEMENT SERVICES

PART 310
PAY PLAN

SUBPART A: NARRATIVE

SUBPART B: SCHEDULE OF RATES

SUBPART C: MERIT COMPENSATION SYSTEM

DEPARTMENT OF CENTRAL MANAGEMENT SERVICES

NOTICE OF PEREMPTORY AMENDMENTS

DEPARTMENT OF CENTRAL MANAGEMENT SERVICES

NOTICE OF PEREMPTORY AMENDMENTS

AUTHORITY: Implementing and authorized by Sections 8 and 8a of the Personnel
Code [20 ILCS 415/8 and 8a].

SOURCE: Filed June 28, 1967; codified at 8 Ill. Reg. 1558; emergency amendment
at 8 Ill. Reg. 1990, effective January 31, 1984, for a maximum of 150 days;
amended at 8 Ill. Reg. 2440, effective February 15, 1984; emergency amendment
at 8 Ill. Reg. 3348, effective March 5, 1984, for a maximum of 150 days;
emergency amendment at 8 Ill. Reg. 4249, effective March 16, 1984, for a
maximum of 150 days; emergency amendment at 8 Ill. Reg. 5704, effective April
16, 1984, for a maximum of 150 days; emergency amendment at 8 Ill. Reg. 7290,
effective May 11, 1984, for a maximum of 150 days; amended at 8 Ill. Reg.
11299, effective June 25, 1984; emergency amendment at 8 Ill. Reg. 12616,
effective July 1, 1984, for a maximum of 150 days; emergency amendment at 8
Ill. Reg. 15007, effective August 6, 1984, for a maximum of 150 days; amended
at 8 Ill. Reg. 15367, effective August 13, 1984; emergency amendment at 8 Ill.
Reg. 21310, effective October 15, 1984, for a maximum of 150 days; amended at 8
Ill. Reg. 21544, effective October 24, 1984; amended at 8 Ill. Reg. 22844,
effective November 14, 1984; emergency amendment at 9 Ill. Reg. 1134, effective
January 16, 1985, for a maximum of 150 days; amended at 9 Ill. Reg. 1320,
effective January 23, 1985; amended at 9 Ill. Reg. 3681, effective March 12,
1985; emergency amendment at 9 Ill. Reg. 4163, effective March 15, 1985, for a
maximum of 150 days; emergency amendment at 9 Ill. Reg. 9231, effective May 31,
1985, for a maximum of 150 days; amended at 9 Ill. Reg. 9420, effective June 7,
1985; amended at 9 Ill. Reg. 10663, effective July 1, 1985; emergency amendment
at 9 Ill. Reg. 15043, effective September 24, 1985, for a maximum of 150 days;
peremptory amendment at 10 Ill. Reg. 3325, effective January 22, 1986; amended
at 10 Ill. Reg. 3230, effective January 24, 1986; emergency amendment at 10
Ill. Reg. 8904, effective May 13, 1986, for a maximum of 150 days; peremptory
amendment at 10 Ill. Reg. 8928, effective May 13, 1986; emergency amendment at
10 Ill. Reg. 12090, effective June 30, 1986, for a maximum of 150 days;
peremptory amendment at 10 Ill. Reg. 13675, effective July 31, 1986; peremptory
amendment at 10 Ill. Reg. 14867, effective August 26, 1986; amended at 10 Ill.
Reg. 15567, effective September 17, 1986; emergency amendment at 10 Ill. Reg.
17765, effective September 30, 1986, for a maximum of 150 days; peremptory
amendment at 10 Ill. Reg. 19132, effective October 28, 1986; peremptory
amendment at 10 Ill. Reg. 21097, effective December 9, 1986; amended at 11 Ill.

DEPARTMENT OF CENTRAL MANAGEMENT SERVICES

NOTICE OF PEREMPTORY AMENDMENTS

Reg. 648, effective December 22, 1986; peremptory amendment at 11 Ill. Reg. 3363, effective February 3, 1987; peremptory amendment at 11 Ill. Reg. 4388, effective February 27, 1987; peremptory amendment at 11 Ill. Reg. 6291, effective March 23, 1987; amended at 11 Ill. Reg. 5901, effective March 24, 1987; emergency amendment at 11 Ill. Reg. 8787, effective April 15, 1987, for a maximum of 150 days; emergency amendment at 11 Ill. Reg. 11830, effective July 1, 1987, for a maximum of 150 days; peremptory amendment at 11 Ill. Reg. 13675, effective July 29, 1987; amended at 11 Ill. Reg. 14984, effective August 27, 1987; peremptory amendment at 11 Ill. Reg. 15273, effective September 1, 1987; peremptory amendment 11 Ill. Reg. 17919, effective October 19, 1987; peremptory amendment at 11 Ill. Reg. 19812, effective November 19, 1987; emergency amendment at 11 Ill. Reg. 20664, effective December 4, 1987, for a maximum of 150 days; amended at 11 Ill. Reg. 20778, effective December 11, 1987; peremptory amendment at 12 Ill. Reg. 3811, effective January 27, 1988; peremptory amendment at 12 Ill. Reg. 5459, effective March 3, 1988; amended at 12 Ill. Reg. 6073, effective March 21, 1988; peremptory amendment at 12 Ill. Reg. 7783, effective April 14, 1988; emergency amendment at 12 Ill. Reg. 7734, effective April 15, 1988, for a maximum of 150 days; peremptory amendment at 12 Ill. Reg. 8135, effective April 22, 1988; peremptory amendment at 12 Ill. Reg. 9745, effective May 23, 1988; emergency amendment at 12 Ill. Reg. 11778, effective July 1, 1988, for a maximum of 150 days; emergency amendment at 12 Ill. Reg. 12895, effective July 18, 1988, for a maximum of 150 days; peremptory amendment at 12 Ill. Reg. 13306, effective July 27, 1988; corrected at 12 Ill. Reg. 13359; amended at 12 Ill. Reg. 14630, effective September 6, 1988; amended at 12 Ill. Reg. 20449, effective November 28, 1988; peremptory amendment at 12 Ill. Reg. 20584, effective November 28, 1988; peremptory amendment at 13 Ill. Reg. 8080, effective May 10, 1989; amended at 13 Ill. Reg. 8849, effective May 30, 1989; peremptory amendment at 13 Ill. Reg. 8970, effective May 26, 1989; emergency amendment at 13 Ill. Reg. 10967, effective June 20, 1989, for a maximum of 150 days; emergency amendment expired on November 17, 1989; amended at 13 Ill. Reg. 11451, effective June 28, 1989; emergency amendment at 13 Ill. Reg. 11854, effective July 1, 1989, for a maximum of 150 days; corrected at 13 Ill. Reg. 12647; peremptory amendment at 13 Ill. Reg. 12887, effective July 24, 1989; amended at 13 Ill. Reg. 16950, effective October 20, 1989; amended at 13 Ill. Reg. 19221, effective December 12, 1989; amended at 14 Ill. Reg. 615, effective January 2, 1990; peremptory amendment at 14 Ill. Reg. 1627, effective January 11, 1990; amended at 14 Ill. Reg. 4455, effective March 12, 1990; peremptory amendment at 14 Ill. Reg. 7652, effective May 7, 1990; amended at 14 Ill. Reg. 10002, effective June 11, 1990; emergency amendment at 14 Ill. Reg. 11330, effective June 29, 1990, for a maximum of 150 days; amended at 14 Ill. Reg. 14361, effective August 24, 1990; emergency amendment at 14 Ill. Reg. 15570, effective September 11, 1990, for a maximum of 150 days; emergency amendment expired on February 8, 1991; corrected at 14 Ill. Reg. 16092; peremptory amendment at 14 Ill. Reg. 17098, effective September 25, 1990; amended at 14 Ill. Reg. 17189, effective October 2, 1990; amended at 14 Ill. Reg. 17189, effective October 19, 1990; amended at 14 Ill. Reg. 18719, effective November 13, 1990; peremptory amendment at 14 Ill. Reg. 18854, effective November 13, 1990; peremptory amendment at 15 Ill. Reg. 663,

DEPARTMENT OF CENTRAL MANAGEMENT SERVICES

NOTICE OF PEREMPTORY AMENDMENTS

effective January 7, 1991; amended at 15 Ill. Reg. 3296, effective February 14, 1991; peremptory amendment at 15 Ill. Reg. 4401, effective March 11, 1991; peremptory amendment at 15 Ill. Reg. 5100, effective March 20, 1991; peremptory amendment at 15 Ill. Reg. 5465, effective April 2, 1991; emergency amendment at 15 Ill. Reg. 10485, effective July 1, 1991, for a maximum of 150 days; amended at 15 Ill. Reg. 11080, effective July 19, 1991; amended at 15 Ill. Reg. 13080, effective August 21, 1991; amended at 15 Ill. Reg. 14210, effective September 23, 1991; emergency amendment at 16 Ill. Reg. 711, effective December 26, 1991, for a maximum of 150 days; amended at 16 Ill. Reg. 3450, effective February 20, 1992; peremptory amendment at 16 Ill. Reg. 5068, effective March 11, 1992; peremptory amendment at 16 Ill. Reg. 7056, effective April 20, 1992; emergency amendment at 16 Ill. Reg. 8239, effective May 19, 1992, for a maximum of 150 days; amended at 16 Ill. Reg. 8382, effective May 26, 1992; emergency amendment at 16 Ill. Reg. 13950, effective August 19, 1992, for a maximum of 150 days; emergency amendment at 16 Ill. Reg. 14452, effective September 4, 1992, for a maximum of 150 days; amended at 17 Ill. Reg. 238, effective December 23, 1992; peremptory amendment at 17 Ill. Reg. 498, effective December 18, 1992; amended at 17 Ill. Reg. 590, effective January 4, 1993; amended at 17 Ill. Reg. 1819, effective February 2, 1993; amended at 17 Ill. Reg. 6441, effective April 8, 1993; emergency amendment at 17 Ill. Reg. 12900, effective July 22, 1993, for a maximum of 150 days; amended at 17 Ill. Reg. 13409, effective July 29, 1993; emergency amendment at 17 Ill. Reg. 13789, effective August 9, 1993, for a maximum of 150 days; emergency amendment at 17 Ill. Reg. 14666, effective August 26, 1993, for a maximum of 150 days; amended at 17 Ill. Reg. 19103, effective October 25, 1993; emergency amendment at 17 Ill. Reg. 21858, effective December 1, 1993, for a maximum of 150 days; amended at 17 Ill. Reg. 22514, effective December 15, 1993; amended at 18 Ill. Reg. 227, effective December 17, 1993; amended at 18 Ill. Reg. 1107, effective January 18, 1994; amended at 18 Ill. Reg. 5146, effective March 21, 1994; peremptory amendment at 18 Ill. Reg. 9562, effective June 13, 1994; emergency amendment at 18 Ill. Reg. 11299, effective July 1, 1994, for a maximum of 150 days; peremptory amendment at 18 Ill. Reg. 13476, effective August 17, 1994; emergency amendment at 18 Ill. Reg. 14417, effective September 9, 1994, for a maximum of 150 days; amended at 18 Ill. Reg. 16545, effective October 31, 1994; peremptory amendment at 18 Ill. Reg. 16708, effective October 28, 1994; amended at 18 Ill. Reg. 17191, effective November 21, 1994; amended at 19 Ill. Reg. 1024, effective January 24, 1995; peremptory amendment at 19 Ill. Reg. 2481, effective February 17, 1995; peremptory amendment at 19 Ill. Reg. 3073, effective February 17, 1995; amended at 19 Ill. Reg. 3456, effective March 7, 1995; peremptory amendment at 19 Ill. Reg. 5145, effective March 14, 1995; amended at 19 Ill. Reg. 6452, effective May 2, 1995; peremptory amendment at 19 Ill. Reg. 6688, effective May 1, 1995; amended at 19 Ill. Reg. 7841, effective June 1, 1995; amended at 19 Ill. Reg. 8156, effective June 12, 1995; amended at 19 Ill. Reg. 9096, effective June 27, 1995; emergency amendment at 19 Ill. Reg. 11954, effective August 1, 1995, for a maximum of 150 days; peremptory amendment at 19 Ill. Reg. 13979, effective September 19, 1995; peremptory amendment at 19 Ill. Reg. 15103, effective October 12, 1995; amended at 19 Ill. Reg. 16160, effective November 28, 1995; amended at 20 Ill. Reg. 308, effective December

DEPARTMENT OF CENTRAL MANAGEMENT SERVICES

NOTICE OF PEREMPTORY AMENDMENTS

22, 1995; emergency amendment at 20 Ill. Reg. 4060, effective February 27, 1996, for a maximum of 150 days; peremptory amendment at 20 Ill. Reg. 6334, effective April 22, 1996; peremptory amendment at 20 Ill. Reg. 7434, effective May 14, 1996; amended at 20 Ill. Reg. 8301, effective June 11, 1996; amended at 20 Ill. Reg. 8657, effective June 20, 1996; amended at 20 Ill. Reg. 9006, effective June 26, 1996; amended at 20 Ill. Reg. 9925, effective July 10, 1996; emergency amendment at 20 Ill. Reg. 10213, effective July 15, 1996, for a maximum of 150 days; amended at 20 Ill. Reg. 10841, effective August 5, 1996; peremptory amendment at 20 Ill. Reg. 13408, effective September 24, 1996; amended at 20 Ill. Reg. 15018, effective November 7, 1996; peremptory amendment at 20 Ill. Reg. 15092, effective November 7, 1996; emergency amendment at 21 Ill. Reg. 1023, effective January 6, 1997, for a maximum of 150 days; amended at 21 Ill. Reg. 1629, effective January 22, 1997; amended at 21 Ill. Reg. 5144, effective April 15, 1997; amended at 21 Ill. Reg. 6444, effective May 15, 1997; amended at 21 Ill. Reg. 7118, effective June 3, 1997; emergency amendment at 21 Ill. Reg. 10061, effective July 21, 1997, for a maximum of 150 days; emergency amendment at 21 Ill. Reg. 12859, effective September 8, 1997, for a maximum of 150 days; peremptory amendment at 21 Ill. Reg. 14267, effective October 14, 1997; peremptory amendment at 21 Ill. Reg. 14589, effective October 15, 1997; peremptory amendment at 21 Ill. Reg. 15030, effective November 10, 1997; amended at 21 Ill. Reg. 16344, effective December 4, 1997; peremptory amendment at 21 Ill. Reg. 16465, effective December 4, 1997; peremptory amendment at 21 Ill. Reg. _____, effective _____ **DEC 0 9 1997**

DEPARTMENT OF CENTRAL MANAGEMENT SERVICES

NOTICE OF PEREMPTORY AMENDMENTS

Section 310.APPENDIX A Negotiated Rates of Pay

Section 310.TABLE O RC-028 (Paraprofessional Human Services Employees, AFSCME)

Effective July 1, 1997

	STEPS					
	1c 3/	1b	1a	1	2	3
Apparel Dry Goods Specialist III	1938	1996	2056	2118	2207	2294
Assistant Reimbursement Officer	1546	1592	1640	1689	1747	1809
Child Development Aide III	1724	1776	1829	1884	1966	2037
Clinical Laboratory Associate	1546	1592	1640	1689	1747	1809
Clinical Laboratory Technician I	1724	1776	1829	1884	1966	2037
Clinical Laboratory Technician I	1885	1942	2000	2060	2148	2228
Clinical Laboratory Technician II	1885	1942	2000	2060	2148	2228
Compliance Officer	2062	2124	2188	2254	2350	2449
Conservation Resource Technician I	1724	1776	1829	1884	1966	2037
Conservation Resource Technician II	1967	2026	2087	2150	2240	2336
Construction Supervisor I	1967	2026	2087	2150	2240	2336
Construction Supervisor II	2262	2330	2400	2472	2586	2704
Crime Scene Investigator	2942	3030	3121	3215	3380	3543
Crime Studies Associate	1724	1776	1829	1884	1966	2037
Data Processing Administrative Specialist	2062	2124	2188	2254	2350	2449
Data Processing Specialist	1885	1942	2000	2060	2148	2228
Data Processing Technician	1660	1710	1761	1814	1882	1955
Data Processing Technician Trainee	1495	1540	1586	1634	1689	1744
Dental Assistant	1599	1647	1696	1747	1814	1879
Dental Hygienist	1885	1942	2000	2060	2148	2228
Electroencephalograph Technician	1599	1647	1696	1747	1814	1879
Environmental Equipment Operator I	1885	1942	2000	2060	2148	2228
Environmental Equipment Operator II	2062	2124	2188	2254	2350	2449
Environmental Protection Technician I	1724	1776	1829	1884	1966	2037
Environmental Protection	1724	1776	1829	1884	1966	2037

DEPARTMENT OF CENTRAL MANAGEMENT SERVICES

NOTICE OF PEREMPTORY AMENDMENTS

Technician II						
Hearing & Speech	1495	1540	1586	1634	1689	1744
Technician I						
Hearing & Speech	1660	1710	1761	1814	1882	1955
Technician II						
Historic Site Interpreter	1660	1710	1761	1814	1882	1955
Historic Site Lead I	1967	2026	2087	2150	2240	2336
Historic Site Lead II	2062	2124	2188	2254	2350	2449
Housekeeper II	1399	1441	1484	1529	1578	1628
Inhalation Therapist	1599	1647	1696	1747	1814	1879
Intermittent Unemployment	9.20	9.48	9.76	10.06	10.39	10.73
Insurance Technician						
Laboratory Assistant	1399	1441	1484	1529	1582	1632
Laboratory Associate I	1724	1776	1829	1884	1966	2037
Laboratory Associate II						
	1885	1942	2000	2060	2148	2228
Legal Research Assistant*	1967	2026	2087	2150	2240	2336
Licensed Practical Nurse I	1709	1760	1813	1867	1936	2015
Licensed Practical Nurse II	1792	1846	1901	1958	2045	2121
Medical Records Assistant	1660	1710	1761	1814	1882	1955
Medical Records Technician	1800	1854	1910	1967	2049	2124
Office Administrative	1885	1942	2000	2060	2148	2228
Specialist						
Office Specialist	1800	1854	1910	1967	2049	2124
Pharmacist Lead Technician	1599	1647	1696	1747	1814	1879
Pharmacist Technician	1495	1540	1586	1634	1689	1744
Public Aid Eligibility Assistant	1599	1647	1696	1747	1814	1879
Radiologic Technologist	1800	1854	1910	1967	2049	2124
Radiologic Technologist						
Program Coordinator	1885	1942	2000	2060	2148	2228
Ranger	1967	2026	2087	2150	2240	2336
Rehabilitation Counselor	1660	1710	1761	1814	1882	1955
Aide I						
Rehabilitation Counselor	1800	1854	1910	1967	2049	2124
Aide II						
Senior Ranger	2062	2124	2188	2254	2350	2449
Site Technician I	1724	1776	1829	1884	1966	2037
Site Technician II	1885	1942	2000	2060	2148	2228
Social Service Community	1800	1854	1910	1967	2049	2124
Planner						
State Police Crime Information	1800	1854	1910	1967	2049	2124
Evaluator						
State Police Evidence	1885	1942	2000	2060	2148	2228
Technician I						
State Police Evidence	1967	2026	2087	2150	2240	2336
Technician II						
Statistical Research Technician	1800	1854	1910	1967	2049	2124

DEPARTMENT OF CENTRAL MANAGEMENT SERVICES

NOTICE OF PEREMPTORY AMENDMENTS

Veterans Service Officer	1885	1942	2000	2060	2148	2228
Vocational Instructor	1885	1942	2000	2060	2148	2228

S T E P S (cont.)			
4	5	6	7
2388	2476	2559	2704
1870	1931	1995	2102
2115	2189	2268	2394
1870	1931	1995	2102
2115	2189	2268	2394
2321	2405	2497	2636
2559	2656	2759	2919
2115	2189	2268	2394
2431	2522	2619	2768
2431	2522	2619	2768
2817	2934	3052	3232
3708	3877	4038	4289
3135	3189	3260	3994
2559	2656	2759	2919
1950	2013	2082	2192
2115	2189	2268	2394
1804	1860	1920	2017
1950	2013	2082	2192
2321	2405	2497	2636
1950	2013	2082	2192
2115	2189	2268	2394
1804	1860	1920	2017
2025	2101	2173	2287
2431	2522	2619	2768
2559	2656	2759	2919
1676	1722	1776	1867
1950	2013	2082	2192
11.10	11.45	11.82	12.41
1678	1735	1782	1874
2115	2189	2268	2394
2321	2405	2497	2636
2431	2522	2619	2768
2088	2170	2340	2360
2204	2285	2367	2519
2025	2101	2173	2287
2211	2293	2371	2504
2321	2405	2497	2636
2211	2293	2371	2504
1950	2013	2082	2192
1804	1860	1920	2017
1950	2013	2082	2192
2211	2293	2371	2504
2321	2405	2497	2636

DEPARTMENT OF CENTRAL MANAGEMENT SERVICES

NOTICE OF PEREMPTORY AMENDMENTS

2431	2522	2619	2768
2025	2101	2173	2287
2211	2293	2371	2504
2559	2656	2759	2919
2115	2189	2268	2394
2321	2405	2497	2636
2211	2293	2371	2504
2211	2293	2371	2504
2321	2405	2497	2636
2431	2522	2619	2768
2211	2293	2371	2504
2321	2405	2497	2636
2321	2405	2497	2636

NOTE: Employees subject to the alternative pension formula will be paid at rates that are 3% higher than those stated above.

Full-time employees who are receiving the flat-rate pension formula will receive a one-time lump sum payment of $565.

Effective July 1, 1998

	STEPS					
	1c	1b	1a	1	2	3
Apparel Dry Goods Specialist III	1996	2056	2118	2182	2273	2363
Assistant Reimbursement Officer	1592	1640	1689	1740	1799	1863
Child Development Aide III	1776	1829	1884	1941	2025	2098
Clinical Laboratory Associate	1592	1640	1689	1740	1799	1863
Clinical Laboratory Technician I	1776	1829	1884	1941	2025	2098
Clinical Laboratory Technician II	1942	2000	2060	2122	2212	2295
Compliance Officer	2124	2188	2254	2322	2421	2522
Conservation Resource Technician I	1776	1829	1884	1941	2025	2098
Conservation Resource Technician II	2026	2087	2150	2215	2307	2406
Construction Supervisor I	2026	2087	2150	2215	2307	2406
Construction Supervisor II	2330	2400	2472	2546	2664	2785
Crime Scene Investigator	3030	3121	3215	3311	3481	3649
Crime Studies Associate	1776	1829	1884	1941	2025	2098
Data Processing Administrative Specialist	2124	2188	2254	2322	2421	2522
Data Processing Specialist	1942	2000	2060	2122	2212	2295
Data Processing Technician	1710	1761	1814	1868	1938	2014
Data Processing Technician	1540	1586	1634	1683	1740	1796

DEPARTMENT OF CENTRAL MANAGEMENT SERVICES

NOTICE OF PEREMPTORY AMENDMENTS

Trainee						
Dental Assistant	1647	1696	1747	1799	1868	1935
Dental Hygienist	1942	2000	2060	2122	2212	2295
Electroencephalograph Technician	1647	1696	1747	1799	1868	1935
Environmental Equipment Operator I	1942	2000	2060	2122	2212	2295
Environmental Equipment Operator II	2124	2188	2254	2322	2421	2522
Environmental Protection Technician I	1647	1696	1747	1799	1868	1935
Environmental Protection Technician II	1776	1829	1884	1941	2025	2098
Hearing & Speech Technician I	1540	1586	1634	1683	1740	1796
Hearing & Speech Technician II	1710	1761	1814	1868	1938	2014
Historic Site Interpreter	1710	1761	1814	1868	1938	2014
Historic Site Lead I	2026	2087	2150	2215	2307	2406
Historic Site Lead II	2124	2188	2254	2322	2421	2522
Housekeeper II	1441	1484	1529	1575	1625	1677
Inhalation Therapist	1647	1696	1747	1799	1868	1935
Intermittent Unemployment Insurance Technician	9.48	9.76	10.06	10.36	10.71	11.05
Laboratory Assistant	1441	1484	1529	1575	1628	1681
Laboratory Associate I	1776	1829	1884	1941	2025	2098
Laboratory Associate II	1942	2000	2060	2122	2212	2295
Legal Research Assistant	2026	2087	2150	2215	2307	2406
Licensed Practical Nurse I	1760	1813	1867	1923	1994	2075
Licensed Practical Nurse II	1846	1901	1958	2017	2106	2185
Medical Records Assistant	1710	1761	1814	1868	1938	2014
Medical Records Technician	1854	1910	1967	2026	2110	2188
Office Administrative Specialist	1942	2000	2060	2122	2212	2295
Office Specialist	1854	1910	1967	2026	2110	2188
Pharmacist Lead Technician	1647	1696	1747	1799	1868	1935
Pharmacist Technician	1540	1586	1634	1683	1740	1796
Public Aid Eligibility Assistant	1647	1696	1747	1799	1868	1935
Radiologic Technologist	1854	1910	1967	2026	2110	2188
Radiologic Technologist Program Coordinator	1942	2000	2060	2122	2212	2295
Ranger	2026	2087	2150	2215	2307	2406
Rehabilitation Counselor Aide I	1710	1761	1814	1868	1938	2014
Rehabilitation Counselor Aide II	1854	1910	1967	2026	2110	2188
Senior Ranger	2124	2188	2254	2322	2421	2522
Site Technician I	1776	1829	1884	1941	2025	2098

DEPARTMENT OF CENTRAL MANAGEMENT SERVICES

NOTICE OF PEREMPTORY AMENDMENTS

Site Technician II	1942	2000	2060	2122	2212	2295
Social Service Community Planner	1854	1910	1967	2026	2110	2188
State Police Crime Information Evaluator	1854	1910	1967	2026	2110	2188
State Police Evidence Technician I	1942	2000	2060	2122	2212	2295
State Police Evidence Technician II	2026	2087	2150	2215	2307	2406
Statistical Research Technician	1854	1910	1967	2026	2110	2188
Veterans Service Officer	1942	2000	2060	2122	2212	2295
Vocational Instructor	1942	2000	2060	2122	2212	2295

STEPS (cont.)

	4	5	6	7
Apparel Dry Goods Specialist III		2460	2550	2636	2785
Assistant Reimbursement Officer	1926	1989	2055	2165
Child Development Aide III	2178	2255	2336	2466
Clinical Laboratory Associate	1926	1989	2055	2165
Clinical Laboratory Technician I	2178	2255	2336	2466
Clinical Laboratory Technician II	2391	2477	2572	2715
Compliance Officer	2636	2736	2842	3007
Conservation Resource Technician I	2178	2255	2336	2466
Conservation Resource Technician II	2504	2598	2698	2851
Construction Supervisor I	2504	2598	2698	2851
Construction Supervisor II	2902	3023	3144	3329
Crime Scene Investigator	3819	3993	4159	4418
~~Crime Studies Associate~~	~~2178~~	~~2255~~	~~2336~~	~~2466~~
Data Processing Administrative Specialist	2636	2736	2842	3007
Data Processing Specialist	2391	2477	2572	2715
Data Processing Technician	2086	2164	2238	2356
Data Processing Technician Trainee	1858	1916	1978	2078
Dental Assistant	2009	2073	2144	2258
Dental Hygienist	2391	2477	2572	2715
Electroencephalograph Technician	2009	2073	2144	2258
Environmental Equipment Operator I	2391	2477	2572	2715
Environmental Equipment Operator II	2636	2736	2842	3007

DEPARTMENT OF CENTRAL MANAGEMENT SERVICES

NOTICE OF PEREMPTORY AMENDMENTS

Environmental Protection Technician I	2009	2073	2144	2258
Environmental Protection Technician II	2178	2255	2336	2446
Hearing & Speech Technician I	1858	1916	1978	2078
Hearing & Speech Technician II	2086	2164	2238	2356
Historic Site Interpreter	2086	2164	2238	2356
Historic Site Lead I	2504	2598	2698	2851
Historic Site Lead II	2636	2736	2842	3007
Housekeeper II	1726	1774	1829	1923
Inhalation Therapist	2009	2073	2144	2258
Intermittent Unemployment Insurance Technician	11.43	11.79	12.17	12.79
Laboratory Assistant	1728	1787	1835	1930
Laboratory Associate I	2178	2255	2336	2466
Laboratory Associate II	2391	2477	2572	2715
Legal Research Assistant	2504	2598	2698	2851
Licensed Practical Nurse I	2151	2235	2307	2431
Licensed Practical Nurse II	2270	2354	2438	2595
Medical Records Assistant	2086	2164	2238	2356
Medical Records Technician	2277	2362	2442	2579
Office Administrative Specialist	2391	2477	2572	2715
Office Specialist	2277	2362	2442	2579
Pharmacist Lead Technician	2009	2073	2144	2258
Pharmacist Technician	1858	1916	1978	2078
Public Aid Eligibility Assistant	2009	2073	2144	2258
Radiologic Technologist	2277	2362	2442	2579
Radiologic Technologist Program Coordinator	2391	2477	2572	2715
Ranger	2504	2598	2698	2851
Rehabilitation Counselor Aide I	2086	2164	2238	2356
Rehabilitation Counselor Aide II	2277	2362	2442	2579
Senior Ranger	2636	2736	2842	3007
Site Technician I	2178	2255	2336	2466
Site Technician II	2391	2477	2572	2715
Social Service Community Planner	2277	2362	2442	2579
State Police Crime Information Evaluator	2277	2362	2442	2579
State Police Evidence Technician I	2391	2477	2572	2715
State Police Evidence Technician II	2504	2598	2698	2851

DEPARTMENT OF CENTRAL MANAGEMENT SERVICES

NOTICE OF PEREMPTORY AMENDMENTS

Statistical Research Technician	2277	2362	2442	2579
Veterans Service Officer	2391	2477	2572	2715
Vocational Instructor	2391	2477	2572	2715

NOTE: Employees subject to the alternative pension formula will be paid at rates that are 3% higher than those stated above.

Effective July 1, 1999

	STEPS					
	1c	1b	1a	1	2	3
Apparel Dry Goods Specialist III	2056	2118	2182	2247	2341	2434
Assistant Reimbursement Officer	1640	1689	1740	1792	1853	1919
Child Development Aide III	1829	1884	1941	1999	2086	2161
Clinical Laboratory Associate	1640	1689	1740	1792	1853	1919
Clinical Laboratory Technician I	1829	1884	1941	1999	2086	2161
Clinical Laboratory Technician II	2000	2060	2122	2186	2278	2364
Compliance Officer	2188	2254	2322	2392	2494	2598
Conservation Resource Technician I	1829	1884	1941	1999	2086	2161
Conservation Resource Technician II	2087	2150	2215	2281	2376	2478
Construction Supervisor I	2087	2150	2215	2281	2376	2478
Construction Supervisor II	2400	2472	2546	2622	2744	2869
Crime Scene Investigator	3121	3215	3311	3410	3585	3758
Crime Studies Associate	1829	1884	1941	1999	2086	2161
Data Processing Administrative Specialist	2188	2254	2322	2392	2494	2598
Data Processing Specialist	2000	2060	2122	2186	2278	2364
Data Processing Technician	1761	1814	1868	1924	1996	2074
Data Processing Technician Trainee	1586	1634	1683	1733	1792	1850
Dental Assistant	1696	1747	1799	1853	1924	1993
Dental Hygienist	2000	2060	2122	2186	2278	2364
Electroencephalograph Technician	1696	1747	1799	1853	1924	1993
Environmental Equipment Operator I	2000	2060	2122	2186	2278	2364
Environmental Equipment Operator II	2188	2254	2322	2392	2494	2598
Environmental Protection Technician I	1696	1747	1799	1853	1924	1993
Environmental Protection Technician II	1829	1884	1941	1999	2086	2161

DEPARTMENT OF CENTRAL MANAGEMENT SERVICES

NOTICE OF PEREMPTORY AMENDMENTS

Hearing & Speech Technician I	1586	1634	1683	1733	1792	1850
Hearing & Speech Technician II	1761	1814	1868	1924	1996	2074
Historic Site Interpreter	1761	1814	1868	1924	1996	2074
Historic Site Lead I	2087	2150	2215	2281	2376	2478
Historic Site Lead II	2188	2254	2322	2392	2494	2598
Housekeeper II	1484	1529	1575	1622	1674	1727
Inhalation Therapist	1696	1747	1799	1853	1924	1993
Intermittent Unemployment Insurance Technician	9.76	10.06	10.36	10.66	11.03	11.38
Laboratory Assistant	1484	1529	1575	1622	1677	1731
Laboratory Associate I	1829	1884	1941	1999	2086	2161
Laboratory Associate II	2000	2060	2122	2186	2278	2364
Legal Research Assistant	2087	2150	2215	2281	2376	2478
Licensed Practical Nurse I	1813	1867	1923	1981	2054	2137
Licensed Practical Nurse II	1901	1958	2017	2078	2169	2251
Medical Records Assistant	1761	1814	1868	1924	1996	2074
Medical Records Technician	1910	1967	2026	2087	2173	2254
Office Administrative Specialist	2000	2060	2122	2186	2278	2364
Office Specialist	1918	1967	2026	2087	2173	2254
Pharmacist Lead Technician	1696	1747	1799	1853	1924	1993
Pharmacist Technician	1586	1634	1683	1733	1792	1850
Public Aid Eligibility Assistant	1696	1747	1799	1853	1924	1993
Radiologic Technologist	2000	2060	2122	2186	2278	2364
Radiologic Technologist Program Coordinator	2087	2150	2215	2281	2376	2478
Ranger	1761	1814	1868	1924	1996	2074
Rehabilitation Counselor Aide I	1910	1967	2026	2087	2173	2254
Rehabilitation Counselor Aide II	2188	2254	2322	2392	2494	2598
Senior Ranger	1829	1884	1941	1999	2086	2161
Site Technician I	2000	2060	2122	2186	2278	2364
Site Technician II	1910	1967	2026	2087	2173	2254
Social Service Community Planner	1910	1967	2026	2087	2173	2254
State Police Crime Information Evaluator	1910	1967	2026	2087	2173	2254
State Police Evidence Technician I	2000	2060	2122	2186	2278	2364
State Police Evidence Technician II	2087	2150	2215	2281	2376	2478
Statistical Research Technician	1910	1967	2026	2087	2173	2254
Veterans Service Officer	2000	2060	2122	2186	2278	2364
Vocational Instructor	2000	2060	2122	2186	2278	2364

DEPARTMENT OF CENTRAL MANAGEMENT SERVICES

NOTICE OF PEREMPTORY AMENDMENTS

	STEPS (cont.)			
	4	5	6	7
Apparel Dry Goods Specialist III	2534	2627	2715	2869
Assistant Reimbursement Officer	1984	2049	2117	2230
Child Development Aide III	2243	2323	2406	2540
Clinical Laboratory Associate	1984	2049	2117	2230
Clinical Laboratory Technician I	2243	2323	2406	2540
Clinical Laboratory Technician II	2463	2551	2649	2796
Compliance Officer	2715	2818	2927	3097
Conservation Resource Technician I	2243	2323	2406	2540
Conservation Resource Technician II	2579	2676	2779	2937
Construction Supervisor I	2579	2676	2779	2937
Construction Supervisor II	2989	3113	3238	3429
Crime Scene Investigator	3934	4113	4284	4551
~~Crime Studies Associate~~	~~2243~~	~~2323~~	~~2406~~	~~2540~~
Data Processing Administrative Specialist	2715	2818	2927	3097
Data Processing Specialist	2463	2551	2649	2796
Data Processing Technician	2149	2229	2305	2427
Data Processing Technician Trainee	1914	1973	2037	2140
Dental Assistant	2069	2135	2208	2326
Dental Hygienist	2463	2551	2649	2796
Electroencephalograph Technician	2069	2135	2208	2326
Environmental Equipment Operator I	2463	2551	2649	2796
Environmental Equipment Operator II	2715	2818	2927	3097
Environmental Protection Technician I	2069	2135	2208	2326
Environmental Protection Technician II	2243	2323	2406	2540
Hearing & Speech Technician I	1914	1973	2037	2140
Hearing & Speech Technician II	2149	2229	2305	2427
Historic Site Interpreter	2149	2229	2305	2427
Historic Site Lead I	2579	2676	2779	2937
Historic Site Lead II	2715	2818	2927	3097
Housekeeper II	1778	1827	1884	1981
Inhalation Therapist	2069	2135	2208	2326

DEPARTMENT OF CENTRAL MANAGEMENT SERVICES

NOTICE OF PEREMPTORY AMENDMENTS

Intermittent Unemployment Insurance Technician	11.78	12.44	12.54	13.17
Laboratory Assistant	1780	1841	1890	1988
Laboratory Associate I	2243	2323	2406	2540
Laboratory Associate II	2463	2551	2649	2796
Legal Research Assistant	2579	2676	2779	2937
Licensed Practical Nurse I	2216	2302	2376	2504
Licensed Practical Nurse II	2338	2425	2511	2673
Medical Records Assistant	2149	2229	2305	2427
Medical Records Technician	2345	2433	2515	2656
Office Administrative Specialist	2463	2551	2649	2796
Office Specialist	2345	2433	2515	2656
Pharmacist Lead Technician	2069	2135	2208	2326
Pharmacist Technician	1914	1973	2037	2140
Public Aid Eligibility Assistant	2069	2135	2208	2326
Radiologic Technologist Program Coordinator	2345	2433	2515	2656
Radiologic Technologist	2463	2551	2649	2796
Ranger	2579	2676	2779	2937
Rehabilitation Counselor Aide I	2149	2229	2305	2427
Rehabilitation Counselor Aide II	2345	2433	2515	2656
Senior Ranger	2715	2818	2927	3097
Site Technician I	2243	2323	2406	2540
Site Technician II	2463	2551	2649	2796
Social Service Community Planner	2345	2433	2515	2656
State Police Crime Information Evaluator	2345	2433	2515	2656
State Police Evidence Technician I	2463	2551	2649	2796
State Police Evidence Technician II	2579	2676	2779	2937
Statistical Research Technician	2345	2433	2515	2656
Veterans Service Officer	2463	2551	2649	2796
Vocational Instructor	2463	2551	2649	2796

NOTE: Employees subject to the alternative pension formula will be paid at rates that are 3% higher than those stated above.

Maximum Security Institutions Schedule
Effective July 1, 1999

	STEPS					
	1c	1b	1a	1	2	3
Apparel Dry Goods						

DEPARTMENT OF CENTRAL MANAGEMENT SERVICES

NOTICE OF PEREMPTORY AMENDMENTS

Specialist III	2233	2299	2366	2435	2535	2634
Assistant Reimbursement Officer	1791	1844	1897	1953	2018	2088
Child Development Aide III	1992	2051	2110	2172	2265	2344
Clinical Laboratory Associate	1791	1844	1897	1953	2018	2088
Clinical Laboratory Technician I	1992	2051	2110	2172	2265	2344
Clinical Laboratory Technician II	2173	2237	2303	2371	2468	2560
Compliance Officer	2373	2443	2515	2589	2698	2808
Conservation Resource Technician I	1992	2051	2110	2172	2265	2344
Conservation Resource Technician II	2266	2333	2401	2471	2572	2680
Construction Supervisor I	2266	2333	2401	2471	2572	2680
Construction Supervisor II	2598	2674	2752	2834	2962	3095
Crime Scene Investigator	3363	3462	3564	3669	3855	4039
~~Crime Studies Associate~~	~~1992~~	~~2051~~	~~2110~~	~~2172~~	~~2265~~	~~2344~~
Data Processing Administrative Specialist	2373	2443	2515	2589	2698	2808
Data Processing Specialist	2173	2237	2303	2371	2468	2560
Data Processing Technician	1920	1976	2033	2093	2169	2252
Data Processing Technician Trainee	1735	1785	1836	1890	1953	2015
Dental Assistant	1851	1904	1960	2018	2093	2166
Dental Hygienist	2173	2237	2303	2371	2468	2560
Electroencephalograph Technician	1851	1904	1960	2018	2093	2166
Environmental Equipment Operator I	2173	2237	2303	2371	2468	2560
Environmental Equipment Operator II	2373	2443	2515	2589	2698	2808
Environmental Protection Technician I	1851	1904	1960	2018	2093	2166
Environmental Protection Technician II	1992	2051	2110	2172	2265	2344
Hearing & Speech Technician I	1735	1785	1836	1890	1953	2015
Hearing & Speech Technician II	1920	1976	2003	2093	2169	2252
Historic Site Interpreter	1920	1976	2033	2093	2169	2252
Historic Site Lead I	2266	2333	2401	2471	2572	2680
Historic Site Lead II	2373	2443	2515	2589	2698	2808
Housekeeper II	1626	1674	1722	1773	1827	1884
Inhalation Therapist	1851	1904	1960	2018	2093	2166
Intermittent Unemployment Insurance Technician	10.68	10.98	11.30	11.63	12.02	12.40
Laboratory Assistant	1626	1674	1722	1773	1827	1884

DEPARTMENT OF CENTRAL MANAGEMENT SERVICES

NOTICE OF PEREMPTORY AMENDMENTS

Laboratory Associate I	1992	2051	2110	2172	2265	2344
Laboratory Associate II	2173	2237	2303	2371	2468	2560
Legal Research Assistant	2266	2333	2401	2471	2572	2680
Licensed Practical Nurse I	1975	2032	2092	2153	2231	2319
Licensed Practical Nurse II	2068	2129	2192	2256	2353	2440
Medical Records Assistant	1920	1976	2033	2093	2169	2252
Medical Records Technician	2078	2138	2201	2266	2357	2443
Office Administrative Specialist	2173	2237	2303	2371	2468	2560
Office Specialist	2078	2138	2201	2266	2357	2443
Pharmacist Lead Technician	1851	1904	1960	2018	2093	2166
Pharmacist Technician	1735	1785	1836	1890	1953	2015
Public Aid Eligibility Assistant	1851	1904	1960	2018	2093	2166
Radiologic Technologist	2078	2138	2201	2266	2357	2443
Radiologic Technologist Program Coordinator	2173	2237	2303	2371	2468	2560
Ranger	2266	2333	2401	2471	2572	2680
Rehabilitation Counselor Aide I	1920	1976	2033	2093	2169	2252
Rehabilitation Counselore Aide II	2078	2138	2201	2266	2357	2443
Senior Ranger	2373	2443	2515	2589	2698	2808
Site Technician I	1992	2051	2110	2172	2265	2344
Site Technician II	2173	2237	2303	2371	2468	2560
Social Service Community Planner	2078	2138	2201	2266	2357	2443
State Police Crime Information Evaluator	2078	2138	2201	2266	2357	2443
State Police Evidence Technician I	2173	2237	2303	2371	2468	2560
State Police Evidence Technician II	2266	2333	2401	2471	2572	2680
Statistical Research Technician	2078	2138	2201	2266	2357	2443
Veterans Service Officer	2173	2237	2303	2371	2468	2560
Vocational Instructor	2173	2237	2303	2371	2468	2560

	STEPS (cont.)			
	4	5	6	7
Apparel Dry Goods Specialist III	2740	2839	2931	3095
Assistant Reimbursement Officer	2157	2225	2298	2417
Child Development Aide III	2431	2516	2604	3746
Clinical Laboratory Associate	2157	2225	2298	2417
Clinical Laboratory Technician I	2431	2516	2604	2746
Clinical Laboratory Technician II	2665	2758	2861	3018

DEPARTMENT OF CENTRAL MANAGEMENT SERVICES

NOTICE OF PEREMPTORY AMENDMENTS

Compliance Officer	2931	3042	3157	3737
Conservation Resource Technician I	2431	2516	2604	2746
Conservation Resource Technician II	2787	2890	2999	3167
Construction Supervisor I	2787	2890	2999	3167
Construction Supervisor II	3223	3354	3487	3689
Crime Scene Investigator	4225	4415	4597	4880
~~Crime Studies Associate~~	~~2431~~	~~2516~~	~~2604~~	~~2746~~
Data Processing Administrative Specialist	2931	3042	3157	3337
Data Processing Specialist	2665	2758	2861	3018
Data Processing Technician	2331	2416	2497	2627
Data Processing Technician Trainee	2082	2144	2212	2322
Dental Assistant	2246	2316	2394	2519
Dental Hygienist	2665	2758	2861	3018
Electroencephalograph Technician	2246	2316	2394	2519
Environmental Equipment Operator I	2665	2758	2861	3018
Environmental Equipment Operator II	2931	3042	3157	3337
Environmental Protection Technician I	2246	2316	2394	2519
Environmental Protection Technician II	2431	2516	2604	2746
Hearing & Speech Technician I	2082	2144	2212	2322
Hearing & Speech Technician II	2331	2416	2497	2627
Historic Site Interpreter	2331	2416	2497	2627
Historic Site Lead I	2787	2890	2999	3167
Historic Site Lead II	2931	3042	3157	3337
Housekeeper II	1937	1990	2051	2153
Inhalation Therapist	2246	2316	2394	2519
Intermittent Unemployment Insurance Technician	12.81	13.19	13.61	14.29
Laboratory Assistant	1937	1990	2051	2153
Laboratory Associate I	2431	2516	2604	2746
Laboratory Associate II	2665	2758	2861	3018
Legal Research Assistant	2787	2890	2999	3167
Licensed Practical Nurse I	2402	2494	2573	2708
Licensed Practical Nurse II	2532	2624	2715	2887
Medical Records Assistant	2331	2416	2497	2627
Medical Records Technician	2539	2633	2719	2870
Office Administrative Specialist	2665	2758	2861	3018

DEPARTMENT OF CENTRAL MANAGEMENT SERVICES

NOTICE OF PEREMPTORY AMENDMENTS

Office Specialist	2539	2633	2719	2870
Pharmacist Lead Technician	2246	2316	2394	2519
Pharmacist Technician	2082	2144	2212	2322
Public Aid Eligibility Assistant	2246	2316	2394	2519
Radiologic Technologist	2539	2633	2719	2870
Radiologic Technologist Program Coordinator	2665	2758	2861	3018
Ranger	2787	2890	2999	3167
Rehabilitation Counselor Aide I	2331	2416	2497	2627
Rehabilitation Counselor Aide II	2539	2633	2719	2870
Senior Ranger	2931	3042	3157	3337
Site Technician I	2431	2516	2604	2746
Site Technician II	2665	2758	2861	3018
Social Service Community Planner	2539	2633	2719	2870
State Police Crime Information Evaluator	2539	2633	2719	2870
State Police Evidence Technician I	2665	2758	2861	3018
State Police Evidence Technician II	2787	2890	2999	3167
Statistical Research Technician	2539	2633	2719	2870
Veterans Service Officer	2665	2758	2861	3018
Vocational Instructor	2665	2758	2861	3018

(Source: Peremptory amendment at 21 Ill. Reg. _____, effective
DEC 0.9 1997)

Section 310.TABLE P RC-029 (Paraprofessional Investigatory and Law Enforcement Employees, IFPE)

Effective July 1, 1994

				S-T-E-P-S			
	1	2	3	4	5	6	7
~~AGRICULTURAL PRODUCTS PROMOTER~~	~~1942~~	~~2084~~	~~2100~~	~~2187~~	~~2267~~	~~2353~~	~~2464~~
~~ANIMAL & ANIMAL PRODUCTS INVESTIGATOR~~	~~2324~~	~~2216~~	~~2309~~	~~2412~~	~~2504~~	~~2601~~	~~2751~~
~~APIARY INSPECTOR~~	~~1441~~	~~1499~~	~~1530~~	~~1582~~	~~1635~~	~~1680~~	~~1766~~
~~ARSON INVESTIGATOR I~~	~~2330~~	~~2438~~	~~2549~~	~~2655~~	~~2766~~	~~2877~~	~~3047~~
~~ARSON INVESTIGATOR II~~	~~2576~~	~~2762~~	~~2827~~	~~2955~~	~~3077~~	~~3199~~	~~3389~~
~~BREATH-ALCOHOL-ANALYSIS TECHNICIAN~~	~~2215~~	~~2321~~	~~2422~~	~~2521~~	~~2624~~	~~2722~~	~~2884~~
~~COMMERCE COMMISSION POLICE OFR I~~	~~2330~~	~~2438~~	~~2549~~	~~2655~~	~~2766~~	~~2877~~	~~3047~~
~~COMMERCE COMMISSION POLICE OFR II~~	~~2576~~	~~2762~~	~~2827~~	~~2955~~	~~3077~~	~~3199~~	~~3389~~
~~COMMODITIES INSPECTOR~~	~~1776~~	~~1853~~	~~1920~~	~~1993~~	~~2063~~	~~2138~~	~~2256~~
~~DANGEROUS DRUGS COMPLIANCE OFFICER I~~	~~2026~~	~~2112~~	~~2202~~	~~2291~~	~~2378~~	~~2469~~	~~2609~~
~~DANGEROUS DRUGS COMPLIANCE~~	~~2210~~	~~2321~~	~~2422~~	~~2521~~	~~2604~~	~~2722~~	~~2884~~

DEPARTMENT OF CENTRAL MANAGEMENT SERVICES

NOTICE OF PEREMPTORY AMENDMENTS

	1	2	3	4	5	6	7
OFFICER-II							
DANGEROUS-DRUGS-COMPLIANCE OFFICER-III	2330	2438	2549	2655	2766	2877	3047
DRUG-COMPLIANCE-INVESTIGATOR	3203	3379	3535	3701	3872	4035	4285
ENVIRONMENTAL-PROTECTION-LEGAL INVESTIGATOR-I	1776	1853	1920	1993	2063	2138	2256
ENVIRONMENTAL-PROTECTION-LEGAL INVESTIGATOR-II	1942	2024	2100	2187	2267	2353	2484
EXPLOSIVES-INSPECTOR-I	2124	2216	2309	2412	2504	2601	2751
EXPLOSIVES-INSPECTOR-II	2444	2561	2680	2792	2906	3024	3204
FINGERPRINT-TECHNICIAN-I	1647	1710	1771	1838	1897	1962	2066
FINGERPRINT-TECHNICIAN-II	1776	1853	1920	1993	2063	2138	2256
FINGERPRINT-TECHNICIAN-III	1942	2024	2100	2187	2267	2353	2484
FIRE-PREVENTION-INSPECTOR-I	2210	2301	2422	2521	2624	2722	2884
FIRE-PREVENTION-INSPECTOR-II	2576	2702	2827	2955	3077	3199	3389
GUARD-I	1490	1540	1591	1642	1690	1740	1826
GUARD-II	1647	1710	1771	1838	1897	1962	2066
GUARD-III	1854	1931	2002	2084	2161	2235	2360
LICENSING-ASSISTANT	1592	1647	1705	1763	1820	1881	1982
LICENSING-INVESTIGATOR-I	1854	1931	2002	2084	2161	2235	2360
LICENSING-INVESTIGATOR-II	2124	2216	2309	2412	2504	2601	2751
LICENSING-INVESTIGATOR-III	2210	2301	2422	2521	2624	2722	2884
LICENSING-INVESTIGATOR-IV	2444	2561	2680	2792	2906	3024	3204
LIQUOR-CONTROL-SPECIAL-AGENT-I	2026	2112	2202	2291	2378	2469	2609
MOTORIST-ASSISTANCE-SPECIALIST	1592	1647	1705	1763	1820	1881	1982
PLANT-&-PESTICIDE-SPECIALIST-I	2210	2301	2422	2521	2624	2722	2884
PLANT-&-PESTICIDE-SPECIALIST-II	2444	2561	2680	2792	2906	3024	3204
PLUMBING-INSPECTOR	2576	2702	2827	2955	3077	3199	3389
POLICE-OFFICER-I	2330	2438	2549	2655	2766	2877	3047
POLICE-OFFICER-II	2576	2702	2827	2955	3077	3199	3389
POLICE-OFFICER III							
POLYGRAPH-EXAMINER-I	2576	2702	2827	2955	3077	3199	3389
POLYGRAPH-EXAMINER-II	2870	3014	3155	3305	3447	3589	3809
POLYGRAPH-EXAMINER-III	3203	3379	3535	3701	3872	4035	4285
PRODUCTS-&-STANDARDS-INSPECTOR	1942	2024	2100	2187	2267	2353	2484
SECURITY-OFFICER	2070	3014	3155	3305	3447	3589	3809
SECURITY-OFFICER-SERGEANT	2026	2112	2202	2291	2378	2469	2609
SEED-ANALYST-I	1854	1931	2002	2084	2161	2235	2360
SEED-ANALYST-II	1942	2024	2100	2187	2267	2353	2484
SITE-SECURITY-OFFICER	1647	1710	1771	1838	1897	1962	2066
TRUCK-WEIGHING-INSPECTOR	1710	1774	1843	1909	1981	2049	2155
VEHICLE-EMISSIONS-COMPLIANCE INSPECTOR	1942	2024	2100	2187	2267	2353	2484
VEHICLE-TESTING-COMPLIANCE-OFFICER	2210	2301	2422	2521	2624	2722	2884
VITAL-RECORDS-QUALITY-CONTROL INSPECTOR	1942	2024	2100	2187	2267	2353	2484
WAREHOUSE-CLAIMS-SPECIALIST	2716	2854	2988	3126	3258	3395	3600

DEPARTMENT OF CENTRAL MANAGEMENT SERVICES

NOTICE OF PEREMPTORY AMENDMENTS

	1	2	3	4	5	6	7
WAREHOUSE-EXAMINER-I	1942	2024	2100	2187	2267	2353	2484
WAREHOUSE-EXAMINER-II	2210	2301	2422	2521	2624	2722	2884
WAREHOUSE-EXAMINER-III	2444	2561	2680	2792	2906	3024	3204
WELL-INSPECTOR-I	2124	2216	2309	2412	2504	2601	2751
WELL-INSPECTOR-II	2444	2561	2680	2792	2906	3024	3204

NOTE: Effective July 1, 1994, employees who have 15 years of service and have 3 or more years of creditable service on Step 7 in the same pay grade shall receive an additional $25.00 monthly.

Effective January 1, 1995

	S-T-E-P-S						
	1	2	3	4	5	6	7
FINGERPRINT-TECHNICIAN	1942	2024	2100	2187	2267	2353	2484
TRUCK-WEIGHING-INSPECTOR	1776	1853	1920	1993	2063	2138	2256

Effective July 1, 1995

	S-T-E-P-S						
	1	2	3	4	5	6	7
AGRICULTURAL-PRODUCTS-PROMOTER	2175	2268	2360	2449	2543	2687	2741
ANIMAL-&-ANIMAL-PRODUCTS INVESTIGATOR	2202	2378	2404	2579	2679	2684	2891
APIARY-INSPECTOR	1535	1584	1629	1684	1730	1819	1855
ARSON-INVESTIGATOR-I	2511	2625	2735	2849	2963	3130	3201
ARSON-INVESTIGATOR-II	2783	2912	3044	3169	3295	3491	3561
BREATH-ALCOHOL-ANALYSIS-TECHNICIAN	2391	2495	2597	2703	2804	2971	3030
COMMERCE-COMMISSION-POLICE-OFR-I	2511	2625	2735	2849	2963	3130	3201
COMMERCE-COMMISSION-POLICE-OFR-II	2783	2912	3044	3169	3295	3491	3561
CONDUCTING-INSPECTOR	1909	1978	2053	2125	2202	2324	2370
DANGEROUS-DRUGS-COMPLIANCE OFFICER-I	2175	2268	2360	2449	2540	2687	2741
DANGEROUS-DRUGS-COMPLIANCE OFFICER-II	2391	2495	2597	2703	2804	2971	3030
DANGEROUS-DRUGS-COMPLIANCE OFFICER-III	2511	2625	2735	2849	2963	3130	3201
DRUG-COMPLIANCE-INVESTIGATOR	3471	3641	3812	3988	4156	4414	4502
ENVIRONMENTAL-PROTECTION-LEGAL INVESTIGATOR-I	1909	1978	2053	2125	2202	2324	2370
ENVIRONMENTAL-PROTECTION-LEGAL INVESTIGATOR-II	2005	2163	2253	2335	2424	2559	2610
EXPLOSIVES-INSPECTOR-I	2202	2378	2404	2579	2679	2884	2891
EXPLOSIVES-INSPECTOR-II	2630	2760	2876	2993	3115	3308	3366
FINGERPRINT-TECHNICIAN	2005	2163	2253	2335	2424	2559	2610
FIRE-PREVENTION-INSPECTOR-I	2391	2495	2597	2703	2804	2971	3030
FIRE-PREVENTION-INSPECTOR-II	2783	2912	3044	3169	3295	3491	3561
GUARD-I	1586	1639	1691	1741	1792	1881	1919

DEPARTMENT OF CENTRAL MANAGEMENT SERVICES

NOTICE OF PEREMPTORY AMENDMENTS

~~GUARD-II~~	~~1761~~	~~1824~~	~~1893~~	~~1954~~	~~2021~~	~~2128~~	~~2171~~
~~GUARD-III~~	~~1989~~	~~2062~~	~~2147~~	~~2226~~	~~2302~~	~~2431~~	~~2480~~
~~LICENSING-ASSISTANT~~	~~1696~~	~~1756~~	~~1816~~	~~1875~~	~~1937~~	~~2041~~	~~2082~~
~~LICENSING-INVESTIGATOR-I~~	~~1989~~	~~2062~~	~~2147~~	~~2226~~	~~2302~~	~~2431~~	~~2480~~
~~LICENSING-INVESTIGATOR-II~~	~~2202~~	~~2278~~	~~2464~~	~~2579~~	~~2679~~	~~2834~~	~~2891~~
~~LICENSING-INVESTIGATOR-III~~	~~2391~~	~~2495~~	~~2597~~	~~2703~~	~~2804~~	~~2971~~	~~3030~~
~~LICENSING-INVESTIGATOR-IV~~	~~2638~~	~~2760~~	~~2876~~	~~2993~~	~~3115~~	~~3300~~	~~3366~~
~~LIQUOR-CONTROL-SPECIAL-AGENT-I~~	~~2175~~	~~2268~~	~~2360~~	~~2449~~	~~2543~~	~~2607~~	~~2741~~
~~MOTORIST-ASSISTANCE-SPECIALIST~~	~~1696~~	~~1756~~	~~1816~~	~~1875~~	~~1937~~	~~2041~~	~~2082~~
~~PLANT-&-PESTICIDE-SPECIALIST-I~~	~~2391~~	~~2495~~	~~2597~~	~~2703~~	~~2804~~	~~2971~~	~~3030~~
~~PLANT-&-PESTICIDE-SPECIALIST-II~~	~~2638~~	~~2760~~	~~2876~~	~~2993~~	~~3115~~	~~3300~~	~~3366~~
~~PLUMBING-INSPECTOR~~	~~2940~~	~~3078~~	~~3220~~	~~3356~~	~~3497~~	~~3708~~	~~3782~~
~~POLICE-OFFICER-I~~	~~2511~~	~~2625~~	~~2735~~	~~2849~~	~~2963~~	~~3138~~	~~3201~~
~~POLICE-OFFICER-II~~	~~2783~~	~~2912~~	~~3044~~	~~3169~~	~~3295~~	~~3491~~	~~3561~~
~~POLICE-OFFICER~~	~~3104~~	~~3250~~	~~3404~~	~~3550~~	~~3697~~	~~3923~~	~~4001~~
~~III~~							
~~POLYGRAPH-EXAMINER-I~~	~~2783~~	~~2912~~	~~3044~~	~~3169~~	~~3295~~	~~3491~~	~~3561~~
~~POLYGRAPH-EXAMINER-II~~	~~3104~~	~~3250~~	~~3404~~	~~3550~~	~~3697~~	~~3923~~	~~4001~~
~~POLYGRAPH-EXAMINER-III~~	~~3471~~	~~3641~~	~~3812~~	~~3988~~	~~4156~~	~~4414~~	~~4502~~
~~PRODUCTS-&-STANDARDS-INSPECTOR~~	~~2085~~	~~2163~~	~~2253~~	~~2335~~	~~2424~~	~~2559~~	~~2610~~
~~SECURITY-OFFICER~~	~~2085~~	~~2163~~	~~2253~~	~~2335~~	~~2424~~	~~2559~~	~~2610~~
~~SECURITY-OFFICER-SERGEANT~~	~~2175~~	~~2268~~	~~2360~~	~~2449~~	~~2543~~	~~2607~~	~~2741~~
~~SHED-ANALYST-I~~	~~1989~~	~~2062~~	~~2147~~	~~2226~~	~~2302~~	~~2431~~	~~2480~~
~~SHED-ANALYST-II~~	~~2085~~	~~2163~~	~~2253~~	~~2335~~	~~2424~~	~~2559~~	~~2610~~
~~.SITE-SECURITY-OFFICER~~	~~1761~~	~~1824~~	~~1893~~	~~1954~~	~~2021~~	~~2128~~	~~2171~~
~~TRUCK-WEIGHING-INSPECTOR~~	~~1909~~	~~1978~~	~~2053~~	~~2125~~	~~2202~~	~~2324~~	~~2370~~
~~VEHICLE-EMISSIONS-COMPLIANCE~~	~~2085~~	~~2163~~	~~2253~~	~~2335~~	~~2424~~	~~2559~~	~~2610~~
~~INSPECTOR~~							
~~VEHICLE-TESTING-COMPLIANCE-OFFICER~~	~~2391~~	~~2495~~	~~2597~~	~~2703~~	~~2804~~	~~2971~~	~~3030~~
~~VITAL-RECORDS-QUALITY-CONTROL~~	~~2085~~	~~2163~~	~~2253~~	~~2335~~	~~2424~~	~~2559~~	~~2610~~
~~INSPECTOR~~							
~~WAREHOUSE-CLAIMS-SPECIALIST~~	~~2940~~	~~3078~~	~~3220~~	~~3356~~	~~3497~~	~~3708~~	~~3782~~
~~WAREHOUSE-EXAMINER-I~~	~~2085~~	~~2163~~	~~2253~~	~~2335~~	~~2424~~	~~2559~~	~~2610~~
~~WAREHOUSE-EXAMINER-II~~	~~2391~~	~~2495~~	~~2597~~	~~2703~~	~~2804~~	~~2971~~	~~3030~~
~~WAREHOUSE-EXAMINER-III~~	~~2638~~	~~2760~~	~~2876~~	~~2993~~	~~3115~~	~~3300~~	~~3366~~
~~WELL-INSPECTOR-I~~	~~2202~~	~~2278~~	~~2464~~	~~2579~~	~~2679~~	~~2834~~	~~2891~~
~~WELL-INSPECTOR-II~~	~~2638~~	~~2760~~	~~2876~~	~~2993~~	~~3115~~	~~3300~~	~~3366~~

~~NOTE: Effective July 1, 1995, the Step 7 longevity clause is terminated for duration of the contract.~~

Effective: July 1, 1997 ~~1996~~

	STEPS						
	1	2	3	4	5	6	7
AGRICULTURAL PRODUCTS PROMOTER	2240	2336	2431	2522	2619	2768	2823
ANIMAL & ANIMAL PRODUCTS INVESTIGATOR	2350	2449	2559	2656	2759	2919	2978

DEPARTMENT OF CENTRAL MANAGEMENT SERVICES

NOTICE OF PEREMPTORY AMENDMENTS

APIARY INSPECTOR	1581	1632	1678	1735	1782	1874	1911
~~ARSON INVESTIGATOR I~~	~~2586~~	~~2704~~	~~2817~~	~~2934~~	~~3052~~	~~3232~~	~~3297~~
~~ARSON INVESTIGATOR II~~	~~2866~~	~~2999~~	~~3135~~	~~3264~~	~~3394~~	~~3596~~	~~3668~~
BREATH ALCOHOL ANALYSIS TECHNICIAN	2463	2570	2675	2784	2888	3060	3121
~~COMMERCE COMMISSION POLICE OFR I~~	~~2704~~	~~2817~~	~~2934~~	~~3052~~	~~3232~~	~~3297~~	~~3363~~
~~COMMERCE COMMISSION POLICE OFR II~~	~~2999~~	~~3135~~	~~3264~~	~~3394~~	~~3596~~	~~3668~~	~~3741~~
COMMODITIES INSPECTOR	1966	2037	2115	2189	2268	2394	2441
DANGEROUS DRUGS COMPLIANCE OFFICER I	2240	2336	2431	2522	2619	2768	2823
DANGEROUS DRUGS COMPLIANCE OFFICER II	2463	2570	2675	2784	2888	3060	3121
DANGEROUS DRUGS COMPLIANCE OFFICER III	2586	2704	2817	2934	3052	3232	3297
DRUG COMPLIANCE INVESTIGATOR	3575	3750	3926	4108	4281	4546	4637
ENVIRONMENTAL PROTECTION LEGAL INVESTIGATOR I	1966	2037	2115	2189	2268	2394	2441
ENVIRONMENTAL PROTECTION LEGAL INVESTIGATOR II	2148	2228	2321	2405	2497	2636	2688
EXPLOSIVES INSPECTOR I	2350	2449	2559	2656	2759	2919	2978
EXPLOSIVES INSPECTOR II	2717	2843	2962	3083	3208	3399	3467
FINGERPRINT TECHNICIAN	2148	2228	2321	2405	2497	2636	2688
FIRE PREVENTION INSPECTOR I	2463	2570	2675	2784	2888	3060	3121
FIRE PREVENTION INSPECTOR II	2866	2999	3135	3264	3394	3596	3668
GUARD I	1634	1688	1742	1793	1846	1937	1977
GUARD II	1814	1879	1950	2013	2082	2192	2236
GUARD III	2049	2124	2211	2293	2371	2504	2554
LICENSING ASSISTANT	1747	1809	1870	1931	1995	2102	2144
LICENSING INVESTIGATOR I	2049	2124	2211	2293	2371	2504	2554
LICENSING INVESTIGATOR II	2350	2449	2559	2656	2759	2919	2978
LICENSING INVESTIGATOR III	2463	2570	2675	2784	2888	3060	3121
LICENSING INVESTIGATOR IV	2717	2843	2962	3083	3208	3399	3467
LIQUOR CONTROL SPECIAL AGENT I	2240	2336	2431	2522	2619	2768	2823
MOTORIST ASSISTANCE SPECIALIST	1747	1809	1870	1931	1995	2102	2144
PLANT & PESTICIDE SPECIALIST I	~~2586~~ 2463	~~2704~~ 2570	~~2817~~ 2675	~~2934~~ 2784	~~3052~~ 2888	~~3232~~ 3060	~~3297~~ 3121
PLANT & PESTICIDE SPECIALIST II	~~2866~~ 2717	~~2999~~ 2843	~~3135~~ 2962	~~3264~~ 3083	~~3394~~ 3208	~~3596~~ 3399	~~3668~~ 3467
PLUMBING INSPECTOR	3028	3170	3317	3457	3602	3819	3895
~~POLICE OFFICER I~~	~~2704~~	~~2817~~	~~2934~~	~~3052~~	~~3232~~	~~3297~~	~~3363~~
~~POLICE OFFICER II~~	~~2999~~	~~3135~~	~~3264~~	~~3394~~	~~3596~~	~~3668~~	~~3741~~
~~POLICE OFFICER III~~	~~3197~~	~~3348~~	~~3506~~	~~3657~~	~~3838~~	~~4041~~	~~4121~~
POLYGRAPH EXAMINER II	2866	2999	3135	3264	3394	3596	3668
POLYGRAPH EXAMINER III	3197	3348	3506	3657	3838	4041	4121
POLYGRAPH EXAMINER III	3575	3750	3926	4108	4281	4546	4637
PRODUCTS & STANDARDS INSPECTOR	~~2350~~ 2148	~~2449~~ 2228	~~2559~~ 2321	~~2656~~ 2405	~~2759~~ 2497	~~2919~~ 2636	~~2978~~ 2688
SECURITY OFFICER	2148	2228	2321	2405	2497	2636	2688

DEPARTMENT OF CENTRAL MANAGEMENT SERVICES

NOTICE OF PEREMPTORY AMENDMENTS

	1	2	3	4	5	6	7
SECURITY OFFICER SERGEANT	2240	2336	2431	2522	2619	2758	2823
SEED ANALYST I	2049	2124	2211	2293	2371	2504	2554
SEED ANALYST II	2148	2228	2321	2405	2497	2636	2688
SITE SECURITY OFFICER	1814	1879	1950	2013	2082	2192	2236
TRUCK WEIGHING INSPECTOR	1966	2037	2115	2189	2268	2394	2441
VEHICLE COMPLIANCE INSPECTOR	2463	2520	2675	2784	2898	3060	3121
VEHICLE EMISSIONS COMPLIANCE INSPECTOR	2148	2228	2321	2405	2497	2636	2688
VITAL RECORDS QUALITY CONTROL INSPECTOR	2148	2228	2321	2405	2497	2636	2688
WAREHOUSE CLAIMS SPECIALIST	3028	3170	3317	3457	3602	3819	3895
WAREHOUSE EXAMINER I	2148	2228	2321	2405	2497	2636	2688
WAREHOUSE EXAMINER II	2463	2570	2675	2784	2888	3060	3121
WAREHOUSE EXAMINER III	2717	2843	2962	3083	3208	3399	3467
WELL INSPECTOR I	2350	2449	2559	2656	2759	2919	2978
WELL INSPECTOR II	2717	2843	2962	3083	3208	3399	3467

~~Effective September 18, 1996~~

Steps

	1	2	3	4	5	6	7
~~Vehicle Compliance Inspector~~	~~2354~~	~~2463~~	~~2570~~	~~2675~~	~~2784~~	~~2888~~	~~3060~~

NOTE: Full-time employees who are receiving the flat-rate pension formula will receive a one-time lump sum payment of $565.00.

RC-029 Alternative Retirement Formula Schedule

Effective July 1, 1997

Steps

	1	2	3	4	5	6	7
Arson Investigator I	2785	2902	3022	3144	3329	3396	3464
Arson Investigator II	3089	3229	3362	3496	3704	3778	3853
Commerce Commission Police Officer I	2785	2902	3022	3144	3329	3396	3464
Commerce Commission Police Officer II	3089	3229	3362	3496	3704	3778	3853
Police Officer I	2785	2902	3022	3144	3329	3396	3464
Police Officer II	3089	3229	3362	3496	3704	3778	3853
Police Officer III	3293	3448	3611	3767	3922	4162	4245
Polygraph Examiner III	3682	3863	4044	4231	4409	4682	4776

Effective: July 1, 1998

DEPARTMENT OF CENTRAL MANAGEMENT SERVICES

NOTICE OF PEREMPTORY AMENDMENTS

	STEPS						
	1	2	3	4	5	6	7
Agricultural Products Promoter	2307	2406	2504	2598	2698	2851	2908
Animal & Animal Products Investigator	2421	2522	2636	2736	2842	3007	3067
Apiary Inspector	1628	1681	1728	1787	1835	1930	1968
Breath Alcohol Analysis Technician	2537	2647	2755	2868	2975	3152	3215
Commodities Inspector	2025	2098	2178	2255	2336	2466	2514
Dangerous Drugs Compliance Officer I	2307	2406	2504	2598	2698	2851	2908
Dangerous Drugs Compliance Officer II	2537	2647	2755	2868	2975	3152	3215
Dangerous Drugs Compliance Officer III	2664	2785	2902	3022	3144	3329	3396
Drug Compliance Investigator	3682	3863	4044	4231	4409	4682	4776
Environmental Protection Legal Investigator I	2212	2295	2391	2477	2572	2715	2769
Environmental Protection Legal Investigator II	2421	2522	2636	2736	2842	3007	3067
Explosives Inspector I	2421	2522	2636	2736	2842	3007	3067
Explosives Inspector II	2799	2928	3051	3175	3304	3501	3571
Fingerprint Technician	2212	2295	2391	2477	2572	2715	2769
Fire Prevention Inspector I	2537	2647	2755	2868	2975	3152	3215
Fire Prevention Inspector II	2952	3089	3229	3362	3496	3704	3778
Guard I	1683	1739	1794	1847	1901	1995	2036
Guard II	1858	1935	2009	2073	2144	2258	2303
Guard III	2110	2188	2277	2362	2442	2579	2631
Licensing Assistant	1799	1863	1926	1989	2055	2165	2208
Licensing Investigator I	2110	2188	2277	2362	2442	2579	2631
Licensing Investigator II	2421	2522	2636	2736	2842	3007	3067
Licensing Investigator III	2537	2647	2755	2868	2975	3152	3215
Licensing Investigator IV	2799	2928	3051	3175	3304	3501	3571
Liquor Control Special Agent I	2307	2406	2504	2598	2698	2851	2908
Motorist Assistance Specialist	1799	1863	1926	1989	2055	2165	2208
Plant & Pesticide Specialist I	2664	2785	2902	3022	3144	3329	3396
Plant & Pesticide Specialist II	2952	3089	3229	3362	3496	3704	3778
Plumbing Inspector	3119	3265	3417	3561	3710	3934	4012
Polygraph Examiner I	2952	3089	3229	3362	3496	3704	3778
Polygraph Examiner II	3293	3448	3611	3767	3922	4162	4245
Polygraph Examiner III	3682	3863	4044	4231	4409	4682	4776
Products & Standards Inspector	2421	2522	2636	2736	2842	3007	3067
Security Officer	2212	2295	2391	2477	2572	2715	2769
Security Officer Sergeant	2307	2406	2504	2598	2698	2851	2908
Seed Analyst I	2110	2188	2277	2362	2442	2579	2631
Seed Analyst II	2212	2295	2391	2477	2572	2715	2769
Site Security Officer	1868	1935	2009	2073	2144	2258	2303
Truck Weighing Inspector	2025	2098	2178	2255	2336	2466	2514
Vehicle Compliance Inspector	2537	2647	2755	2868	2975	3152	3215

DEPARTMENT OF CENTRAL MANAGEMENT SERVICES

NOTICE OF PEREMPTORY AMENDMENTS

Vehicle Emissions Compliance Inspector	2212	2295	2391	2477	2572	2715	2769
Vital Records Quality Control Inspector	2212	2295	2391	2477	2572	2715	2769
Warehouse Claims Specialist	3119	3265	3417	3561	3710	3934	4012
Warehouse Examiner	2537	2647	2755	2868	2975	3152	3215
Warehouse Examiner Specialist	2799	2928	3051	3175	3304	3501	3571
Well Inspector I	2421	2522	2636	2736	2842	3007	3067
Well Inspector II	2799	2928	3051	3175	3304	3501	3571

NOTE: Those employees (non-sworn) on Step 7 who have attained 15 years of service and have 3 or more years of creditable service on Step 7 in the same pay grade shall receive a longevity increase of $50 per month.

RC-029 Alternative Retirement Formula Schedule

Effective: July 1, 1998

	STEPS						
	1	2	3	4	5	6	7
Arson Investigator I	2869	2989	3113	3238	3429	3498	3568
Arson Investigator II	3182	3326	3463	3601	3815	3891	3969
Commerce Commission Police Officer I	2869	2989	3113	3238	3429	3498	3568
Commerce Commission Police Officer II	3182	3326	3463	3601	3815	3891	3969
Police Officer I	2869	2989	3113	3238	3429	3498	3568
Police Officer II	3182	3326	3463	3601	3815	3891	3969
Police Officer III	3392	3551	3719	3980	4040	4287	4372
Polygraph Examiner III	3792	3979	4165	4358	4541	4822	4919

LONGEVITY		
10 Yrs	13 Yrs	u15 Yrs
3618	3668	3718
4019	4069	4119
3618	3668	3718
4019	4069	4119
3618	3668	3718
4019	4069	4119
4422	4472	4522
0000	0000	0000

Effective: July 1, 1999

	STEPS						
	1	2	3	4	5	6	7
Agricultural Products Promoter	2376	2478	2579	2676	2779	2937	2995

DEPARTMENT OF CENTRAL MANAGEMENT SERVICES

NOTICE OF PEREMPTORY AMENDMENTS

Animal & Animal Products Investigator	2494	2598	2715	2818	2927	3097	3159
Apiary Inspector	1677	1731	1780	1841	1890	1988	2027
Breath Alcohol Analysis Technician	2613	2726	2838	2954	3064	3247	3311
Commodities Inspector	2086	2161	2243	2323	2406	2540	2589
Dangerous Drugs Compliance Officer I	2376	2478	2579	2676	2779	2937	2995
Dangerous Drugs Compliance Officer II	2613	2726	2838	2954	3064	3247	3311
Dangerous Drugs Compliance Officer III	2744	2869	2982	3113	3238	3429	3498
Drug Compliance Investigator	3792	3979	4165	4358	4541	4822	4919
Environmental Protection Legal Investigator I	2278	2364	2463	2551	2649	2796	2852
Environmental Protection Legal Investigator II	2494	2598	2715	2818	2927	3097	3159
Explosives Inspector I	2494	2598	2715	2818	2927	3097	3159
Explosives Inspector II	2883	3016	3143	3270	3403	3606	3678
Fingerprint Technician	2278	2364	2463	2551	2649	2796	2852
Fire Prevention Inspector I	2613	2726	2838	2954	3064	3247	3311
Fire Prevention Inspector II	3041	3182	3326	3463	3601	3815	3891
Guard I	1733	1791	1848	1902	1958	2055	2097
Guard II	1924	1993	2069	2135	2208	2326	2372
Guard III	2173	2254	2345	2433	2515	2656	2710
Licensing Assistant	1853	1919	1984	2049	2117	2230	2274
Licensing Investigator I	2173	2254	2345	2433	2515	2656	2710
Licensing Investigator II	2494	2598	2715	2818	2927	3097	3159
Licensing Investigator III	2613	2726	2838	2954	3064	3247	3311
Licensing Investigator IV	2883	3016	3143	3270	3403	3606	3678
Liquor Control Special Agent I	2376	2478	2579	2676	2779	2937	2995
Motorist Assistance Specialist	1853	1919	1984	2049	2117	2230	2274
Plant & Pesticide Specialist I	2744	2869	2982	3113	3238	3429	3498
Plant & Pesticide Specialist II	3041	3182	3326	3463	3601	3815	3891
Plumbing Inspector	3213	3363	3520	3668	3821	4052	4132
Polygraph Examiner I	3041	3182	3326	3463	3601	3815	3801
Polygraph Examiner II	3392	3551	3719	3980	4040	4287	4372
Polygraph Examiner III	3792	3979	4165	4358	4541	4822	4919
Products & Standards Inspector	2494	2598	2715	2818	2927	3097	3159
Security Officer	2278	2364	2463	2551	2649	2796	2852
Security Officer Sergeant	2376	2478	2579	2676	2779	2937	2995
Seed Analyst I	2173	2254	2345	2433	2515	2656	2710
Seed Analyst II	2278	2364	2463	2551	2649	2796	2852
Site Security Officer	1924	1993	2069	2135	2208	2326	2372
Truck Weighing Inspector	2086	2161	2243	2323	2406	2540	2589
Vehicle Compliance Inspector	2613	2726	2838	2954	3064	3247	3311
Vehicle Emissions Compliance Inspector	2278	2364	2463	2551	2649	2796	2852
Vital Records Quality Control	2278	2364	2463	2551	2649	2796	2852

DEPARTMENT OF CENTRAL MANAGEMENT SERVICES

NOTICE OF PEREMPTORY AMENDMENTS

Inspector							
Warehouse Claims Specialist	3213	3363	3520	3668	3821	4052	4132
Warehouse Examiner	2613	2726	2838	2954	3064	3247	3311
Warehouse Examiner Specialist	2893	3016	3143	3270	3403	3606	3678
Well Inspector I	2494	2598	2715	2818	2927	3097	3159
Well Inspector II	2893	3016	3143	3270	3403	3606	3678

RC-029 Alternative Retirement Formula Schedule

Effective: July 1, 1999

				S T E P S			
	1	2	3	4	5	6	7
Arson Investigator I	2955	3079	3206	3335	3532	3603	3675
Arson Investigator II	3277	3426	3567	3709	3929	4008	4088
Commerce Commission Police Officer I	2955	3079	3206	3335	3532	3603	3675
Commerce Commission Police Officer II	3277	3426	3567	3709	3929	4008	4088
Police Officer I	2955	3079	3206	3335	3532	3603	3675
Police Officer II	3277	3426	3567	3709	3929	4008	4088
Police Officer III	3494	3658	3831	3996	4161	4416	4503
Polygraph Examiner III	3906	4098	4290	4489	4677	4967	5067

	LONGEVITY	
10 Yrs	13 Yrs	15 Yrs
3725	3775	3825
4138	4188	4238
3725	3775	3825
4138	4188	4238
3725	3775	3825
4138	4188	4238
4553	4603	4653
0000	0000	0000

(Source: Peremptory amendment 21 Ill. Reg. 17167 , effective
DEC 0 9 1997)

DEPARTMENT OF NATURAL RESOURCES

NOTICE OF PUBLIC HEARING ON PROPOSED RULES

1) Heading of the Part: Commercial Fishing and Musseling in Certain Waters of the State

2) Code Citation: 17 Ill. Adm. Code 830

3) Register Citation to Notice of Proposed Amendments:

   21 Ill. Reg. ; December 26, 1997

4) Date, Time and Location of Public Hearing:

   Tuesday, January 20, 1998
   10:00 a.m.
   Illinois Department of Agriculture Disease Laboratory
   Second Floor Conference Room
   2100 South Lake Story Road
   Galesburg, Illinois
   (1 mile west of U.S. 150 on the northwest edge of Galesburg)

5) Other Pertinent Information:

   Individuals who are unable to attend the public hearings but wish to comment on the Proposed Amendments should submit written comments by February 10, 1998, to:

   Jack Price
   Department of Natural Resources
   524 S. Second Street
   Springfield, IL 62701-1787
   Telephone: 217/782-1809
   Fax: 217/524-9640

All comments received will be fully considered by the agency.

HEALTH FACILITIES PLANNING BOARD

NOTICE OF EXPEDITED CORRECTION

1) Heading of the Part: Narrative and Planning Policies

2) Code Citation: 77 Ill. Adm. Code 1100

3) Section Numbers: 1100.530

4) Date Proposal published in Illinois Register: July 19, 1996, 20 Ill. Reg. 9470

5) Date Adoption published in Illinois Register: May 30, 1997, 21 Ill. Reg. 6220

6) Date Request for Expedited Correction published in Illinois Register: October 24, 1997, 21 Ill. Reg. 14108

7) Adoption Effective Date: December 19, 1997

8) Correction Effective Date: December 19, 1997

9) Reason for Approval of Expedited Correction: The Illinois Health Facilities Planning Board originally proposed changing a factor in determining bed need for obstetrics in 2 different subsections from 3.5 days to 2.5 days. Although both changes were included in the Planning Board's original proposal of the rulemaking, the change was inadvertently omitted from Section 1100.530(e)(3) in the version that was filed and published.

The full text of the Corrected Rule begins on the following page:

HEALTH FACILITIES PLANNING BOARD

NOTICE OF EXPEDITED CORRECTION

TITLE 77: PUBLIC HEALTH
CHAPTER II: HEALTH FACILITIES
PLANNING BOARD
SUBCHAPTER a: ILLINOIS HEALTH CARE FACILITIES PLAN

PART 1100
NARRATIVE AND PLANNING POLICIES

SUBPART A: GENERAL NARRATIVE

HEALTH FACILITIES PLANNING BOARD

NOTICE OF EXPEDITED CORRECTION

Policies
1100.520   Medical-Surgical/Pediatric Categories of Service
1100.530   Obstetric Category of Service
1100.540   Intensive Care Category of Service
1100.550   Comprehensive Physical Rehabilitation Category of Service
1100.560   Acute Mental Illness Categories of Service
1100.570   Substance Abuse Category of Service
1100.580   Neonatal Intensive Care Category of Service
1100.590   Burn Category of Service
1100.600   Therapeutic Radiology Equipment
1100.610   Open Heart Surgery Category of Service
1100.620   Cardiac Catheterization Services
1100.630   Chronic Renal Dialysis Category of Service
1100.640   Non-Hospital Based Ambulatory Surgery
1100.650   Computer Systems (Repealed)
1100.660   General Long-Term Care Category of Service
1100.670   Specialized Long-Term Care Categories of Service
1100.680   Magnetic Resonance
1100.690   High Linear Energy Transfer (L.E.T.)
1100.700   Positron Emission Tomographic Scanning (P.E.T.)
1100.710   Extracorporeal Shock Wave Lithotripsy
1100.720   Selected Organ Transplantation
1100.730   Kidney Transplantation
1100.740   Subacute Care Hospital Model
1100.750   Postsurgical Recovery Care Center Alternative Health Care Model
1100.760   Children's Respite Care Center Alternative Health Care Model

APPENDIX A   Applicable Codes and Standards Utilized in 77 Ill. Adm.
Code: Chapter II, Subchapter a

AUTHORITY: Implementing and authorized by the Illinois Health Facilities
Planning Act (20 ILCS 3960).

SOURCE: Fourth Edition adopted at 3 Ill. Reg. 30, p. 194, effective July 28,
1979; amended at 4 Ill. Reg. 4, p. 129, effective January 11, 1980; amended at
5 Ill. Reg. 4895, effective April 22, 1981; amended at 5 Ill. Reg. 10297,
effective September 30, 1981; amended at 6 Ill. Reg. 3079, effective March 8,
1982; emergency amendments at 6 Ill, Reg. 6895, effective May 20, 1982, for a
maximum of 150 days; amended at 6 Ill. Reg. 11574, effective September 9, 1982;
Fifth Edition adopted at 7 Ill. Reg. 5441, effective April 15, 1983; amended at
8 Ill. Reg. 1633, effective January 31, 1984; codified at 8 Ill. Reg. 15476;
amended at 9 Ill. Reg. 3344, effective March 6, 1985; amended at 11 Ill. Reg.
7311, effective April 1, 1987; amended at 12 Ill. Reg. 16079, effective
September 21, 1988; amended at 13 Ill. Reg. 16055, effective September 29,
1989; amended at 16 Ill. Reg. 16074, effective October 2, 1992; amended at 18
Ill. Reg. 2986, effective February 10, 1994; amended at 18 Ill. Reg. 8448,
effective July 1, 1994; emergency amendment at 19 Ill. Reg. 1941, effective
January 31, 1995, for a maximum of 150 days; amended at 19 Ill. Reg. 2985,

HEALTH FACILITIES PLANNING BOARD

NOTICE OF EXPEDITED CORRECTION

effective March 1, 1995; amended at 19 Ill. Reg. 10143, effective June 30,
1995; recodified at 20 Ill. Reg. 2594; amended at 20 Ill. Reg. 14778, effective
November 15, 1996; amended at 21 Ill. Reg. 6220, effective May 30, 1997;
expedited correction at 21 Ill. Reg. _____, effective May 30, 1997.

SUBPART D: NEED FORMULAS/UTILIZATION TARGETS

Section 1100.530 Obstetric Category of Service

a) Planning Areas: Same as M-S
b) Age Groups: Female 15-44; Female 15 and over
c) Occupancy Targets:

    1-10 beds   60%   Gynecology
    11-25 beds   75%   Utilization
    26+ beds   78%   within
                            Obstetrics 90%

d) Bed Capacity: Obstetrics bed capacity is the lesser of measured bed
    capacity or functional bed capacity per individual room.
e) Total Bed Need for Obstetrics and the number of additional beds needed
    are determined by:
    1) multiplying the projected female 15-44 population by the current
        fertility rate of the health planning area to obtain projected
        births;
    2) multiplying the projected number of births by a hospitalization
        factor of .99 (99%) to determine number of projected births
        occurring in hospitals;
    3) multiplying projected births occurring in hospitals by length of
        stay factor of 2.5 3-5 days to obtain projected maternity patient
        days;
    4) dividing the gynecology utilization (of the base year) within
        obstetric units by the current female 15+ population to obtain a
        use rate;
    5) multiplying the use rate of gynecology patients by the projected
        female 15+ population to obtain projected gynecology patient
        days;
    6) dividing the projected maternity patient days by 365 to obtain a
        maternity average daily census;
    7) dividing the projected gynecology patient days by 365 to obtain a
        gynecology average daily census;
    8) dividing the gynecology patient days by .9 (90%) to determine
        obstetric beds needed for gynecology patients;
    9) dividing the maternity average daily census by the occupancy
        target for new construction to obtain obstetric beds needed for
        maternity patients;
    10) adding the maternity bed need (step 9) with the gynecology need
        (step 8) to determine total unadjusted obstetric bed need.
    11) determine the number of patients entering the planning area from

outside and the number of area residents leaving the planning area for obstetrics service;

12) multiplying the total number of patients entering the area and those leaving the area by 2.5 to determine a patient day estimate for in-migration and out-migration;

13) multiplying the patient totals for area in-migration and out-migration by a .85 (85%) adjustment factor;

14) subtracting the resulting in-migration adjusted patient day total from the out-migration adjusted patient day total to determine the net in or out patient day migration estimate;*

AGENCY NOTE: *Patient migration adjustment is for a one year period and the base year shall be the date of the latest available patient origin data.

15) dividing the net in or out patient day estimate by 365 to determine the average daily census for migration;

16) adding to net in-migration areas the average daily census for migration to the unadjusted bed need to determine the migration adjusted obstetric bed need; in net out-migration areas subtract the average daily census for migration to determine adjusted obstetric bed need.

17) calculating the number of beds which should be added in each area by subtracting the number of beds in existing facilities from the number of beds needed.

(Source: Expedited correction at 21 Ill. Reg. 7207, effective May 30, 1997)

a) Part(s) (Heading and Code Citation): Claims, Adjudication, Appeals and Hearings, 56 Ill. Adm. Code 2720

1) Rulemaking(s):

A) The Department is considering an amendment to Section 2720.130 to eliminate the provision that the timeliness of a protest is determined by the postmark date of the envelope containing the protest (or the time imprinted by the Department's facsimile machine) only if it is mailed (or telefaxed) to the local office designated in the notice of claim to the employer. If the protest is mailed to an address (or telefaxed to a telephone number) other than the designated address (or telephone number), timeliness is determined by the date of receipt by the designated local office. Such an amendment would provide that the timeliness of the protest would be measured from the postmark date on the envelope containing the protest (or time imprinted by the Department's facsimile machine) as long as it is sent to a Department of Employment Security facility.

B) Statutory Authority: 820 ILCS 405/239, 409, 500, 604, 700, 701, 702, 703, 705, 706, 800, 801, 803, 804, 805, 1000, 1001, 1002, 1004, 1200, 1700, 1701, 2300, 2301, 2302, and 2304.

C) Schedule of date(s) for hearings, meetings or other opportunities for public participation: Specific criticisms, suggestions and/or comments can be forwarded to the Department of Employment Security in writing by interested persons during the First Notice Period.

D) Date(s) agency anticipates First Notice(s): It is expected that First Notice for all amendments will be filed around February, 1998.

E) Affect on small business, small municipalities or not for profit corporations: These rules would have an impact on all employers in the state.

F) Agency contact person for information:

Gregory J. Ramel, Deputy Legal Counsel
Illinois Department of Employment Security
401 South State Street - 7th Floor South
Chicago, IL 60605
312-793-4240

DEPARTMENT OF EMPLOYMENT SECURITY

JANUARY 1998 REGULATORY AGENDA

G) Related rulemakings and other pertinent information: None

b) Part(s) (Heading and Code Citation): Administrative Hearings and Appeals, 56 Ill. Adm. Code 2725

1) Rulemaking(s):

A) The Department is considering amendments to several Sections to specify that the timeliness of a protest, appeal, objection or similar tax document filed with the Department is measured by the postmark date of the envelope containing such document (or the time imprinted by the Department's facsimile machine) as long as it is sent to a Department of Employment Security facility, even if that facility is not the office designated to receive such filings.

B) Statutory Authority: 820 ILCS 405/701, 702, 703, 705, 706, 1501, 1501.1, 1502, 1502.1, 1508, 1508.1, 1509, 1510, 1700, 1701, 2200, 2201, 2203, 2300, 2301, 2302, 2304 and 2305.

C) Schedule of date(s) for hearings, meetings or other opportunities for public participation: Specific criticisms, suggestions and/or comments can be forwarded to the Department of Employment Security in writing by interested persons during the First Notice Period.

D) Date(s) agency anticipates First Notice(s): It is expected that First Notice for all amendments will be filed around February, 1998.

E) Affect on small business, small municipalities or not for profit corporations: These rules would have an impact on all employers in the state.

F) Agency contact person for information:

Gregory J. Ramel, Deputy Legal Counsel
Illinois Department of Employment Security
401 South State Street - 7th Floor South
Chicago, IL 60605
312-793-4240

G) Related rulemakings and other pertinent information: None

c) Part(s) (Heading and Code Citation): Wages, 56 Ill. Adm. Code 2730

1) Rulemaking(s):

DEPARTMENT OF EMPLOYMENT SECURITY

JANUARY 1998 REGULATORY AGENDA

A) In the past, the Department's practice has been to disallow a reduction in an employer's wages subject to the payment of contributions for reimbursement of expenses unless the employer could present evidence that the reimbursement represented a dollar for dollar reimbursement for actual expenses paid by the worker. The Department is considering acceptance of "per diem" reimbursements which meet the federal regulatory requirements for exclusion from the definition of wages under the Federal Unemployment Tax Act (FUTA).

B) Statutory Authority: 820 ILCS 405/234, 235, 245, 1700 and 1701.

C) Schedule of date(s) for hearings, meetings or other opportunities for public participation: Specific criticisms, suggestions and/or comments can be forwarded to the Department of Employment Security in writing by interested persons during the First Notice Period.

D) Date(s) agency anticipates First Notice(s): It is expected that First Notice for this amendment will be filed around February, 1998.

E) Affect on small business, small municipalities or not for profit corporations: This rule would have an impact on all employers that provide "per diem" reimbursement of employee expenses.

F) Agency contact person for information:

Gregory J. Ramel, Deputy Legal Counsel
Illinois Department of Employment Security
401 South State Street - 7th Floor South
Chicago, IL 60605
312-793-4240

G) Related rulemakings and other pertinent information: None

d) Part(s) (Heading and Code Citation): Employment, 56 Ill. Adm. Code 2732

1) Rulemaking(s):

A) The owner of a fleet of trucks (or of a single truck) may lease the truck(s), along with a driver(s), to a carrier. In that case, an issue arises as to whether the fleet owner or the carrier is the driver's employing unit. The

DEPARTMENT OF EMPLOYMENT SECURITY

JANUARY 1998 REGULATORY AGENDA

Department is considering a rule to establish guidelines on the matter.

The Department will also revise Section 2732.205 to correct minor drafting errors.

B) Statutory Authority: 820 ILCS 405/205, 206, 211.5, 212, 212.1, 215, 217, 218, 225, 234, 1700 and 1701.

C) Schedule of date(s) for hearings, meetings or other opportunities for public participation: Specific criticisms, suggestions and/or comments can be forwarded to the Department of Employment Security in writing by interested persons during the First Notice Period.

D) Date(s) agency anticipates First Notice(s): It is expected that First Notice for this amendment will be filed around January, 1998.

E) Affect on small business, small municipalities or not for profit corporations: This rulemaking would have an impact on all fleet owners and carriers.

F) Agency contact person for information:

Gregory J. Ramel, Deputy Legal Counsel
Illinois Department of Employment Security
401 South State Street - 7th Floor South
Chicago, IL 60605
312-793-4240

G) Related rulemakings and other pertinent information: None

e] Part(s) (Heading and Code Citation): Notices, Records, Reports, 56 Ill. Adm. Code 2760

1) Rulemaking(s):

A) Section 301 of the Act was recently amended to allow the Director to terminate an employer's account on her own initiative when the employer has permanently ceased to pay wages and permanently ceased to have individuals performing services for it. The Department is seeking public input into establishing standards for the exercise of the Director's initiative.

A proposed amendment to Section 2760.140 is intended to clarify the ramifications of an employer's failure to comply

DEPARTMENT OF EMPLOYMENT SECURITY

JANUARY 1998 REGULATORY AGENDA

with this rule. The new example would explain that a reporting penalty will be imposed monthly even if the employer submits its report on paper. When each penalty is imposed, the employer's contribution payment is reallocated to cover the penalty, and this will increase the balance of its unpaid contributions.

The second change to Section 2760.140 would clarify that, if the Internal Revenue Service grants an employer an exemption from its electronic reporting requirements for a particular year, the exemption will apply to the employer's compliance with this rule for the next year. For example, if the IRS exempts an employer from electronically filing W-2 forms for tax year 1997 (the forms must be filed in 1998), the employer need not file wage reports electronically or magnetically for any quarter in 1998.

The Department is also considering a change in the certification requirements for electronic reporters.

A recent amendment to Section 1507 of the Act eliminates the requirement that an employer report a succession within 120 days of the succession in order to succeed to the predecessor's contribution rate if that rate is lower than that of the successor. Rules need to be adjusted to accommodate this amendment.

B) Statutory Authority: 820 ILCS 405/204, 234, 245, 300, 301, 302, 700, 1400, 1401, 1402, 1404, 1405, 1507, 1700, 1701, 1706, 1800, 1801, 2201 and 2208.

C) Schedule of date(s) for hearings, meetings or other opportunities for public participation: Specific criticisms, suggestions and/or comments can be forwarded to the Department of Employment Security in writing by interested persons during the First Notice Period.

D) Date(s) agency anticipates First Notice(s): It is expected that First Notice for this amendment will be filed around February, 1998.

E) Affect on small business, small municipalities or not for profit corporations: The rule on electronic reporting affects only entities with more than 250 employees. The other amendments affect all employers.

F) Agency contact person for information:

DEPARTMENT OF EMPLOYMENT SECURITY

JANUARY 1998 REGULATORY AGENDA

Gregory J. Ramel, Deputy Legal Counsel
Illinois Department of Employment Security
401 South State Street - 7th Floor South
Chicago, IL 60605
312-793-4240

G) Related rulemakings and other pertinent information: None

f) Part(s) (Heading and Code Citation): Payment Of Unemployment
Contributions, Interest and Penalties, 56 Ill. Adm. Code 2765

1) Rulemaking(s):

A) Recent amendments to the Unemployment Insurance Act allow
the Director to disregard credit balances of less than $2.00
in an employer's account and debit balances of less than
$2.00 in an employer's account for a particular quarter.
The Department is soliciting public input into rules to
administer these provisions.

B) Statutory Authority: 820 ILCS 405/212, 302, 500, 601, 602,
603, 612, 701, 1400, 1401, 1402, 1403, 1404, 1405, 1502.1,
1503, 1507, 1508, 1509, 1700, 1701, 2201, 2201.1 and 2600

C) Schedule of date(s) for hearings, meetings or other
opportunities for public participation: Specific
criticisms, suggestions and/or comments can be forwarded to
the Department of Employment Security in writing by
interested persons during the First Notice Period.

D) Date(s) agency anticipates First Notice(s): It is expected
that First Notice for this amendment will be filed around
February, 1998.

E) Affect on small business, small municipalities or not for
profit corporations: This rule affects all employers.

F) Agency contact person for information:

Gregory J. Ramel, Deputy Legal Counsel
Illinois Department of Employment Security
401 South State Street - 7th Floor South
Chicago, IL 60605
312-793-4240

G) Related rulemakings and other pertinent information: None

g) Part(s) (Heading and Code Citation): Claimant's Reason For Separation

---

DEPARTMENT OF EMPLOYMENT SECURITY

JANUARY 1998 REGULATORY AGENDA

From Work, 56 Ill. Adm. Code 2840

1) Rulemaking(s):

A) The Department would like to promulgate a rule clarifying
the necessary elements for the introduction of the results
of a drug or alcohol test at a benefit hearing.

In a recent decision, the Illinois Supreme Court held that
intervening employment will make an individual no longer
subject to the provisions of Section 604 of the Act (labor
dispute) only if the intervening employment is taken in
"good faith". The Department solicits the public's view on
how it should determine "good faith" in such cases.

B) Statutory Authority: 820 ILCS 405/601, 602, 604, and 1701.

C) Schedule of date(s) for hearings, meetings or other
opportunities for public participation: Specific
criticisms, suggestions and/or comments can be forwarded to
the Department of Employment Security in writing by
interested persons during the First Notice Period.

D) Date(s) agency anticipates First Notice(s): It is expected
that First Notice for this amendment will be filed around
January, 1998.

E) Affect on small business, small municipalities or not for
profit corporations: This rule would affect all employers.

F) Agency contact person for information:

Gregory J. Ramel, Deputy Legal Counsel
Illinois Department of Employment Security
401 South State Street - 7th Floor South
Chicago, IL 60605
312-793-4240

G) Related rulemakings and other pertinent information: None

b) Part(s) (Heading and Code Citation): General Provisions, 56 Ill. Adm.
Code 2960

1) Rulemaking(s):

A) Responsibility for the Veterans Employment Act Program was
transferred to the Department of Employment Security in
1993, and these rules provide guidelines for the Program's

DEPARTMENT OF EMPLOYMENT SECURITY

JANUARY 1998 REGULATORY AGENDA

administration. The Department is considering an amendment to clarify the requirements for financial record keeping and to eliminate the requirement for an annual audit by the Department.

B) Statutory Authority: 330 ILCS 25/1-25/7.

C) Schedule of date(s) for hearings, meetings or other opportunities for public participation: Specific criticisms, suggestions and/or comments can be forwarded to the Department of Employment Security in writing by interested persons during the First Notice Period.

D) Date(s) agency anticipates First Notice(s): It is expected that First Notice for this amendment will be filed around February, 1998.

E) Affect on small business, small municipalities or not for profit corporations: This rule has no direct effect on employers.

F) Agency contact person for information:

Gregory J. Ranel, Deputy Legal Counsel
Illinois Department of Employment Security
401 South State Street - 7th Floor South
Chicago, IL 60605
312-793-4340

G) Related rulemakings and other pertinent information: None

DEPARTMENT OF HUMAN RIGHTS

JANUARY 1998 REGULATORY AGENDA

Part(s) (Heading of Code Citation): Procedures Applicable to All Agencies; 44 Ill. Adm. Code 750.

1) Rulemaking:

A) Description: The Department intends to amend its existing regulations in order to clarify the regulations, to update statutory citations, and to implement new procedures for obtaining Bidder Eligibility Numbers.

B) Statutory Authority Implementing Section 2-105 and authorized by Section 7-101(A) of the Illinois Human Rights Act [775 ILCS 2-105 and 7-101(A)].

C) Schedule of dates for hearings, meetings, or other opportunities for public participation: None scheduled at this time.

D) Date agency anticipates submitting to the Index Department a Notice of Proposed Rules: (Amendments, Repealer) for publication in the Illinois Register: February 28, 1997.

E) Information Concerning the regulatory agenda shall be directed to:

Name: David T. Rothal
Address: Illinois Department of Human Rights
           100 West Randolph Street
           Suite 10-100
           Chicago, IL 60601
Telephone: 312-814-6242
           T.D.D.: 213-263-1579

F) Will this rule (amendment, repealer) affect small business, small municipalities or not for profit corporations: All public contractors and eligible bidders are subject to the Illinois Human Rights Act and its regulations on public contacts.

G) Other pertinent information concerning this rule (amendment, repealer): not applicable.

JOINT COMMITTEE ON ADMINISTRATIVE RULES
ILLINOIS GENERAL ASSEMBLY

SECOND NOTICES RECEIVED

The following second notices were received by the Joint Committee on
Administrative Rules during the period of December 9, 1997 through December 15,
1997 and have been scheduled for review by the Committee at its January 14,
1998 meeting in Springfield. Other items not contained in this published list
may also be considered. Members of the public wishing to express their views
with respect to a rule should submit written comments to the Committee at the
following address: Joint Committee on Administrative Rules, 700 Stratton
Bldg., Springfield IL 62706.

Second Notice Expires	Agency and Rule	Start of First Notice	JCAR Meeting
1/22/98	Pollution Control Board, Effluent Standards (35 Ill Adm Code 304)	10/10/97 21 Ill Reg 13500	1/14/98
1/24/98	Illinois Racing Board, Medication (11 Ill Adm Code 603)	10/3/97 21 Ill Reg 13281	1/14/98

PROCLAMATIONS

97-668
FRANCIS RAYMOND SHEEHAN DAY

Whereas, Francis Raymond Sheehan is celebrating his 75th birthday this
year, 1997; and
Whereas, Francis Raymond Sheehan served his country valiantly as a SeaBee
during World War II in the South Pacific; and
Whereas, Francis Raymond Sheehan married Doris Buehler and together they
have raised seven lovely children; and
Whereas, Francis Raymond Sheehan has instructed three generations of
Sheehan children in the art of the SNIPE hunt; and
Whereas, Francis Raymond Sheehan, though living in South Carolina, is an
avid Cubs fan thanks in part to Chicago's own WGN; and
Whereas, Francis Raymond Sheehan is loved by his nieces and nephews in
Illinois;
Therefore, I, Jim Edgar, Governor of the State of Illinois, proclaim
December 15, 1997, as FRANCIS RAYMOND SHEEHAN DAY in Illinois.
Issued by the Governor November 21, 1997.
Filed by the Secretary of State December 1, 1997.

97-669
AIDS AWARENESS DAY

Whereas, the global spread of HIV infection and AIDS necessitates a
worldwide effort to increase communication, education and action to stop the
spread of HIV/AIDS; and
Whereas, the joint United Nations Programme on HIV/AIDS (UNAIDS) estimates
that 21.8 million people are living with HIV/AIDS, with children younger than
15 years old accounting for 830,000 of the cases; and
Whereas, in Illinois, the number of AIDS cases has reached 20,000, of whom
229 are children younger than 13 years old; and
Whereas, the American Association for World Health is encouraging a better
national understanding of the challenge of HIV/AIDS, since the number of people
diagnosed with HIV/AIDS in the United States continues to increase, with
612,078 cases reported as of June 30, 1997; and
Whereas, UNAIDS observes December 1 of each year as World AIDS Day, a day
to expand and strengthen the worldwide effort to stop the spread of HIV/AIDS;
and
Whereas, the 1997 World AIDS Day theme, "Give Children Hope in a World
With AIDS," urges all individuals to contemplate the long-term repercussions of
the AIDS pandemic; recognizes that everyone can do something about the pandemic
through prevention, education and compassion; and emphasizes the hope of
finding the means to prevent and cure HIV/AIDS as the ultimate prospect of
minimizing the impact of the pandemic on children, their families and their
communities; and
Whereas, this day in Illinois is commemorated by a number of events across
the state, including the dimming of the lights atop the Illinois State Capitol
dome and at the James R. Thompson Center in Chicago during the evening hours to
offer a tribute to those infected and affected by HIV and AIDS;
Therefore, I, Jim Edgar, Governor of the State of Illinois, proclaim

December 1, 1997, as AIDS AWARENESS DAY in Illinois.
   Issued by the Governor November 24, 1997.
   Filed by the Secretary of State December 1, 1997.

97-670
COLLEGE AND UNIVERSITY DAY

   Whereas, more than 760,000 citizens attend the over 180 public and private colleges, universities and community colleges in the State of Illinois every year; and

   Whereas, students who earn a college degree are the future of our state and the inner strength of our economic system; and

   Whereas, colleges and universities in Illinois play an important role in providing the skills necessary for a productive Illinois workforce. This training helps both Illinois citizens preparing for careers and those returning to refine or focus their skills; and

   Whereas, the instruction provided by institutions of higher learning is essential to ensure the quality of the labor market in the State of Illinois for the 21st century and beyond; and

   Whereas, the education provided by Illinois colleges and universities helps shape responsible and self-sufficient citizens with the tools to financially provide for and raise healthy families; and

   Whereas, strong graduate education programs contribute to the cultural, social, and economic well being and progress of the citizens of the state; and

   Whereas, Illinois colleges and universities share the common goals of instruction, research, training and public service. Each has distinctive strengths and makes an important contribution to the state and its citizens; and

   Whereas, hardworking and dedicated staffs fuel the success of the higher education institutions in Illinois and are essential to the education these institutions provide to Illinois citizens;

   Therefore, I, Jim Edgar, Governor of the State of Illinois, proclaim September 16, 1998, as COLLEGE AND UNIVERSITY DAY in Illinois.
   Issued by the Governor November 24, 1997.
   Filed by the Secretary of State December 1, 1997.

97-671
MS. VERA A. WILT DAY

   Whereas, Ms. Vera A. Wilt was elected as the National Fraternal Congress of America Vice President in September 1997; and

   Whereas, the National Fraternal Congress of America (NFCA) has been the central voice of the fraternal insurance industry, including monitoring issues and events relevant to fraternal benefit societies and serving as an information clearinghouse; and

   Whereas, Ms. Wilt graduated from the University of Illinois-Chicago in 1974, and received her Juris Doctor (with distinction) from The John Marshall Law School in 1982; and

   Whereas, Ms. Wilt is married and the proud mother of one son and one daughter; and

   Whereas, Ms. Wilt is the President/CEO of the CSA Fraternal Life, a fraternal life insurance company founded in 1854. The CSA Fraternal Life has its headquarters in Oak Brook, Illinois, and conducts business in 20 states; and

   Whereas, Ms. Wilt currently serves on the Illinois State Board of Health, the State Treasurer's Ethnic Advisory Council and the Citizens Bank of Illinois Board of Directors;

   Therefore, I, Jim Edgar, Governor of the State of Illinois, proclaim November 27, 1997, as MS. VERA A. WILT DAY in Illinois.
   Issued by the Governor November 24, 1997.
   Filed by the Secretary of State December 1, 1997.

Rules acted upon during the quarter of April 1 through June 30, 1997 (Issues 17-28) are listed in the Issues Index by Title number, Part number and Issue number. For example, 50 Ill. Adm. Code 4401 published in Issue 40 will be listed as 50-4401-40. The letter "R" designates a rule that is being repealed. The quarterly Sections Affected Index and Cumulative Index will be published in Issue 29 (July 15); Issue 42 (October 17); and Issue 3 (January 16, 1998). Inquiries about the Issues Index may be directed to the Administrative Code Division at 217-782-4414 or jnatale@ccgate.xos.state.il.us (Internet address).

PROPOSED				
11-300-52	50-4430-52	92-522-51	59-111-49	89-434-49
11-415-52	50-5421-48	92-1205-43	68-590-52	89-1200-52
11-1411-49	50-8100-42	92-1710-43	68-610-52	
17-130-44	68-1283-44	92-1720-43	68-1247-50	EMERGENCY
17-810-49	68-1285-48	92-1730-43	68-1252-42	50-4404-51
17-830-52	68-1300-45	92-1740-43	68-1270-44	50-4430-52
17-3040-50	68-1310-44		68-1320-50	50-5421-48
23-252-49	68-1350-44		68-1380-42	77-290-42
23-451-49	68-1470-44	ADOPTED	68-1400-48	77-845-46
26-100-42,46	77-300-49	2-1975-42	68-1420-48	80-1650-52
26-125-42	77-330-49	8-40-52	68-1480-42	83-757-51
26-216-42	77-350-49	8-75-52	71-400-45	86-3000-45
32-360-45	77-390-49	8-80-52	71-2005-45	
32-406-47	77-463R-44	8-85-52	77-300-47	PEREMPT.
35-183-44	77-465-44	8-105-52	77-350-47	8-125-45
35-201-50	77-750-42	8-110-52	77-830-47	77-290-42
35-611-52	77-515-47	8-115-52	77-1120-49	77-2090-43
35-703-47	77-1130-47	14-130-49	80-150-44	80-310-
35-720-47	80-150-42,49	14-150-50	80-302-49	44,45,47,51,52
35-721-47	80-310-46	14-165-50	80-303-49	89-140-42
35-724-47	80-1650-52	14-170-50	80-310-51	
35-725-47	83-505-48	14-178-50	83-765-52	
35-728-47	83-605-51	17-685-45	86-1910-45	
35-733-47	83-757-51	17-2010-48	89-10-49	
35-742-52	86-130-42	17-4190-48	89-50-47	
38-180-42	89-140-42	20-1285-52	89-104-47	
38-500-53	89-146-42	23-275-45	89-112-49	
38-1000-51	89-302-48	35-205-49	89-114-49	
38-1075-51	89-332-45	35-241-49	89-116-49	
41-180-42	92-102-47	35-742-51	89-117-49	
44-5010-47	92-107-47	35-810-49	89-148-50	
47-220-42	92-171-47	35-811-49	89-152-50	
47-250-42	92-172-47	38-610-52	89-160-50	
47-260-42	92-173-47	50-2018-44	89-165-49	
47-310-42	92-177-47	50-2051-51	89-250-46	
47-360-42	92-178-47	50-3119-42	89-305-46	
47-365-42	92-179-47	56-2520-43	89-326-49	
50-4404-51	92-180-47	56-2770-49	89-360-49	
	92-441-48	56-6000-47	89-428-49	

ILLINOIS REGISTER
ADMINISTRATIVE CODE ORDER FORM

EASE USE THIS FORM FOR ALL ORDERS OR TO NOTIFY US OF A CHANGE
ADDRESS. ALL ORDERS MUST BE PAID IN ADVANCE BY CHECK, MONEY
DER, VISA, MASTER CARD OR DISCOVER CARD. CHECKS AND MONEY
DERS MUST BE PAYABLE TO THE "SECRETARY OF STATE".

CROFICHE SETS OF THE ILLINOIS REGISTER @$200.00 PER SET.
1977-1978 _1979 _1980 _1981 _1982 _1983 _1984 _1985 _1986
1987 _1988 _1989 _1990 _1991 _1992 _1993 _1994 _1995 _1996

MULATIVE INDICES TO THE ILLINOIS REGISTER @$1.00 EACH.
1981 _1982 _1983 _1984 _1985 _1986 _1987 _1988 _1989

CTIONS AFFECTED INDICES TO THE ILLINOIS REGISTER @$1.00 EACH.
1984 _1985 _1986 _1987 _1988 _1989

MULATIVE/SECTIONS AFFECTED INDICES @$5.00 EACH.
1990 _1991 _1992 _1993 _1994 _1995 _1996

CK ISSUES OF THE ILLINOIS REGISTER (CURRENT YEAR ONLY) @$10.00
CH. _____ _____ _____
    (VOLUME #)   (ISSUE #)   (ISSUE DATE)

NUAL SUBSCRIPTION TO THE ILLINOIS REGISTER @$290.00 (52 ISSUES)
_NEW _RENEWAL

JUAL SUBSCRIPTION TO THE ILLINOIS ADMINISTRATIVE CODE ON
-ROM; COMPLETELY UPDATED EDITION PUBLISHED QUARTERLY
:90.00 FOR 4 QUARTERLY EDITIONS

:AL AMOUNT OF ORDER: $_____
:HECK _VISA _MC _DISCOVER CARD#:_____

:IRATION DATE:_____ SIGNATURE:_____
= CHANGE OF ADDRESS, PLEASE LIST BOTH THE OLD AND NEW ADDRESS:

ME, PLEASE TYPE OR PRINT)

)DRESS)

[TY, STATE, ZIP CODE AND TELEPHONE #)

:L TO: GEORGE H. RYAN   OR FAX: (217) 854-0308
              SECRETARY OF STATE
              INDEX DEPARTMENT
              111 E. MONROE
              SPRINGFIELD, IL 62756

JOINT COMMITTEE ON ADMINISTRATIVE RULES
ILLINOIS GENERAL ASSEMBLY

SECOND NOTICES RECEIVED

The following second notices were received by the Joint Committee on Administrative Rules during the period of December 9, 1997 through December 15, 1997 and have been scheduled for review by the Committee at its January 14, 1998 meeting in Springfield. Other items not contained in this published list may also be considered. Members of the public wishing to express their views with respect to a rule should submit written comments to the Committee at the following address: Joint Committee on Administrative Rules, 700 Stratton Bldg., Springfield IL 62706.

Second Notice Expires	Agency and Rule	Start of First Notice	JCAR Meeting
1/22/98	Pollution Control Board, Effluent Standards (35 Ill Adm Code 304)	10/10/97 21 Ill Reg 13500	1/14/98
1/24/98	Illinois Racing Board, Medication (11 Ill Adm Code 603)	10/3/97 21 Ill Reg 13281	1/14/98

PROCLAMATIONS

97-668
FRANCIS RAYMOND SHEEHAN DAY

Whereas, Francis Raymond Sheehan is celebrating his 75th birthday this year, 1997; and

Whereas, Francis Raymond Sheehan served his country valiantly as a SeaBee during World War II in the South Pacific; and

Whereas, Francis Raymond Sheehan married Doris Buehler and together they have raised seven lovely children; and

Whereas, Francis Raymond Sheehan has instructed three generations of Sheehan children in the art of the SNIPE hunt; and

Whereas, Francis Raymond Sheehan, though living in South Carolina, is an avid Cubs fan thanks in part to Chicago's own WGN; and

Whereas, Francis Raymond Sheehan is loved by his nieces and nephews in Illinois;

Therefore, I, Jim Edgar, Governor of the State of Illinois, proclaim December 15, 1997, as FRANCIS RAYMOND SHEEHAN DAY in Illinois.

Issued by the Governor November 21, 1997.
Filed by the Secretary of State December 1, 1997.

97-669
AIDS AWARENESS DAY

Whereas, the global spread of HIV infection and AIDS necessitates a worldwide effort to increase communication, education and action to stop the spread of HIV/AIDS; and

Whereas, the Joint United Nations Programme on HIV/AIDS (UNAIDS) estimates that 21.8 million people are living with HIV/AIDS, with children younger than 15 years old accounting for 830,000 of the cases; and

Whereas, in Illinois, the number of AIDS cases has reached 20,000, of whom 229 are children younger than 13 years old; and

Whereas, the American Association for World Health is encouraging a better national understanding of the challenge of HIV/AIDS, since the number of people diagnosed with HIV/AIDS in the United States continues to increase, with 612,078 cases reported as of June 30, 1997; and

Whereas, UNAIDS observes December 1 of each year as World AIDS Day, a day to expand and strengthen the worldwide effort to stop the spread of HIV/AIDS; and

Whereas, the 1997 World AIDS Day theme, "Give Children Hope in a World With AIDS," urges all individuals to contemplate the long-term repercussions of the AIDS pandemic; recognizes that everyone can do something about the pandemic through prevention, education and compassion; and emphasizes the hope of finding the means to prevent and cure HIV/AIDS as the ultimate prospect of minimizing the impact of the pandemic on children, their families and their communities; and

Whereas, this day in Illinois is commemorated by a number of events across the state, including the dimming of the lights atop the Illinois State Capitol dome and at the James R. Thompson Center in Chicago during the evening hours to offer a tribute to those infected and affected by HIV and AIDS;

Therefore, I, Jim Edgar, Governor of the State of Illinois, proclaim

December 1, 1997, as AIDS AWARENESS DAY in Illinois.
  Issued by the Governor November 24, 1997.
  Filed by the Secretary of State December 1, 1997.

97-670
COLLEGE AND UNIVERSITY DAY

  Whereas, more than 760,000 citizens attend the over 180 public and private
colleges, universities and community colleges in the State of Illinois every
year; and
  Whereas, students who earn a college degree are the future of our state
and the inner strength of our economic system; and
  Whereas, colleges and universities in Illinois play an important role in
providing the skills necessary for a productive Illinois workforce. This
training helps both Illinois citizens preparing for careers and those returning
to refine or focus their skills; and
  Whereas, the instruction provided by institutions of higher learning is
essential to ensure the quality of the labor market in the State of Illinois
for the 21st century and beyond; and
  Whereas, the education provided by Illinois colleges and universities
helps shape responsible and self-sufficient citizens with the tools to
financially provide for and raise healthy families; and
  Whereas, strong graduate education programs contribute to the cultural,
social, and economic well being and progress of the citizens of the state; and
  Whereas, Illinois colleges and universities share the common goals of
instruction, research, training and public service. Each has distinctive
strengths and makes an important contribution to the state and its citizens;
and
  Whereas, hardworking and dedicated staffs fuel the success of the higher
education institutions in Illinois and are essential to the education these
institutions provide to Illinois citizens;
  Therefore, I, Jim Edgar, Governor of the State of Illinois, proclaim
September 16, 1998, as COLLEGE AND UNIVERSITY DAY in Illinois.
  Issued by the Governor November 24, 1997.
  Filed by the Secretary of State December 1, 1997.

97-671
MS. VERA A. WILT DAY

  Whereas, Ms. Vera A. Wilt was elected as the National Fraternal Congress
of America Vice President in September 1997; and
  Whereas, the National Fraternal Congress of America (NFCA) has been the
central voice of the fraternal insurance industry, including monitoring issues
and events relevant to fraternal benefit societies and serving as an
information clearinghouse; and
  Whereas, Ms. Wilt graduated from the University of Illinois-Chicago in
1974, and received her Juris Doctor (with distinction) from The John Marshall
Law School in 1982; and
  Whereas, Ms. Wilt is married and the proud mother of one son and one
daughter; and
  Whereas, Ms. Wilt is the President/CEO of the CSA Fraternal Life, a
fraternal life insurance company founded in 1954. The CSA Fraternal Life has
its headquarters in Oak Brook, Illinois, and conducts business in 20 states;
and
  Whereas, Ms. Wilt currently serves on the Illinois State Board of Health,
the State Treasurer's Ethnic Advisory Council and the Citizens Bank of Illinois
Board of Directors;
  Therefore, I, Jim Edgar, Governor of the State of Illinois, proclaim
November 27, 1997, as MS. VERA A. WILT DAY in Illinois.
  Issued by the Governor November 24, 1997.
  Filed by the Secretary of State December 1, 1997.

Rules acted upon during the quarter of April 1 through June 30, 1997 (Issues 17-28) are listed in the Issues Index by Title number, Part number and Issue number. For example, 50 Ill. Adm. Code 4401 published in Issue 40 will be listed as 50-4401-40. The letter "R" designates a rule that is being repealed. The quarterly Sections Affected Index and Cumulative Index will be published in Issue 29 (July 15); Issue 42 (October 17); and Issue 3 (January 16, 1998). Inquiries about the Issues Index may be directed to the Administrative Code Division at 217-782-4414 or jnairale@ccgate.sos.state.il.us (Internet address).

PROPOSED			
	50-4430-52	92-522-51	59-111-49
11-300-52	50-5421-48	92-1205-43	68-590-52
11-415-52	50-8100-42	92-1710-43	68-610-52
11-1411-49	68-1283-44	92-1720-43	68-1247-50
17-130-44	68-1285-48	92-1730-43	68-1252-42
17-810-49	68-1300-45	92-1740-43	68-1270-44
17-830-52	68-1310-44		68-1320-50
17-3040-50	68-1350-44		68-1380-42
23-252-49	68-1470-44	ADOPTED	68-1400-48
23-451-49	77-300-49	2-1975-42	68-1420-48
26-100-42,46	77-330-49	8-40-52	68-1480-42
26-125-42	77-350-49	8-75-52	71-400-45
26-216-42	77-390-49	8-80-52	71-2005-45
32-360-45	77-463R-44	8-85-52	77-300-47
32-406-47	77-465-44	8-105-52	77-350-47
35-183-44	77-750-42	8-110-52	77-830-47
35-201-50	77-515-47	8-115-52	77-1120-49
35-611-52	77-1130-47	14-130-49	80-150-44
35-703-47	80-150-42,49	14-150-50	80-302-49
35-720-47	80-310-46	14-165-50	80-303-49
35-721-47	80-1650-52	14-170-50	80-310-51
35-724-47	83-505-48	14-178-50	83-765-52
35-725-47	83-605-51	17-685-45	86-1910-45
35-728-47	83-757-51	17-2010-48	89-10-49
35-733-47	86-130-42	17-4190-48	89-50-47
35-742-52	89-140-42	20-1285-52	89-104-47
38-180-42	89-146-42	23-275-45	89-112-49
38-500-52	89-302-48	35-205-49	89-114-49
38-1000-51	89-332-45	35-241-49	89-116-49
38-1075-51	92-102-47	35-742-51	89-117-49
41-180-42	92-107-47	35-810-49	89-148-50
44-5010-47	92-171-47	35-811-49	89-152-50
47-220-42	92-172-47	38-610-52	89-160-50
47-250-42	92-173-47	50-2018-44	89-165-49
47-260-42	92-177-47	50-2051-51	89-290-46
47-310-42	92-178-47	50-3119-42	89-305-46
47-360-42	92-179-47	56-2520-43	89-326-49
47-365-42	92-180-47	56-2770-49	89-360-49
50-4404-51	92-441-48	56-6000-47	89-428-49

89-434-49	
89-1200-52	
EMERGENCY	
50-4404-51	
50-4430-52	
50-5421-48	
77-290-42	
77-845-46	
80-1650-52	
83-757-51	
86-3000-45	
PEREMPT.	
8-125-45	
77-290-42	
77-2090-43	
80-310-	
44,45,47,51,52	
89-140-42	

CPSIA information can be obtained
at www.ICGtesting.com
Printed in the USA
BVHW041103190219
540639BV00007B/118/P